The Literate Communist

Major Concepts in Politics and Political Theory

Garrett Ward Sheldon
General Editor

Vol. 16

PETER LANG
New York • Washington, D.C./Baltimore • Boston
Bern • Frankfurt am Main • Berlin • Vienna • Paris

Donald Clark Hodges

The Literate Communist

150 Years of the
Communist Manifesto

PETER LANG
New York • Washington, D.C./Baltimore • Boston
Bern • Frankfurt am Main • Berlin • Vienna • Paris

Library of Congress Cataloging-in-Publication Data

Hodges, Donald Clark.
The literate communist: 150 years of the Communist manifesto /
Donald Clark Hodges.
p. cm. — (Major concepts in politics and political theory; v. 16)
Includes bibliographical references and index.
1. Marx, Karl, 1818–1883. Manifest der Kommunistischen Partei.
2. Communism. 3. Socialism. 4. Historical materialism.
5. Marxist criticism. I. Title. II. Series.
HX39.5.H59   335.4'22—dc21   98-30633
ISBN 0-8204-4187-2
ISSN 1059-3535

Die Deutsche Bibliothek-CIP-Einheitsaufnahme

Hodges, Donald Clark:
The literate communist: 150 years of the Communist manifesto /
Donald Clark Hodges. –New York; Washington, D.C./Baltimore; Boston;
Bern; Frankfurt am Main; Berlin; Vienna; Paris: Lang.
(Major concepts in politics and political theory; Vol. 16)
ISBN 0-8204-4187-2

Cover design by James F. Brisson

The paper in this book meets the guidelines for permanence and durability
of the Committee on Production Guidelines for Book Longevity
of the Council of Library Resources.

Printed in the United States of America

Contents

Introduction: Understanding the Manifesto

> The secret history of the *Communist Manifesto* is not its conscious materialism and Marx's own opinion of it.
>
> Karl Löwith, *Meaning in History* (1949)

> "All history," as the...*Manifesto* proclaims, "has been the history of class struggles." The matter bears emphasis because the class struggle would become the cardinal article of Marxist doctrine for the Soviets.
>
> Martin Malia, *The Soviet Tragedy* (1994)

The Manifesto, whose 150th birthday we celebrate in this work, is reputedly the Magna Carta of modern communism. As a classic of Western political culture, it shares with Marx's *Capital* a distinguished niche in the *Encyclopedia Britannica's* 60-volume series on the "Great Books of the Western World,"[1] and with good reason, because it may be read as an informal prelude to *Capital*—the so-called bible of the working class. Not for nothing does the chapter that constitutes the logical conclusion to volume one—the penultimate chapter—end with a quotation from the opening section of the Manifesto.

An anniversary is hardly a sufficient call for a new reading of this important work. Why, then, a scrutiny of the Manifesto at the close of the second millennium? Because the Manifesto contains a clue, if only an ideological one, to the 1991 collapse of Soviet Communism. That alone is reason enough to take another look at this literary masterpiece, a document both perplexing and consequential, that continues to be controversial and is still misunderstood.

For a full understanding of this influential tract, a close reading of the text is only a starter. Unraveling its concealed as well as publicly proclaimed meanings requires more than a formal analysis of its language at the time of composition. One needs to grasp the manuscript as a whole, as a

---

[1] *Marx*, vol. 50 in the series Great Books of the Western World, ed. John Maynard Hutchins (Chicago: Encyclopedia Britannica, 1990; orig. pub. 1952). All direct quotations from the Manifesto are from the 1888 authorized English translation by Samuel Moore, revised and edited by Frederick Engels.

revolutionary document based not only on its assimilation of the mainstream of Western culture, but also on the various side currents that shaped it. The Manifesto has an historical beginning, middle, and end—a movement through both time and space.

Just as one gets to know a person by what he does as well as by what he says, so the Manifesto is best understood not just through a reading of its text, but also through an examination of its historical influence—the uses to which it has been put. Whether or not the shapers of Soviet domestic policy believed in the words of the Manifesto, the fact that they periodically cited it in support of their policies is sufficient evidence of its consequentiality. Thus Part I of the present study deals with the Manifesto's fragile consensus among the competing radical tendencies during Marx and Engels' lifetime; Part II, with the text's political uses and abuses by Anarchists, Social Democrats, and Communists of different persuasions—all of which have a bearing on the rise and fall of Soviet Communism.

The Manifesto is a literary masterpiece, not just a masterwork of propaganda in the intellectual arsenal of a revolutionary movement. Besides its novel theses presented with forceful arguments, the Manifesto is written with a fresh voice that effectively arouses the reader's emotions. "If he were going to influence and move people," observes one commentator, "Marx realized that he would have to use all available means of persuasion, including what Aristotle called the 'good style' in the *Rhetoric*, parts of which Marx had translated in his university days." An omnivorous reader of plays, poetry, and novels, Marx was thoroughly familiar with the devices used by rhetoricians and outstanding orators. As Wilhelm Liebknecht, a devoted follower, writes in his reminiscences, "Marx attached extraordinary value to pure, correct expression; and in Goethe, Lessing, Shakespeare, Dante, and Cervantes, whom he read every day, he had chosen the greatest masters."[2]

Steeped in the humanist tradition of classical Greek, Latin, and Renaissance literature, Marx was the literate communist par excellence—a model for those who followed in his footsteps. But not all literate communists have shared his humanist revision of the communist legacy, which also has Biblical roots and extends back more than two thousand years. Nor are those who speak in his name the Vergils equipped to steer us through the labyrinths of the Manifesto's vast secondary literature. Self-

---

[2] Quoted by Haig A. Bosmajian, "A Rhetorical Approach to the *Communist Manifesto*," in Frederic L. Bender, ed., *Karl Marx. The Communist Manifesto* (New York/London: Norton, 1988), 190–191.

deception, half-truths, and imaginary outcomes are interwoven with most revolutionary gospels—and the Manifesto is no exception.

It would be a mistake, therefore, to interpret Marx's literate communist—made in his own image—as representing a general type. Unlike Machiavelli's report on princely behavior, Castiglione's depiction of life at court, and Peacham's portrait of the educated gentleman, Marx's prototype of the "Communist" is not a mirror of typical working-class communists in action.[3]

If we are to understand both the "meltdown" of communism in the Soviet bloc and the emerging Marxist critique of Soviet society after Stalin's death, we must do more than examine the "long line of attempts to turn the authority of Marx against what was claimed to be the most perfect social embodiment of his ideas."[4] To understand communism, we need to situate ourselves, imaginatively, in 1848, and then look backward and forward from 1848; we need to consider not only the contemporary expressions of Marxism-Leninism, but also the Manifesto's forerunners.

Marxists dispute the religious origins of their faith. Although Christian theology has succeeded even better than Marxist ideology in spreading confusion about a particular brand of communism—as if it alone were authentic and worthy of belief—the fact remains that the Christian Bible is the principal fountainhead of communist ideas in the West. Thus in the ingenious but misunderstood man from Nazareth one finds the perfect image of the communist before Marx arrived on the scene.[5]

For the past two millennia the Roman Catholic Church has professed communism in one form or another. Among the Fathers of the Church who defended communism one need only mention St. Cyprian, St. Zeno of Verona, St. Ambrose, St. John Chrysostom, and the communist author of the Fifth Epistle of Clement. The Church consistently maintained that a life of voluntary poverty was the best way to salvation—a doctrine that found

---

[3] Niccolò Machiavelli, *The Prince* and *The Discourses*, trans. Luigi Ricci and revised by E. R. P. Vincent (New York: Modern Library, 1940; orig. pub. 1532); Baldassare Castiglione, *The Book of the Courtier*, trans. Sir Thomas Hoby (London: J. M. Dent & Sons/New York: Dutton, 1948; orig. pub. 1528); and Henry Peacham, *Peacham's Compleat Gentleman* (Oxford: Clarendon Press, 1906; orig. pub. 1622).

[4] Raymond Taras, ed., "The 'Meltdown' of Marxism in the Soviet Bloc: An Introduction," *The Road to Disillusion: From Critical Marxism to Postcommunism in Eastern Europe* (Armonk, NY: M. E. Sharpe, 1992), 3–5, 8–9; and in the same volume the essay by James P. Scanlan, "From Samizdat to Perestroika: The Soviet Marxist Critique of Soviet Society," 19–21.

[5] On Jesus as an "illiterate" carpenter and "radical egalitarian" communist, see John Dominic Crossan, *Jesus: A Revolutionary Biography* (New York: HarperCollins, 1994), 25–26, 73–74.

institutionalized expression in the monastic movement and its orders of monks, nuns, friars, and sorores. From the eleventh century onward there were also to be found in the more populated regions of Europe groups of laymen living in quasi-monastic communities, holding all property in common. The vernacular literature was another medium in which the communist idea found expression, as in that great exemplar of medieval literature, Jean de Meun's *Romance of the Rose* (ca. 1280).[6]

The spread of the communist idea in Western civilization owes less to Plato's *Republic* (ca. 380 B.C.) and Iamblichus' *On the Pythagorean Life* (ca. 300 A.D.) than to the Christian Bible. The New Testament became a breeding ground of communism, thanks to Matt. 19:20–24 and Acts 2:44–45 and 4:32–35, while the early Christian communities put the Bible's communist teachings into practice. So, to identify communism with Marxism, says the former Jesuit Priest José Porfirio Miranda in his provocative *Communism in the Bible*, is to show the crassest ignorance of history.[7]

Those raised in the Protestant tradition may recall its origins among the millenarian sects of the fourteenth and fifteenth centuries. The sermons of John Ball electrified the English peasants during the Peasants' Revolt of 1381 in a text that was already a communist proverb:

> When Adam delved and Eve span,
> Who was then a gentleman?

Ball was a follower of John Wycliffe (ca. 1330–1384), an Oxford scholar and forerunner of the Reformation. Known as Lollards, his followers came under heavy persecution by the Church. So they went underground.

Under constant harassment, communists became adept at lying, at concealing their beliefs in Aesopian language. In Jesus' parables they found a model of how to preserve their secret doctrine. "Cast not your pearls before swine, lest they trample them under their feet and turn and rend you" (Matt. 7:6). From the Lollards to the Illuminati, communists survived thanks to their secret societies. Compelled to hide, they turned to conspiracies.

The modern equivalent of Wycliffe was Adam Weishaupt (1748–1830), a professor of canon law at the University of Ingolstadt in Bavaria. The founder of the Illuminati in 1776, his impact on the French Revolution and on the secret communist societies that arose in its wake had no equal.

---

[6] Norman Cohn, *The Pursuit of the Millennium* (New York: Harper, 1961), 202–212.
[7] José Porfirio Miranda, *Comunismo en la biblia* (Mexico City: Siglo XXI, 1981), 17, 26.

Through his immediate disciples he shaped both the theory and practice of François Noël "Gracchus" Babeuf (1760–1797), of Babeuf's mentor Sylvain Maréchal (1750–1803), and of Babeuf's alter ego and premier disciple, Filippo Michele Buonarroti (1761–1837).[8]

That Weishaupt did not call himself a communist is of little moment. He was the first of the moderns to target the sinister trinity of Prince, Priest, and Property—Caesar, Loyola, and Shylock.[9] He was the gray eminence behind a line of communist manifestos culminating in Babeuf's November 1795 *Manifesto of the Plebeians* and Maréchal's April 1796 *Manifesto of the Equals*. And he was the inspiration behind Buonarroti's 1828 manual of communism entitled *Babeuf's Conspiracy for Equality*.

Buonarroti's manual was the first communist bible. No less a flaming revolutionary than Michael Bakunin (1814–1876), the father of anarcho-Marxism and Marx's principal rival for control of the First International, called it the "communist testament of Babeuf."[10] Its program was radically egalitarian: through leveling downward instead of upward, through the imposition of equal burdens and equal benefits, its acolytes hoped to achieve economic equality. Its strategy was murderous: seizure of power by a conspiratorial vanguard followed by a revolutionary dictatorship, abolition of private property, and annihilation of the class enemy.

What made Babeuf's communism modern was its appeal to wage earners in the ranks of the laboring poor and its depiction of capitalists as "enemies of the people."[11] The social question would henceforth focus not only on the plight of the laboring poor opposite the idle rich, but increasingly on the exploitation of the new class of proletarians.

This historical sketch has a direct bearing on how one interprets the Manifesto. The Manifesto was written and published as the authorized statement of a political party whose members were still under the influence of Babeuf's plebeian communism. If we wish to understand the Manifesto,

---

8   Elizabeth L. Eisenstein, *The First Professional Revolutionist: Filippo Michele Buonarroti (1761–1837)* (Cambridge: Harvard University Press, 1957), 11, 35–49.

9   John Robison, *Proofs of a Conspiracy* (Boston: Western Islands, 1967; orig. pub. 1798), 77, 92–93.

10   Philippe (Filippo) Buonarroti, *Babeuf's Conspiracy for Equality*, trans. Bronterre O'Brien (New York: Augustus M. Kelley, 1965; orig. pub. 1828); and Michael Bakunin, "To the Comrades of the International Workingmen's Association of Locle and Chaux-des-Fonds (1869)," in Albert Fried and Ronald Sanders, eds., *Socialist Thought: A Documentary History*, rev. ed. (New York: Columbia University Press, 1992), 336–337.

11   "Analysis of the Doctrine of Babeuf by the Babouvists" (1796), and "Babeuf's Defense" (from the Trial at Vendôme, February–May 1797), in Fried and Sanders, *Socialist Thought*, 56, 63–64.

we had therefore better add the "first revolutionary communist" (Babeuf) and the "first professional revolutionist" (Buonarroti) to our reading list.[12] Such is the stage setting for understanding the Manifesto, which presented not the first nor the most consistent version of communism, but surely the most influential among the communist manifestos going back to the French Revolution of 1789–1794.

Thus, in brief, runs the road from a faraway past to the Manifesto. The Manifesto is the principal station on the road from the French Revolution to the Russian Bolshevik Revolution, from French communism to its Russian counterpart (Marxism–Leninism). Its tour de force was to make communism scientific, while preserving the mainstream of Western civilization and culture. In this capacity it included a critique of the French conspiratorial and vanguardist precursors of bolshevism—but in the name of communism instead of anticommunism. The account offered in Part I shows the Manifesto to have effectively repudiated the French legacy.

The Manifesto presents communism as the fulfillment of socialism, while socialism is presented as the fulfillment of liberalism and democracy. It equates communism with fully developed humanism, with a society in which the free development of each is the condition for the free development of all. Free development of all? That means the mass production of a Renaissance man—a prince, courtier, and gentleman rolled into one and translated into the middle of the nineteenth century!

What is one to make of the Manifesto as a respectable addition to the collection of Western cultural artifacts and, at the same time, a manual of subversion? For the Manifesto speaks for a party of discontents and for an ideology vilified by its enemies as a Red Specter haunting the earth. Its professed goal is summarized in a single sentence: "Abolition of private property"—meaning bourgeois property in the means of production. Communism is depicted in the Manifesto as not only the most radical rupture with traditional property relations, but also as "the most radical rupture with traditional ideas." What is respectable about *that*?

Was this radical rupture with the past Marx's communism, or was it part of the communist legacy that he felt obliged to insert into the Manifesto against his best wishes? For the Manifesto expressly challenges that legacy for having "inculcated universal asceticism and social leveling in its crudest form," for having a "reactionary" and "purely Utopian character"—as if the

---

[12] B. Rose, *Gracchus Babeuf: The First Revolutionary Communist* (Stanford: Stanford University Press, 1978); and Eisenstein, *The First Professional Revolutionist*. One might also include Albert L. Weeks, *The First Bolshevik: A Political Biography of Peter Tkachev* (New York: New York University Press, 1968).

Manifesto's communism was any less utopian despite its claim to being scientific!

How, then, should one understand this little masterpiece—a work that is enmeshed in a thicket of contradictions within a world of exegesis at once contemptuous of the Manifesto's precursors and skeptical about its posthistory?

To understand the Manifesto one needs to recognize, first of all, that it is a protean document with a universal appeal. It can be read not only as a brief for humanism, but also as a demoliberal revolutionary tract, as a technocratic manifesto, and for its socialist as well as communist and anarchist message. If it were not so misleading, there would not be so many different interpretations of it.

Although the manifesto of a Communist party, is it primarily a *communist* manifesto? If so, why did Engels later call it a "*Socialist* Manifesto"? Why did Austrian Social Democrats believe it was a Humanist Manifesto for the "reform of consciousness"? What prompted Eduard Bernstein, Engels' literary executor, to describe the Manifesto as an ambiguous document, at once committed to a communist "violent revolution" and to the liberal winning of power rather by "lawful than by unlawful means"? What led Russian anarchists to revile it as the "Bible of legal revolutionary democracy"? Why did Bakunin translate it into Russian?[13] The answers to these questions will disclose the elusive as well as ambiguous character of this important document.

Among the thorniest obstacles to understanding the Manifesto are its understatements and its author's efforts to get it accepted by Communists with different political views. The Manifesto would have us believe that "Communists do not...set up any sectarian principles of their own, by which to shape and mould the proletarian movement." In fact, Marx sought to reshape the proletarian movement according to his own lights. Admittedly, he said things he only partly believed and misled his readers by resorting to ambiguity. There is a diplomatic cast to the Manifesto designed to bridge major differences of opinion and to cover over patent contradictions. As I show at length in Part I, the Manifesto is not a reliable guide to what most Communists believed when it first appeared.

---

[13] Frederick Engels, "Preface to the English Edition of 1888," in Bender, 48; Rondel V. Davidson, "Reform versus Revolution: Victor Considérant and the *Communist Manifesto*," in Bender, 94; Max Adler, "Socialism and Communism," in Bender, 138. See also Eduard Bernstein, *Evolutionary Socialism*, trans. Edith C. Harvey (New York: Schocken, 1961; orig. pub. 1899), xxiv–xxvii; and G. P. Maximoff, ed., *The Political Philosophy of Bakunin: Scientific Anarchism* (Glencoe, IL: Free Press, 1953), 286–287, 289.

One should beware of confusing Marx and Engels' programmatic and group-sponsored statements issued in the name of the Communist and workers' movement, and therefore not signed by them personally, with their own pronouncements. Their group-sponsored statements were by far the more influential pieces they wrote on political matters. Besides the Manifesto, the most important of these were Engels' "Communist Credo" and "Principles of Communism" (1847), Marx and Engels' "Address of the Central Authority to the Communist League" (1850), and Marx's "Inaugural Address and General Rules of the International Working Men's Association" (1864) and "Address of the General Council of the International on the Civil War in France" (1871). To say that Marx and Engels minced words in these documents is to understate their achievement.

In the preparatory materials leading up to the Manifesto and in the Manifesto itself, they presented communism as the means to universal humanism—the goal. Pressured to make concessions, however they later inverted that means-end relation by defining themselves as "socialist" and by avoiding the word "humanist." As they repeatedly acknowledged in their correspondence, they tried to formulate their position "in a form in which there will at least be nothing contrary to our views." But they were obliged to insert phrases with which they disagreed, although "in such a way that they can do no harm." As Marx noted in a letter to Engels (4 November 1864), he had to be *"fortiter in re, suaviter in modo"*—firm in principle, accommodating in manner. In another letter he explained that, as a political broker for the General Council pressured from all sides, he could not write the same way as he could in his own name.[14]

It was no easy task. As aptly summed up by two British authors apropos of Marx's 1864 Inaugural Address, "Marx's task was to reconcile the irreconcilable." That he did so with finesse is evident from a letter by his daughter Jenny to Ludwig Kugelmann and spouse concerning the French translation of Marx's *Civil War in France*. The translation, she wrote, "made a very good impression on the [Communard] refugees, for it has equally satisfied all parties—Blanquists, Proudhonists, and Communists."[15]

Beginning with the Inaugural Address, Marx stopped importing humanist philosophy into his group-sponsored political documents. In the

---

[14] Karl Marx and Frederick Engels, *Selected Correspondence* (Moscow: Foreign Languages Publishing House, 1953), 53, 182; and Marx to Engels, 14 September 1870, cited by Hal Draper, *Karl Marx's Theory of Revolution*, 4 vols. (New York: Monthly Review Press, 1977–1990), 2:601.

[15] Cited by Draper, 2:601. The two British authors are Henry Collins and C. Abramsky, *Karl Marx and the British Labour Movement. Years of the First International* (London: Macmillan, 1965), also cited by Draper, 2:601 n.

General Rules of the International, Marx's concessions to English and French Communists and to proletarians generally are evident in his slogan, "The emancipation of the working class must be conquered by the working classes themselves." By what means? By "the conquest of political power." To what end? The triumph of the social revolution—"the abolition of classes."[16] Not a word about the enrichment of human nature and the flowering of individual talents!

Marx's desire to reserve a place in the International for all working-class parties accounts for the myriad of contradictory readings of the documents he issued in its name. The pundits of the Second International read into them what they wanted to see, as did competing factions of the Third International. Because the Manifesto's ideas clashed with one another, each competing "communism" and "socialism" settled on what it could agree with and bracketed out the rest. Engels' quip in a letter to Marx (27 November 1851), "You must cast a sprat to catch a Mackerel," aptly sums up the policy Marx followed in getting his views endorsed.[17]

The Manifesto seemingly contains a well-chiseled set of ideas. But what appears to be a coherent text has sown confusion and contention. As a continuing source of controversy, its mix of incompatible ideas can only be described as Janus-faced. Thus, not only communists, but also humanists and liberals, democrats and socialists have found sustenance at the ideological smorgasbord set out in the pages of the Manifesto.[18]

Yet the fare was not easily faulted. The deception was not apparent. Rather than conceal the aims of an underground movement, Marx prefaced the Manifesto with the disengaging declaration: "It is high time that Communists should openly, in the face of the whole world, publish their views, their aims, their tendencies, and meet this nursery tale of the Specter of Communism with a Manifesto." Faced with such a seemingly forthright preface, the Manifesto's readers were taken off guard.

Everything in the Manifesto suggests that, like the International Working Men's Association that succeeded it in 1864, the Communist League was a democratic association with an unscreened membership open to public scrutiny. But as Part I of the present work reveals, the League had yet to cast off its conspiratorial legacy.

---

[16] Karl Marx, "Inaugural Address and Rules of the International Working Men's Association," idem and Frederick Engels, *Selected Works*, 2 vols. (Moscow: Foreign Languages Publishing House, 1958), 1:386, 383–388.

[17] Karl Marx and Frederick Engels, *Collected Works*, 46 vols. (New York: International Publishers, 1975–1992), 38: 495.

[18] See Michael Harrington, "The Democratic Essence of Socialism," in Bender, *Karl Marx. The Communist Manifesto*, 107–108.

Consider a few telling examples. The rules adopted in December 1847 included among the conditions of membership not only revolutionary energy and zeal in propaganda, but also "Observance of secrecy concerning the existence of all League affairs." The rules required that members bear League names to conceal their identities, that the various communities "do not know each other and do not conduct any correspondence with each other." Moreover, the League was hierarchically organized so that the lower bodies were subordinated to circles comprising at least two and not more than ten communities under a leading circle, in its turn subordinated to the Central Authority, the League's governing body responsible only to the annual congress.[19]

Since Marx and Engels were in principle opposed to secret societies, these rules amounted to concessions in keeping with the League's conspiratorial origins. After the sectarians were expelled in November 1850, one might have expected Marx and Engels to adopt a new set of rules entirely to their liking. Sectarianism, however, was rife not only in ideology but also in the League's organizational structure. Indeed, the new set of rules was even more sectarian than its predecessor. Article 1 declared that "as long as the proletarian revolution has not attained its ultimate goal the League shall remain secret and indissoluble," while Article 2 announced that members had to be "emancipated from all religion" and could not "participate in any ceremony not required by civil law." Members were required to maintain the strictest secrecy and to "swear to abide unconditionally by the decisions of the League." Whoever violated the rules would be expelled, including "whole communities where expulsion has been proposed by a district community."[20]

So the Communist League was a conspiratorial organization despite all protests to the contrary. Although it stopped short of being a party of professional revolutionaries, it was the party of a chosen elect and not the kind of electoral, mass-based political party to which Marx and Engels later gave support. Marx hoped to build a mass movement that by sheer numbers and superior knowledge might steamroll its way to power. But the League was hardly the most effective vehicle for that purpose.

The Manifesto was to be the League's guiding light, the embodiment of Communist political intelligence. It could not afford to be exclusive. Overcoming the ideological divisions within the working class might best be achieved by an ideological mix that accounts for the Manifesto's growing

---

[19] Marx and Engels, *Collected Works*, 6:633–634, 636.
[20] Ibid., 10:634–635.

readership and popularity. That the number of copies eventually ran into the tens of millions may be attributed to this ecumenicism.

Our account would be incomplete without research into Marx and Engels' second thoughts—their commentaries on the original manuscript, which they refrained from altering because it had become a historical document with a life of its own. The history of the Manifesto is the history not only of a document in the making, but also of its subsequent amendments and adaptations that fueled the revolutionary fires and forged the major programs of the various Socialist and Communist parties. Designed to bring the Manifesto up to date in response to changing circumstances, the resolutions of party congresses and the successive manuals of communism for building cadres helped to spread a revolutionary message with multiple faces. For the elites, Marx's Heraclitean Manifesto flowed with the current; for the masses who barely understood it, it remained frozen in time.

Lenin revived the communist legacy spurned by the Manifesto. He thereby returned communism to its original, nonhumanist path—but in the name of Marxism. Thus Lenin turns out to be the true keeper of the flame— seconded by Stalin, not to mention Trotsky—whereas Marx was almost exactly what twentieth-century Western Marxists claimed he was—the enemy within, the mortal enemy of Communism. The account offered in Part II brings to light the Manifesto's unintended consequences contributing to this compounded irony and to Communism's recent demise.

The limited resources of the real world and the dog-eat-dog competition for them inevitably frustrate any attempt to apply the Manifesto's humanist credo. Yet such an attempt was nominally made in the wake of Stalin's death. The humanist component in the Manifesto thus indirectly contributed to the so-called Communist malaise.

The crusaders against Stalinism within the Bolshevik Party, led by Khrushchev, Gorbachev, and Shevardnadze, proclaimed from the rooftops their faith in universal humanism and in the technocratic means thereto through economic modernization.[21] They redefined socialism in terms of

---

[21] Nikita S. Khrushchev, "Report on the Program of the Communist Party of the Soviet Union," in *Documents of the 22nd Congress of the CPSU*, 2 vols. (New York: Crosscurrents Press, 1961), 2:30–33, 118–120, 123; Mikhail Gorbachev, *Perestroika: New Thinking for Our Country and the World* (New York: Harper, 1987), 34, 47, 144–147; and Eduard Shevardnadze, *The Future Belongs to Freedom*, trans. Catherine Fitzpatrick (New York: Free Press, 1991), 24–26, 63, 66–68, 117, 126, 166–167, 191. See also the essay by Gorbachev's main advisor, Alexander Yakovlev, "The Humanistic Choice of Perestroika," *World Marxist Review* 32 (February 1989), 8–13.

humanist, liberal, and democratic values, while identifying the enemy within as pseudo-socialism—the legacy of Stalinism and a command economy. They may have given mostly lip-service to other features of the Manifesto, but they assuredly swallowed its humanist bait and its demoliberal and technocratic hook.

The road from Soviet communism gained momentum with these reformers—the misnamed "radicals" within the socialist camp—thanks in part to the translations into Russian of Marx's 1844 *Economic and Philosophic Manuscripts*—the most elaborate statement of his humanism, which he incorporated into the Manifesto. Having been closeted in the Party's archives for some three decades, it was suddenly released on the eve of Stalin's death—with his imprimatur. Who knows why? Possibly, to trap the unsuspecting, the spoiled brats of the Revolution and those he suspected of treachery—the budding "radicals"—in the final purge he was preparing at the time.[22]

Among the factors underlying the Soviet Communist party's loss of legitimacy, ideology is clearly to be included. In 1992, a team of experts specializing in Russian and Eastern European studies concluded that Marxism-Leninism became discredited under the prodding of critical Marxists whose humanist handle opened the door to liberal and democratic values.[23] If critical Marxists can be *credited* for the Soviet ideological meltdown, we are told, it is because Stalin's policy of relentless class struggle can be *blamed* for the systematic violation of universal human values.

In this conventional wisdom of the West it is Soviet Marxism that self-destructs. Although Lenin gave birth to the Soviet Union and Stalin built it into a superpower, their ideologies were defective to the point of being self-dissolving. In retrospect, say the critics, it was only a matter of time for the self-destructive elements in Soviet Marxism to prevail. To this extent, the conventional wisdom is right.

But did Soviet Marxism self-destruct because of its communist legacy or because of its Marxist component? Influenced by French communism and by Lenin's heterodoxy in 1917, the Bolshevik left wing called for leveling from the top down, thereby heading on a collision course with the privileges of party bureaucrats and of the "Red intelligentsia" spawned by the Revolution. At the same time, following Marx and the Manifesto, the Bolshevik right wing called for leveling from the bottom up, thereby

---

[22] Stuart Kahan, *The Wolf of the Kremlin* (New York: William Morrow, 1987), 250–257, 284, 291.

[23] Taras, "The 'Meltdown' of Marxism in the Soviet Bloc," *The Road to Disillusion*, 3.

spurning the interests of ordinary workers who were told to wait—because there were not enough privileges to go around. There was no way of resolving this clash of interests. Thus Soviet Marxism disintegrated owing to the Marxist reaction from on high to the communist pressures from below.

What Lenin and later Stalin termed the "right" and "left" deviations from the Communist party's main line may be found in the Manifesto. Stalin's middle course—scourged by Trotsky for staggering between left and right—also had its counterpart in the Manifesto. The right deviation has its roots in the Manifesto's humanist and demoliberal cluster; the left deviation, in its communist and anarchist elements; centrism, in its technocratic and socialist mix. Thus all the inner-party struggles from 1917 to 1991—from class struggle to class conciliation—are concentrated in capsule form in this historic document.

A balanced view of the Soviet tragedy obliges one to take both "deviations" into account. Indeed, Marx and the Manifesto—not just Lenin's revival of French communism and Stalin's synthesis known as Marxism-Leninism—played a key role not only in building socialism in the Soviet Union, but also in bringing about the Soviet collapse.

The present work describes the multiple, often contradictory roles the Manifesto has played in the history of modern Socialist and Communist movements. Part I traces the prehistory and the birth of the Manifesto, dissects its manifold meanings, and assesses its subsequent updatings, amplifications, and amendments at the hands of Marx and Engels. Part II outlines its posthistory in the hands of the most consequential revisionists of Marxism, both pre-Soviet and Soviet, along with those Soviet leaders who returned to the Marxist fold. Finally, the conclusion assesses how the Manifesto has stood the test of time.

The present work thus aims to fulfill tasks akin to those the Bolshevik historian David Ryazanoff set for himself more than seven decades ago in what is still considered to be the foremost commentary on the Manifesto. To nearly two hundred pages of explanatory notes, he hoped—but failed—to add a second volume, which would satisfy the following conditions: "First of all, it would...give the history of the social and revolutionary movement which called the Manifesto into life as the program of the first international communist organization. Next it would...trace the genesis, the source, of the basic ideas contained in the Manifesto, and would...bring out that which was new in the philosophy of Marx and Engels, that which differentiated them from the thinkers who had gone before. In the third place, the commentary would...indicate to what extent the Manifesto stands the test of historical criticism, and would...amplify and correct it in certain points."[24]

In the preface to the second Russian edition of his work, Ryazanoff again addressed the need for further research. The Manifesto cannot be understood, he noted, without a knowledge of its precursors, including the development of socialist literature and the history of the struggles of the proletariat since the great French Revolution. Otherwise, it is impossible to know what the Manifesto contributed that was original and why it broke new ground. In addition to giving a full account of its genesis as the starting-point of a new era in human history, he proposed to trace all the ideas contained in the Manifesto to their sources and also to explore their consequences. "Some day, such a commentary will have to be written—at the cost of an immense amount of preliminary labor."[25] It was an ambitious and still uncompleted project when he was expelled from the party, fired from his position as Director of the Marx-Engels Institute in Moscow, and his research cut short by one of Stalin's purges.

---

[24] David V. Ryazanoff, *The Communist Manifesto of Karl Marx and Friedrich Engels*, trans. Eden and Cedar Paul (New York: Russell & Russell, 1963; orig. pub. 1922), Appendix A. Preface to the first Russian edition, 255–256.

[25] Ibid., Appendix B. Preface to the second Russian edition, 257–258. See, for example, the monumental work of German scholarship, Karl Marx and Friedrich Engels, *Das Kommunistische Manifest*, ed. Thomas Kuczynski (Trier: Karl-Marx-Haus, 1995).

Part I. A Perplexing Document

I have become all things to all men, that I might by all means save some.

St. Paul, I Corinthians, 9:22.

The prince who has best known how to act as a fox has come out best. But one who has this capacity must understand how to keep it covered, and be a skillful pretender and dissembler.

Machiavelli, The Prince, 18

The great strength of our Order lies in its concealment; let it never appear in any place in its own name, but always covered by another name.

Adam Weishaupt to Baron Knigge,
Neueste Arbeitung des Spartacus und Philo in der
Illuminaten Orden (ca. 1795)

1. The League of the Just

On May 12, 1839, there took place in Paris the unsuccessful revolt organized by the French secret revolutionary Société des Saisons; with the latter was linked the League of the Just...[which] began increasingly to assume the character of a propagandist society, because experience had made clear the hopelessness of plots isolated from the masses.

V. Adoratsky, *The History of the Communist Manifesto of Marx and Engels* (1938)

Elements of this tradition nonetheless lingered on into the 1850s, giving rise to further dissensions, which in the end resulted in the dissolution of the Communist League.

George Lichtheim, *The Origins of Socialism* (1969)

In his 1885 "History of the Communist League," Engels traced the origins of the Communist League to 1836 when the "most extreme, chiefly proletarian elements of the secret democratic-republican Outlaws' League...founded by German refugees in Paris in 1834, split off and formed the new secret League of the Just." Although the parent league went to sleep and disappeared altogether after the police scented its presence in 1840, the new league showed signs of continuing vitality. Engels described it as a "German outlier of the French worker communism, reminiscent of Babouvism and taking shape in Paris at this time." A supporter of the Reign of Terror during the Great French Revolution of 1789–1794, Babeuf planned to revive the revolution and to implement a communist program through a conspiratorial armed uprising. His successors in the Parisian secret societies of the 1830s, the Society of the Families founded in 1834 and its 1836 reorganization as the Society of the Seasons, also relied on a conspiratorial uprising to establish a "community of goods...the necessary consequence of 'equality'."[1]

---

[1] Frederick Engels, "On the History of the Communist League," in Marx and Engels, *Selected Works*, 2:339.

The League's Ideologist

Since Paris continued to be the revolutionary capital of Europe, the League of the Just at that time was little more than the German branch of the Society of the Seasons, "with which a close connection was maintained." Among its top leaders was Karl Schapper (1812–1870), the founder in 1840 of its legal front, the German Workers' Educational Society, and a "model of the professional revolutionist." But the League's ideologist was the tailor Wilhelm Weitling (1808–1871). Engels described his egalitarian communism as the "first independent theoretical striving of the German proletariat." Marx also highly praised Weitling's 1842 *Guarantees of Harmony and Freedom* as a "vehement and brilliant literary debut of the German workers" but was highly critical of its 1845 successor, *The Poor Sinner's Gospel.*[2]

Weitling believed that nineteenth-century communism was the modern equivalent of the social doctrine of early Christianity and that its goal was to implement Christ's teaching through the establishment of the most perfect communism. His poor sinner's gospel called for "the victory of the poor and oppressed, the overthrow of the rich and the oppressors...the abolition of property [as] the necessary condition for putting the teaching of Jesus into practice." In the conviction that "All men are brothers"—the League of the Just's motto—Weitling championed a program of economic equality regardless of differences in skill, education, and responsibility. Marx, however, had no use for this strain of sentimentality in the proletarian movement or for Weitling's reliance on criminal elements to launch a mass uprising. And he was just as repelled by Weitling's call for a messianic dictatorship and intellectual vanguard to guide the proletariat during the transition to a classless society.[3]

Weitling's communism was a curious blend of ideas taken from the leading French communists at the time, Etienne Cabet (1788–1856) and Louis Auguste Blanqui (1805–1881), but mainly from their teacher Buonarroti and his manual of revolution, *Babeuf's Conspiracy for Equality,*

---

[2] Ibid. 339–341. See Marx and Engels, *Collected Works*, 3:201, 402; and P. N. Fedoseyev et al., eds. *Karl Marx: A Biography*, trans. Yuri Sdobnikov (Moscow: Progress Publishers, 1973), 111–112.

[3] Wilhelm Weitling, *The Poor Sinner's Gospel*, trans. Dinah Livingstone (London: Sheed & Ward, 1969), 17, 75, 79, 186; and Max Nomad, *Aspects of Revolt* (New York: Bookman, 1959), 55, 144. On Weitling's communist utopia, ruled "from the top down in the name of *Intelligenz*," see Draper, *Karl Marx's Theory of Revolution*, 2:656–657.

a two-volume chronicle interwoven with documents of Bab
and selections from Babeuf's writings.[4] Published in Brusse
followed by a first French edition in 1830, by several in
abridgments, and by an English translation in 1836 that aluʋ ....
50,000 copies according to one authority.[5] For two decades from 1828 to
1848, Buonarroti's classic was the single most influential work by a
European revolutionary and the principal disseminator of Babeuf's
communist doctrine.

Weitling's claim to originality was to have identified Babeuf's teaching
with the elements of communism in the New Testament and to have
presented it in quasi-religious figures of speech that made a profound
impression on the nascent German proletariat brought up in the spirit of
evangelical Christianity. So influential was Weitling's gospel when he began
preaching it in 1844 that he won over to his beliefs most of the Swiss
members of the League. The Paris branch also consisted overwhelmingly of
Weitlingians until the League's headquarters, originally in Paris, were
transferred to London in November 1846.[6]

Schapper was the first among the League's authorities to challenge
Weitling's communism. Although he initially subscribed to what Engels
called the narrow-minded "communism which bases itself exclusively on the
demand for equality," he told Weitling to his face at a meeting of the
German Workers' Educational Society in June 1845 that the League had no
longer any use for his pseudoreligious utopia. By 1846 the "tracing of
modern communism back to primitive Christianity...had resulted in
delivering the movement in Switzerland to a large extent into the hands of
fools," wrote Engels, while according to Schapper the League's members in
Paris wasted time chewing over fragments of Weitling's writings to the point
of boredom.[7] As the League's new president after it moved from Paris to
London in November 1846, Schapper was instrumental not only in purging
Weitling's followers, but also in reconstructing the League once Marx and
Engels joined it and Weitling's influence began to wane.

---

[4] Max Nomad, *Apostles of Revolution* (New York: Collier, 1961; orig. pub. 1933), 26,
95; and George Lichtheim, *The Origins of Socialism* (New York: Praeger, 1969), 27–
30, 167–170.
[5] Eisenstein, *The First Professional Revolutionist*, 65–67.
[6] Marx and Engels, *Collected Works*, 6:707 n.334.
[7] Engels, "On the History of the Communist League," in *Selected Works*, 2:340–341,
346–347; Lichtheim, *The Origins of Socialism*, 169–171; and Marx and Engels,
Collected Works, 6:590.

Chapter One

Sources of the League's Ideology

The word "communism" appropriated by Weitling and the League was not used by any of the early socialist schools and did not gain currency in France until 1841, when it came to designate the project for a total revolution inspired by Blanqui. During the 1830s Blanqui's followers and the German émigrés influenced by them described themselves as communists but had yet to use the word "communism." Actually, the word "communism" had a prior but forgotten origin in a work by the Parisian journalist Nicolas Restif de la Bretonne, who first used it in 1793 for a system of community of goods governed by the principle of equal work and equal pay. Under the patronage of the egalitarian Sylvain Maréchal, Babeuf coined the term *communitist* for the community of goods to be established by his revolutionary brotherhood.[8] Such was the doctrine bequeathed to Weitling by Blanqui's followers and by Buonarroti's manual of revolution.

The tracing of modern communism to Christianity was not original to Weitling. There are hints of it in Babeuf's defense speech during his trial at Vendôme and also in Buonarroti's account of Babeuf's doctrine. Buonarroti traced Babeuf's communism back to Jean-Jacques Rousseau (1712–1778), whose "Discourse on the Origin of Inequality" and *The Social Contract* lent themselves to a communist interpretation. Babeuf's other major source was the "law-giver of the Christians (Jesus Christ)."[9] As he justified egalitarianism during his trial, "It entirely sums up the Law of Moses and the Prophets."[10] That placed him in the company of Jesus, who said "Think not that I come to destroy the law or the prophets; I am not come to destroy, but to fulfill" (Matt. 5:17).

Rousseau endeared himself to Babeuf through his philosophy of history. Its sequence of stages borders on the Miltonesque. Rousseau's "state of nature" corresponds to Milton's "paradise" in *Paradise Lost*. It was lost when mankind became civilized and people sought to surpass themselves and others by the introduction of agriculture, "fields that had to be watered with the sweat of men, where one could soon see slavery and misery germinating and ripening along with the crops." From the cultivation of the land followed its partitioning. "The first man who, having enclosed a piece of ground, bethought himself of saying 'This is mine,' and found people

---

[8] James H. Billington, *Fire in the Minds of Men: Origins of the Revolutionary Faith* (New York: Basic Books, 1980), 6, 82–83.

[9] Babeuf, "Babeuf's Defense," in Fried and Sanders, 61–62; and Buonarroti, *Babeuf's Conspiracy for Equality*, 10, 57n.

[10] Babeuf, "Babeuf's Defense," in Fried and Sanders, 61, 69–70.

simple enough to believe him, was the real founder of civil society. From how many crimes, wars, and murders, from how many horrors and misfortunes might not any one have saved mankind, by pulling up the stakes." You are undone, said Rousseau, if you forget that "the fruits of the earth belong to us all, and the earth itself to nobody." In almost the same words, Babeuf defended himself at his trial: "By its origins the land belongs to no one, and its fruits are for everyone."[11] That it had become private property is the Fall from which mankind is redeemed and paradise regained.

Babeuf cited the French encyclopedist Denis Diderot (1713–1784) as another influential source of his political philosophy. The complete edition of Diderot's work included the *Code of Nature* (1755), which Babeuf judged to be the most important. However, it was later discovered that the author was not Diderot, but an obscure French tutor named Morelly whose first name and other biographical details are still unknown.

"The only vice that I perceive in the universe is *Avarice*," wrote Morelly, all the others being variations on the "desire to have." Again, this is the Fall and mankind's foremost task is to overcome it. What is the cause of this universal plague? Is it intrinsic to human nature or something external? Morelly's ingenuous answer is that *"where no property exists, none of its pernicious consequences could exist."* Property is the source of evil, so that to remove evil is to abolish private ownership, an "usurpation of the resources that should belong in common to all humanity." Babeuf too called private property an usurpation.[12]

Babeuf's doctrine was anticipated by the so-called Clementine Gospel, according to which possessions are sins and salvation is achieved by selling one's property and distributing the proceeds among the poor. But what is to be done should the rich hold on to their ill-gotten property? Babeuf replied, "It is therefore just to take it back from them"![13]

The Biblical origins of Babeuf's communism can also be traced through Freemasonry. Babeuf, Maréchal, and Buonarroti were Freemasons, and the Masonic legacy counted Jesus among its prophets. In 1796 Babeuf attempted to found a revolutionary Masonic order, the "Order of Equals," whose title tells us something of his intentions. Buonarroti was one of its instigators.

---

[11] Jean-Jacques Rousseau, *The Social Contract* and *Discourses*, trans. G. D. H. Cole (New York: E. P. Dutton, 1950), 208–209, 234, 244, 246; and Babeuf, "Babeuf's Defense," in Fried and Sanders, 63.

[12] Morelly, "Code of Nature," and Babeuf, "Babeuf's Defense," in Fried and Sanders, *Socialist Thought*, 18–19; 64, 66.

[13] See the "Clementine Recognitions and Homilies," in S. Baring-Gould, ed., *The Lost and Hostile Gospels* (London: Williams and Norgate, 1874), 194–195; and Babeuf, "Babeuf's Defense," 66.

The Conspiratorial Legacy

Babeuf has been described as the first revolutionary communist, but Buonarroti went a step further by becoming the first professional revolutionary. In 1809, he founded a revolutionary but secret international aimed at spreading Babeuf's communism under the cover of modern Masonry. The "Sublime Perfect Masters" included a lower and an intermediate degree crowned by a higher degree known as the Areopagites, who alone were privy to Jesus' secret teachings about the Kingdom of God and the advent of universal communism. The lowest degree contained a profession of liberalism based on the Masonic credo that all men are created equal and bound to defend human liberty. The second degree went beyond liberalism to a profession of democracy, for the sake of which "no means are criminal which are employed to obtain this sacred end." The third degree, that of the Areopagites, made the final step to communism. Its confession of faith called for breaking down the barriers of private property: "Let the Republic be the sole Proprietor: like a mother it will afford to each of its members equal education, food, and labor."[14]

After the dissolution of his first secret society in 1823, Buonarroti founded a second one, the Monde. As he described its structure and principles: "The secret society...is a democratic institution in its principles and its end; but...it is absolutely necessary that the impulse come from above and that all the rest obey." That is because it is really a "secret army, destined to fight a powerful enemy." Buonarroti conceived of the Monde as the secular equivalent of the Society of Jesus with himself as a kind of Loyola. If the end is just and reasonable, he wrote, what does it matter if the means are evil. "The Jesuitical congregation can be compared to an army full of enthusiasm and submissive by conviction to a homogeneous and absolute authority. It is precisely an equivalent army that the Monde has attempted to establish against tyranny."[15] Such was the specter of communism that the *Communist Manifesto* sought to exorcise.

What was the principal source of this conspiratorial communism? It could hardly have been Rousseau, Morelly, or even Babeuf. In her biography of Buonarroti, Elizabeth Eisenstein traces his conspiratorial legacy to the founder of revolutionary Masonry, Dr. Adam Weishaupt.

---

[14] Rose, *Gracchus Babeuf*, 199; Billington, *Fire in the Minds of Men*, 97, 100; Eisenstein, *The First Professional Revolutionist*, 36; J. M. Roberts, *The Mythology of the Secret Societies* (London: Secker & Warburg, 1972), 235, 264–266; and Arthur Lehning, *From Buonarroti to Bakunin* (Leiden: Brill, 1970), 43–46.

[15] Eisenstein, *The First Professional Revolutionist*, 35, 37, 40.

Founded in 1776, his Order of the Illuminati became the archetype for the Masonic lodges in France that initially conspired to make the revolution of 1789 and then drove it steadily leftward, culminating in the "revolution in the revolution" of 1792–1794. There is some evidence that Buonarroti may have become an Illuminatus as early as 1786. In any event, "his later familiarity with it [Weishaupt's Order] is certain and was to be of paramount importance in his future development." Although the Order was formally dissolved when its connections with French revolutionary clubs and its principal secrets were unveiled by the Abbé Barruel in 1797, "Buonarroti was to exploit the idea of being linked to a select and secret company, who had set in motion the Great Revolution, and...bequeathed to surviving colleagues the task of bringing it to its ultimate conclusion."[16]

The Illuminati aimed at nothing less than the complete destruction of the three-headed hydra of Church, State, and Capital. "Equality and Liberty are the natural rights of man," wrote Weishaupt. "The first attempt against Equality was that of property; the first against Liberty was that by political societies and governments. The sole support of property and governments were religious and civil laws. Therefore, to reestablish man's original rights of equality and liberty, one must begin by destroying all religion, all civil society, and finally, all property."[17] In carrying out this project, the Illuminati targeted the First Estate (clergy), the Second Estate (nobility), and the Third Estate (bourgeoisie).

Weishaupt attributed his revolutionary doctrine to the secret teachings of Jesus. "Let us take Liberty and Equality as the great aim of his doctrines and Morality as the way to attain it, and everything in the New Testament will be comprehensible." The key to the Scriptures is the loss of liberty and equality. "This is the Fall and ORIGINAL SIN. The KINGDOM OF GOD is that restoration which may be brought about by Illumination.... By subduing our passions or limiting their cravings, we may recover a great deal of our original worth and live in a state of grace. This is the redemption of man...and when this is spread over the world we have THE KINGDOM OF THE JUST." What is this if not the doctrinal source of the League of the Just and of Weitling's identification of the core of Jesus' teachings with the doctrine of equality?[18]

---

[16] Ibid., 11, 42–44.

[17] Cited by Augustin de Barruel, *Mémoires pour servir a l'histoire du jacobinisme*, 5 vols. (Hamburg: Fauche, 1798–1799), 3:24–25.

[18] Robison, *Proofs of a Conspiracy*, 92–93; original emphasis. See Weitling, *The Poor Sinner's Gospel*, 75, 79, 185–186.

Taking the nom de plume of Spartacus, who headed an insurrection of slaves in 73–71 B.C., Weishaupt wrote to his fellow Illuminatus Cato: "How can the weak obtain protection?" Only through organization, he claimed. "Nothing can bring this about but hidden societies. Hidden schools of wisdom are the means which one day will free men from their bonds.... Princes and nations will vanish from the earth. The human race will then become one family." In an allusion to Matthew 7:6, Weishaupt claimed that "Freemasonry is concealed Christianity," that pearls of wisdom are unfit for swine. As his foremost disciple, Baron Knigge explained the Christian doctrine of the elect: "To these elect were entrusted the most important secrets...thus the doctrines of Christianity were committed to the *Adepti*...in hidden societies, who handed them down to posterity; and they are now possessed by the genuine Free Masons [Illuminati]."[19]

Thanks to Buonarroti, Blanqui too bears traces of Weishaupt's influence. A staunch atheist and master conspirator, he was not averse to using Biblical parallels in as near to a full exposition of his communism as he ever made, "The Man Who Makes the Soup Should Get to Eat It" (1834). An adaptation of Buonarroti's manual to the conditions of the nascent French proletariat at the time, it contained the substance of Weishaupt's ideology and Weitling's gospel without the professed faith. Each step on the road to equality, wrote Blanqui, crushed the guide who encouraged that step. "Christ expired on the cross...and, only lately, the defenders of equality [Babeuf and his principal coconspirator] died on the scaffold of the Revolution through the stupidity and ingratitude of the people." In "seeing the hand that exploits him only as the hand that feeds him," the duped human beast of burden has perennially betrayed his would-be liberators. Yet in the final account the friends of equality proved successful in disputing the right to property. "The Essenian principle of equality [Jesus was an Essene] has been gradually undermining it for centuries, through the successive abolition of the various forms of servitude." Thus Blanqui summarized his Babouvist credo in an 1835 handbill: "The end for us is the equal distribution of the burdens and benefits of society—it is the complete establishment of the reign of equality."[20]

Under the influence of Buonarroti's manual of the Equals, the League of the Just helped to spread egalitarian communism in Paris, Lyons, Toulouse,

---

[19] Cited by Robison, *Proofs of a Conspiracy*, 85, 87, 91.

[20] Louis Auguste Blanqui, "The Man Who Makes the Soup Should Get to Eat It," in Fried and Sanders, *Socialist Thought*, 196, 198; Patrick H. Hutton, *The Cult of the Revolutionary Tradition: The Blanquists in French Politics, 1864–1893* (Berkeley/Los Angeles/London: University of California Press, 1981), 45–47, 107, 118; and Alan B. Spitzer, *The Revolutionary Theories of Louis Auguste Blanqui* (New York: Columbia University Press, 1957), 89.

and other manufacturing centers. The revolutionary movement that sparked Babeuf's conspiracy but was momentarily defeated, wrote Marx and Engels, "gave rise to the *communist* idea which...*Buonarroti* reintroduced in France after the Revolution of 1830." Buonarroti's influence also spread to Germany, "thanks to which the essential principles of French socialism came to the attention of German workers."[21] Buonarroti's manual became the bible of French communism, and because of its importance, Marx began making plans for a German translation.

A Republic of Equals

As the German republican Karl Heinzen accurately depicted Babeuf's communism and that of the League of the Just, it "discerns the core of the communist doctrine simply in...the abolition of private property (including that earned though labor) and in the principle of the communal utilization of the earth's riches which follows inseparably from that abolition."[22] In the conviction that property is theft, those Heinzen labeled "real communists" believed that individual talents and the capacity to labor should be owned in common, not just physical assets, and that individuals should be bound by ties resembling kinship, a mutual fellowship of "One for all, and all for one." This accounts for the fundamental difference between the League's communism and that of Marx and his followers.

Yet Babeuf entertained no illusions about the prospects for equality. As he confessed during his trial, the odds against the possibility of realizing such a project are more than a hundred to one. Nonetheless, he believed that the duty of the revolutionary is to make the revolution. The would-be liberator must trace for the oppressed the "outlines of the plan that he feels could end their woes for all time." For a myth by which to mobilize them, Babeuf summoned the specter of a final solution to the social question. For a mystique to inspire them, he invoked the Biblical figure of Moses, prototype of the hero who would lead them out of bondage. The travails imposed by revolution are not easily borne, so that the final goal had to measure up to the sacrifices. As the "Oath of Membership" into Blanqui's Society of the

---

[21] Marx and Engels, *Collected Works*, 4:119; and Maurice Dommanget, *Babeuf et la conjuration des egaux*, 2nd ed. (Paris: Spartacus, 1969), 73.
[22] Marx and Engels, *Collected Works*, 6:303.

Seasons states, "I promise to give my life, even to climb the scaffold, if this sacrifice is necessary to bring the reign of equality."[23]

In November 1795, Babeuf published the first of the communist manifestos in the new genre later made famous by Marx and Engels. Entitled the *Manifesto of the Plebeians*, it demanded real equality, a "system in which the burdens and benefits of society are divided equally." Unlike equality of opportunity, which has citizens begin on an equal footing but end as winners or losers, Babeuf's real equality has everyone end as a winner. Underpinning Babeuf's "system" are three theses: first, that the work of the head is no more deserving than that of the body; second, that there are no more grounds for superior compensation for the more intelligent and industrious than for those less so; and third, that "everything possessed by those who have more than their individual quota of society's goods is theft and usurpation." As Buonarroti summarized and transmitted this legacy to posterity, "labor is evidently for each citizen an essential condition of the social compact; and as each, in entering into society carries with him an equal stake and contribution (the totality of his strength and means), it follows that the burdens, the productions, and the advantages ought to be equally divided."[24]

An extremist version of this doctrine was articulated by Maréchal in April 1796. Known as the *Manifesto of the Equals*, this second communist document called for "real equality or death"—equality at any price. "We consent to everything for the sake of this, and will renounce everything else in order to have this alone. Let all the arts perish, if necessary, as long as real equality remains!" Maréchal made a point of obliterating the differences not just between the rich and poor, masters and servants, but also between governors and governed.[25] And to make equality perfect he demanded an equal share of all products, rather than equal wages to be spent at one's discretion. "Let there be no differences between human beings other than those of age and sex. Everyone is satisfied with having the sun and the air in common. Why could not the same portion and the same quality of food suffice for all?"

---

[23] Babeuf, "Babeuf's Defense," in Fried and Sanders, 68, 69; and idem, "Le Manifeste des plébéiens," in Babeuf, *Textes Choisis* (Paris: Editions Sociales, 1965), 212; and Louis Auguste Blanqui, "Oath of Membership into the Société des Saisons," in Paul E. Corcoran, ed., *Before Marx: Socialism and Communism in France, 1830–48* (New York: St. Martin's Press, 1983), 35.

[24] Babeuf, "Le Manifeste des plébéiens," in *Textes Choisis*, 208–210, 213–215; and Buonarroti, *Babeuf's Conspiracy for Equality*, 69–70.

[25] Sylvain Maréchal, "Manifesto of the Equals," in Fried and Sanders, *Socialist Thought*, 52, 53.

For Maréchal, equality was the final goal; it was not the final goal for Babeuf. The final goal was the "common welfare," meaning the "welfare of all," or the "happiness of all." Yet the principle of equalization, or leveling from the top down, was no ordinary means to this end. It was both the necessary and sufficient condition of the "welfare of the greatest number"— in opposition to institutions that would "place the burden of toil upon the greatest number." Relief from toil rather than self-cultivation was what Babeuf understood by welfare. Thus equality became the guarantee of the happiness of the greatest number as opposed to the happiness of a privileged few. Even the "equal distribution of knowledge" was presented as mainly defensive—as protection against the abuse of knowledge when unequally distributed.[26]

Because of its narrow preoccupation with economic and political matters, as if these were ends in themselves instead of means to a fuller life, Babeuf's doctrine was periodically reviled as antihuman and antihumanistic. According to the political economists whose bible was Adam Smith's *Wealth of Nations*, the multiplication and satisfaction of human needs encouraged by economic development in turn encouraged economic development. Greater wealth and its gradual diffusion spelled happiness; the abolition of private property and downward leveling spelled misery. As both a companion in arms and the principal disseminator of Babeuf's doctrine, Buonarroti disputed this humanist credo.

For Buonarroti, love and fraternity are more important to individual and collective happiness than the wealth required for self-cultivation. Short of a fictitious postscarcity economy, the development of one's capacities and the satisfaction of one's desires are an excuse to enrich oneself. "Every development of our faculties is not necessarily progressive; and to see in this unlimited development the perfection of civilization seems to me to be an error." A little industry unites citizens, but a lot of wealth divides them and makes them hostile and unhappy. "Happiness is more in the moderation of desires…than in the multiplication of needs, the refinement of pleasures, and the satisfaction of truth, of…care about dress, good living, fashions, and luxuries."[27] But in this controversy Marx and Engels sided with the political economists.

Discredited by Engels as a rough set, the Egalitarians, a split-off from the Society of Seasons, aimed at "making the world a working-men's community, putting down every refinement of civilization, science, the fine

---

[26] Babeuf, "Babeuf's Defense," in Fried and Sanders, 58, 61–62, 67.
[27] Cited by Eisenstein, *The First Professional Revolutionist*, 107, 113.

arts, etc., as useless, dangerous, and aristocratic luxuries." A secret society, the Egalitarian Workers were disciples of Maréchal under the immediate influence of Théodore Dézamy's "Code of Community" (1842). They believed in "absolute equality; promising at the same time the fullest satisfaction of all moral, physical and intellectual needs." But they took humanism to be a consequence of egalitarianism rather than their first principle or goal.

The communism of Marx and Engels was of a different kind. The party of philosophical communists in Germany led by Dr. Karl Marx, Engels noted, was "unconnected in its *origins* with either French or English Communists...[and it arose] from that philosophy which, since the last fifty years, Germany has been so proud of."[28] It was eminently humanistic, but at the same time realistic. Thanks to Marx's "second essentially different communism...developing alongside that of the League," wrote Engels, "communism now no longer meant the concoction, by means of the imagination, of an ideal society as perfect as possible, but insight into the nature, the conditions, and the consequent general aims of the struggle waged by the proletariat." Prior to joining forces with this earlier communism, "we influenced the theoretical views of the most important members of the League by word of mouth, by letter, and through the press...until the inadequacy of the previous conception of communism...became more and more clear."[29]

---

[28] Marx and Engels, *Collected Works*, 3:397, 403–404. See also Eisenstein, *The First Professional Revolutionist*, 180. Here, as elsewhere, all italics in quotations are in the original.

[29] Engels, "On the History of the Communist League," in *Selected Works,* 2:344–345, 346–347.

2. Marx's Communist Correspondence Committees

> Marx and Engels launched a practical project to create a chain of international correspondence committees whose purpose was to give the industrial proletariat...the means for self-education.
>
> Maximilien Rubel and Margaret Manale,
> *Marx Without Myth* (1975)

> Marx described communism...as necessary for the sake not of equality but of the full self-actualization of the human essence—that is, for the sake of freedom...a process of liberating humankind from the domination of things...[by] conscious rational control over their natural environment and over their own social forces.
>
> Andrzej Walicki, *Marxism and the Leap to the Kingdom of Freedom* (1995)

At the age of twenty-four Marx entered political life as a liberal democratic journalist, a "champion of political democracy" and an "uncompromising democratic extremist."[1] That he became a convinced democrat and remained one throughout his life is amply documented in the Manifesto and his later writings. But to what extent was he a liberal and what bearing did this have on his communism?

Marx's first articles on politics were almost single-mindedly devoted to defending freedom of the press. Hundreds of pages were spent on it, including its liberal spin-offs aimed at demolishing the vestiges of political absolutism. In the course of these polemics, Marx attacked "pseudo-liberalism" and "cautious liberalism" for being unequal to the task, for not being radical enough, and for playing into the hands of the censors' "*most frightful terrorism...the jurisdiction of suspicions.*"[2] These "illiberal liberals" of the so-called "*liberal opposition...*have never come to know freedom of the press as a *vital need.*" By making it ancillary to other freedoms, they reduced it to a mere means. They feared its "*popular* character," and warned that it was the cause of "revolution." That was not Marx's brand of liberalism, for his was both popular and revolutionary.

---

[1] Draper, *Karl Marx's Theory of Revolution*, 1:31, 57.
[2] Marx and Engels, *Collected Works*, 1:110, 115, 119, 137, 143, 173–174.

There is nothing wrong with liberalism, according to Engels, except for its practitioners. As he summed up his criticism of illiberal liberals in England, if not Germany, the so-called rights of the citizen to freedom of the press, association, habeas corpus, and trial by jury were a living fraud in pretending to equality under the law, while showing "favoritism towards the rich." In England hypocrisy reigns supreme, since "everywhere theory and practice [are] in flagrant contradiction with each other." Civil liberties boil down to "an outward show," with a legal foundation that the state periodically violates. If one can really say that he is free, the "Englishman is not free on account of the law but despite the law." The entire English constitution, the "whole of constitutional public opinion is nothing but a big lie which is constantly supported and concealed by a number of smaller lies." Short of full democracy, Engels concluded, liberalism is a sham. But "democracy itself is not capable of curing social ills...[without] the principle of socialism." "Democracy has become the proletarian principle," precisely because "*Democracy nowadays is communism.*"[3]

Where is one to find a more passionate and audacious defense of liberalism than that of the young Marx and Engels? They were not just fervent democrats, but also flaming liberals, with only one exception—their rejection of the bourgeois right to property and its corollary, free buying and selling.

Two Questions

Marx became a politically influential figure in the nineteenth century because of his journalistic efforts in defense of freedom and democracy combined with his organizing activities on behalf of the proletariat. It was the spread of his ideas through the Communist Correspondence Committees and then the Communist League that paved the way toward the founding of the International Working Men's Association (First International) and the united Social-Democratic Workers' Party of Germany during his lifetime, followed by the Socialist International (Second International) while Engels was still alive. Although Marx was an outstanding propagandist in his own right—the 1848 Manifesto testifies to that—the dissemination of Marxism would have been gravely hampered without the workers' organizations he founded.

---

[3]   Ibid., 3:504–513; and 6:5.

Early in 1846 Marx launched his first political party, a chain of Communist Correspondence Committees whose purpose was to acquaint workers with communist and socialist ideas and activities on an international scale. The first of these committees was that in Brussels. In a discussion of political propaganda at a meeting of the Brussels committee on March 30, Marx launched an attack on Weitling's communism and called for a purge of Weitling's supporters.

Weitling attended the meeting. In a letter to Moses Hess (31 March 1846), he quoted Marx as saying: "As yet there can be no talk of realizing communism; the bourgeoisie must first assume the helm." According to a report by a Russian observer at the meeting, Marx said that to rouse the workers to action without a constructive and scientific theory to guide them "assumes an inspired prophet on the one hand and only gaping asses on the other."[4]

Stung by these remarks, Weitling replied that the "advocates of revolutionary theory were armchair scholars, out of touch with life, doctrinaires indifferent to the people's suffering." But Marx got his way in purging his Correspondence Committees of sectarian communists. Although Weitling had more followers than Marx among Swiss and French Communists, Marx's liberal line was supported not only by Communists in Belgium and Germany, but also by the London leaders of the League of the Just.[5]

The Brussels Committee steered a middle course between Weitling's class struggle line detached from humanism and Karl Grün's philosophical humanism detached from class struggle, so-called True Socialism committed to universal human values. Against Weitling's instant communism it urged German Communists to "sign and push forward bourgeois petitions for freedom of the press, a constitution, and so on...[to] support everything which helps toward progress." Against Grün's appeals to all reasonable persons regardless of class, it urged French Communists to struggle *against* instead of *with* the bourgeoisie![6]

"True Socialism" had more followers in Germany than Marx and Weitling combined. Marx, however, succeeded in also expelling its followers from his Correspondence Committees. As Engels noted in his third

---

[4] Cited by Maximilien Rubel and Margaret Manale, *Marx Without Myth: A Chronological Study of His Life and Work* (New York: Harper, 1976), 58–59.

[5] Fedoseyev et al., *Karl Marx*, 111–112. For a first-hand report of the proceedings of the meeting, see Pavel Annenkov's 1880 "Memoires," Institute of Marxism-Leninism, ed., *Reminiscences of Marx and Engels* (Moscow: Foreign Languages Publishing House, 1957), 270–272.

[6] Marx and Engels, *Collected Works*, 6:56, 667 n.44.

letter from Paris to the Brussels Committee (23 October 1846), the chief point in his polemics against the "True Socialists" was "to prove the necessity for revolution by force and in general to demonstrate that Grün's true socialism…was anti-proletarian," to demonstrate that "community of goods *ruled out* peaceableness, tenderness, or consideration for the bourgeoisie." Thus Engels summed up the aims of the Correspondence Committees in opposition to "True Socialism": (1) "To achieve the interests of the proletariat in opposition to those of the bourgeoisie"; (2) "to do this through the abolition of private property and its replacement by community of goods"; and (3) "to recognize no means of carrying out these objectives other than a democratic revolution by force."[7]

That is how Engels defined communism in his polemic with the Grünians, but it was admittedly a highly simplified definition that hardly did justice to Marx's philosophical humanism. To counter the Grünians' preoccupation with the "good of mankind," Engels deliberately stressed the class content of Marx's communism. That is not to say that Marx was disinterested in universal human values. The thorny question was how to bring them about, the issue on which Marx and the Grünians parted company.

The communism of the Correspondence Committees had its origins in the young Marx's unique responses to two questions: the so-called social question and the much less controversial "human question." The Weitlingians underscored the first question, while the Grünians had eyes mainly for the second. Marx's claim to originality was to give equal weight to both questions, with the result that his communism differed from theirs in being not unidimensional, but multidimensional. That is the generous way of putting it. Less generously, Marx's was a communism with divided loyalties.

Marx's dual focus on the "social" and "human" questions dates from his August 1835 essay, "Reflections of a Young Man on the Choice of a Profession." The chief guide to such a choice, he proclaimed, is "the welfare of mankind and our own perfection," collective as well as individual well-being. "It should not be thought that these two interests could be in conflict, that one would have to destroy the other; on the contrary, man's nature is so constituted that he can attain his own perfection only by working for the perfection, for the good, of his fellow men." The prize held out by both is happiness. For "experience acclaims as happiest the man who has made the greatest number of people happy." Such was Marx's composite ideal of the hero "ennobled…by working for the common good," who finds happiness

---

[7]   Marx and Engels, *Selected Correspondence*, 36–37.

because he has "sacrificed himself for the sake of mankind." As he confessed in a Gymnasium examination that same August, the "love for Christ is not barren, it...causes us to keep His commandments by sacrificing ourselves for one another."[8]

His 1841 doctoral dissertation, on the "Difference Between the Democritean and Epicurean Philosophy of Nature," presents these youthful reflections in a different key unalloyed with the evangelical Christianity he had since outgrown. Having replaced Christ with Epicurus in his pantheon of sages, he takes practical wisdom for a guide. Such is the knowledge necessary to personal freedom, to control over one's environment as the means, and to peace of mind as the goal. In no uncertain terms, Marx acknowledges not sacrifice for others but "human self-consciousness as the highest divinity." We are constantly reminded, he wrote, that "the desire of being is the oldest love...the love of self, the love of one's particular being."[9]

But did Marx's replacement of the "consciousness of sin" with the philosophical celebration of "self-consciousness" mean that he no longer believed that the happiness of each is inextricably tied to the happiness of all? On the contrary, he would remain convinced of their compatibility throughout his adult life.

In January 1843 Marx wrote a series of articles on the distress of the Moselle vine-growers in the neighborhood of his birthplace Trier. His first published essay on the social question, it underscored the "*ruthless* voice of want," the "cry of distress of the vine-growers" that the authorities regarded as "*insolent shrieking*." He returned to the theme of distress in an August 1844 essay on the uprising of the Silesian weavers, victims of increasing pauperism. There can be no alleviation of widespread distress, he argued, without a social revolution. Public charity and administrative reforms are not the answer. "Nothing less [is required] than the abolition of the *proletariat*...the *overthrow* of the existing powers and *dissolution* of the old relationships." A change in the form of ownership is their precondition. Thus Marx concluded that the only real solution to the social question is socialism, but "socialism cannot be realized without a revolution."[10]

What had prompted this concern for a radical solution to the social question? Marx's early experiences and education provide a clue. In the Trier region, reports of increasing hunger and poverty marked the entire three decades from his birth in 1818 to the revolution of 1848. The director

---

[8]　Marx and Engels, *Collected Works*, 1:8–9, 638.
[9]　Ibid., 1:30, 45, 51, 72, 75–76.
[10]　Ibid., 1:332, 337; and 3:196, 206.

of the Gymnasium he attended drew on Rousseau, Kant, and the tradition of Christian morality in response to the distress, arguing that "our duty to humanity never ends." Ludwig Gall, a local official influenced by the philosophy of Henri Comte de Saint-Simon (1760–1825), also addressed the problem of helping the poor as did Marx's future father-in-law under the spell of the Saint-Simonian school. So it is not surprising that Marx's first political utterances "addressed exactly the political and social issues that agitated his native town while he was growing up."[11]

Together these youthful reflections and Marx's study of philosophy and history "engendered his protest against the prevailing social system and his determination to serve the cause of what Saint-Simon called 'la classe le plus nombreuse et la plus misérable.'"[12] It was only later that he turned to political economy in order to support his solution to the social question with scientific arguments, a solution he first identified with "socialism" and then with "communism."

The young Engels also highlighted the need for a solution to the social question. Unlike political patch-up remedies, "the future social revolution will deal with the real causes of want and poverty, of ignorance and crime…it will therefore carry through a real social reform." He defined social revolution as "the open war of the poor against the rich"; and he took the real cause of the social question to be threefold: the division of society into rich and poor, the expansion of poverty in the face of plenty, and the unsupportable tensions resulting from this state of affairs. In such general terms the social question was also posed by his and Marx's predecessors.[13]

Marx and Engels' focus on the social question was not a passing fancy. But with their formulation of the materialist-economic interpretation of history in 1845–1846, they reinterpreted it as a class struggle of the proletariat against the bourgeoisie rather than a war of the poor against the rich. A literary representative of republican ideals, Karl Heinzen objected to Marx's formulation for attaching too much importance to economic matters. "You are trying to make *social questions* the central concern of our age," he

---

[11] Jerrold Seigel, *Marx's Fate: The Shape of a Life* (Princeton: Princeton University Press, 1978), 40–41, 43.

[12] Rubel and Manale, *Marx Without Myth*, x-xi; and Henri Comte de Saint-Simon, "New Christianity" (1825), *Selected Writings*, ed. and trans. F. M. H. Markham (Oxford: Blackwell, 1952), 83, 87, 94, 99–100. On the impact of Saint-Simon's writings on the young Marx, see Draper, *Karl Marx's Theory of Revolution*, 4:2, 3–5.

[13] Marx and Engels, *Collected Works*, 4:262–264; and Corcoran, *Before Marx: Socialism and Communism in France 1830–1848* (New York: St. Martin's Press, 1983), 4–5.

complained, but "you fail to see that there is *no more important social question* than that of *monarchy* or *republic.*"[14]

To this criticism Marx responded that the replacement of rule by princes with republican government "did not mean that even a single 'social question' has been solved in the interests of the proletariat," and that a communist formulation of the social question becomes increasingly relevant once the republican question finds its historical solution in the abolition of monarchy. The more advanced a society, the more glaringly does the communist version of the social question acquire "world-historical significance." In the seventeenth and eighteenth centuries "the point at issue was the abolition of feudal property relations," but in the nineteenth century "it is a matter of abolishing bourgeois property relations." The question of property had become not only a vital question for the proletariat, but also "the most important 'social question.'"[15]

Yet even more important was the human question to which it was closely related. In his 1835 essay on choosing a profession Marx wrote that God gave each man "a general aim...[to] uplift himself and society." To uplift oneself and others implies something more than to redeem the poor and save workers from the scourge of exploitation. The issue was "not that *their* emancipation alone was at stake but...[that] the emancipation of the workers contains universal *human* emancipation." In this perspective, socialism has for its final goal not the overcoming of social distress but rather the "enrichment of human nature." Ideally, it would raise everybody to the status of gods. As the young Hegel anticipated the outcome of human emancipation: "Then for the first time we can expect the *equal* cultivation of *all* abilities, both of single individuals and of all individuals."[16]

In a letter to Arnold Ruge (September 1843), Marx dismissed the communism taught by Weitling and the League of the Just as a "dogmatic abstraction...[as] only a special expression of the humanistic principle...[and] only a special one-sided realization of the socialist principle." Socialism in turn was said to be "only one aspect that concerns the *reality* of the true human being."[17] In other words, communism is a narrow-minded expression of socialism, which is in turn a narrow-minded adaptation of the principle that ranks the emancipation of humanity above all other goals.

---

[14] Marx and Engels, *Collected Works*, 6:321.
[15] Ibid., 6:322–324.
[16] Ibid., 1:3, 3:280, 300; and Seigel, *Marx's Fate*, 23.
[17] Marx and Engels, *Collected Works*, 3:143.

Overcoming Self-Alienation

By the emancipation of humanity Marx understood the unmasking and
overcoming of self-alienation. As he described the new task of philosophy
once the gods have been dethroned, we "merely show to the world what it is
really fighting for"—happiness on earth not as it is in heaven. "Hence our
motto must be: reform of consciousness...self-clarification." By that Marx
meant that, having unmasked self-estrangement in its holy forms, the
"immediate *task of philosophy*, which is in the service of history...is to
unmask self-estrangement in its unholy forms." Thus the criticism of the
otherworld turns into a criticism of this world, into a critique of secular
ideologies ensconced in law, ethics, politics, and economics.[18]

Marx arrived at this position through immersing himself in the writings
of Hegel's most prominent successor, the philosopher Ludwig Feuerbach
(1804–1872). While G. W. F. Hegel (1770–1831) was the undisputed voice
of German philosophy during the period from 1820 to 1840, Feuerbach was
its disputatious voice during the decade that followed. It was Feuerbach, not
Marx, who first turned Hegel on his head with the thesis that it is not the
consciousness of men that determines their being, but their being that
determines their consciousness. "Philosophy is the knowledge of *what
exists*," wrote Feuerbach in his 1842 "Theses on the Reform of Philosophy."
"To think and know things...*as they are* is the...highest task of philosophy."
"Materialism" (naturalism) was one name he gave to this philosophy;
"humanism" was another.[19]

That Marx owed a major debt to Feuerbach is evident from his defense
of Feuerbach's "real humanism" in his *Economic and Philosophic
Manuscripts of 1844*. In the preface he notes that the critique of political
economy has as its foundation the philosophy of Feuerbach. To this
encomium he adds that "It is only with *Feuerbach* that *positive*, humanistic
and naturalistic criticism begins...a real theoretical revolution." In a letter to
Feuerbach (11 August 1844), he says "Your works have provided—I don't
know whether intentionally—a philosophical basis for socialism and the
Communists have immediately understood them in this way."

But Feuerbach's humanism was still mainly theoretical rather than
practical. So one year later we find Marx breaking with his mentor over two
basic issues: first, Feuerbach's reliance on the physical and biological

---

[18]   Ibid., 3:144–145, 176, 186.
[19]   Cited by Seigel, *Marx's Fate*, 98, 99.

sciences instead of human history as the basis of social criticism; second, Feuerbach's preference for the weapons of criticism instead of the criticism of weapons as the decisive means of changing the world.[20]

Besides Feuerbach's focus on knowing the world for man's sake, Marx was concerned with both knowing and transforming it in the interests of the submerged proletariat. Starting from Feuerbach's humanism that was static and contemplative, Marx's humanism became dynamic and revolutionary. Humanism, or "the *emancipation of the human being*," he argued, cannot be realized without abolishing the proletariat as a class, without establishing a classless society. As he noted in a critique of Feuerbach's reform of consciousness for not going far enough, "philosophers have only interpreted the world in various ways; the point...is to change it."[21]

Human emancipation for Marx depends on the emancipation of the proletariat. So the practical question is to understand and overcome the self-alienation of workers in particular, not just humanity in general. Communism too had to be unmasked and transcended as a particular expression of self-alienation, that of the "*preconceived minimum.*" By this Marx understood the "abstract negation of the entire world of culture and civilization [Weitling], the regression to the *unnatural* simplicity of the *poor* and crude man who has few needs." The proletarian is emancipated only by becoming a "*rich* man *profoundly endowed with all the senses.*" This "enrichment of *human* nature" is possible only through the "multiplication of needs and of the means" of satisfying them. This revised and transformed communism equals humanism. It would become the task of the Correspondence Committees to liberate man's "essential powers," this "richness of man's essential being," by putting philosophy into practice.[22]

The liberation of man's essential powers, according to Marx, would have to take place gradually. In general, "people cannot be liberated as long as they are unable to find food and drink, housing and clothing in adequate quality and quantity." But once these basics are provided, the next step is to break free of the division of labor, the stunting of human growth and personal freedom because "each man has a particular, exclusive sphere of activity, which is forced upon him and from which he cannot escape." Communist society would put an end to this social arrangement in which man is a mere cog in a machine that blocks his free development and

---

[20] Marx and Engels, *Collected Works*, 3:232, 354; and 5:3–5. See Sidney Hook, *From Marx to Hegel: Studies in the Intellectual Development of Karl Marx* (New York: Humanities Press, 1958; orig. pub. 1936), 272.
[21] Marx and Engels, *Collected Works*, 3:187; and 5:8.
[22] Ibid., 3:295, 296, 301–302, 306, 308.

reduces him to a dwarf. Thus, "in communist society, where nobody has one exclusive sphere of activity but each can become accomplished in any branch he wishes, society...makes it possible for him to do one thing today and another tomorrow, to hunt in the morning, fish in the afternoon, rear cattle in the evening, criticize after dinner, just as I have a mind, without ever being hunter, fisherman, shepherd, or critic"![23]

These examples reveal one of the unsavory features of Marx and Engels' humanism that has escaped the critic's eye. The underside of their idyllic picture of the future is the cold-blooded, large-scale slaughtering of animals aimed at whetting the palates of the proletariat in imitation of the diet of the successful bourgeois. Such is the butcher's reality underlying the bucolic activities of *hunter, fisherman, shepherd*. As Saint-Simon wrote approvingly of the condition of the English working class in 1803, "Everybody in England knows how to read, write, and add [knows how to criticize, and]...workers in the towns and even in the country eat meat every day."[24]

Nothing, Marx and Engels believed, is too good for a member of the working class who should have the means to develop his particular talents. What they failed to clarify was that to have a well-rounded education and freedom to work as one pleases is an idyllic picture that harkens back to the Renaissance and its "Mirrors for Princes." Castiglione set forth his model of the complete man in *The Book of the Courtier*. In the same vein *Peacham's Compleat Gentleman* stressed the gentleman's list of accomplishments, his familiarity with the classics, his knowledge of music and of musical instruments.[25] Such is the logical consequence of a humanist credo when pushed to extremes. But even a moderate version of it, such as that of Marx and Engels, suggests a utopia when applied to humankind.

Marx and Engels were too wedded to Feuerbach's humanism to sacrifice their philosophical basis of communism to the narrow-minded outlook of Weitling and company.[26] Following Feuerbach's critique of religious descriptions of God as veiled accounts of man's essential being, Marx concluded that only man exists to be worshipped. "Man is seen to have adored his own nature," wrote Feuerbach.[27] So why not adore it without the ghostly excuse of religion?

---

[23] Ibid., 5:38, 47.
[24] Saint-Simon, "Letter from an Inhabitant of Geneva" (1803), *Selected Writings*, 5–6.
[25] Castiglione, *The Book of the Courtier*, 41; and Henry Peacham, *Peacham's Compleat Gentleman*, 2.
[26] Marx and Engels, *Collected Works*, 3:232.
[27] Ludwig Feuerbach, *The Essence of Christianity*, trans. Marian Evans from the 2nd German ed. (London, 1893; orig. pub. 1841), 13.

If Marx had a blind spot, it was his failure to perceive that the highest form of greed consists in self-cultivation, that one man is knowledgeable because others are ignorant. The supreme act of selfishness is not storing up worldly goods that "moth and dust doth corrupt, and where thieves break through and steal" (Matt. 6:19). It consists of accumulating the fruits of human culture that exalt the spirit without end, that dispel fear and ignorance, that bestow peace of mind. The human brain is an unassailable storehouse of such treasures with no rival worth speaking of. But it takes leisure to acquire them; and in this world of scarcity the more leisure anyone has, the less will be available to others. Although in principle accessible to all through public libraries, museums, art galleries, and concert halls, an exceptional dose of education is required to absorb them in full, and private as well as public servants in addition to family members to perform the chores. What is this, if not the "Avarice" Morelly warned against?

It is noteworthy that the young Marx expressed little support for workers' communism except to note that it was an *"important question of the time."* Accused by critics of presenting communism to the public in all its *"unwashed* nakedness," he assured his readers that to draw attention to communism did not mean he recommended it. He advised only that it be studied, so that it might be criticized intelligently and not condemned out of hand. As he wrote in the newspaper he edited, "The *Rheinische Zeitung*...does not admit that communist ideas in their present form possess even *theoretical reality*, and therefore can still less desire their *practical realization.*" The danger of communism, he concluded, does not reside in street mobs and mass demonstrations that can be answered with cannon. The "real *danger* lies...in the *theoretical elaboration* of communist ideas...which have conquered our intellect and taken possession of our minds."[28]

By 1844 Marx had completed his studies of French and German communism. But he had yet to find anything of theoretical substance in the French and German communist parties, which consisted mainly of workers. He characterized their horny-handed communism as "crude," narrowly "political," and fundamentally "negative." What he tentatively called *"positive"* communism, or the "real *appropriation* of the *human essence* by and for man," he identified with "humanism." "Socialism" was still his preferred term for this atypical communism rooted in German philosophy. As he concluded his discussion of communism in his 1844 *Manuscripts*, "socialism is man's *positive self-consciousness*...no longer mediated

---

[28] Marx and Engels, *Collected Works*, 1:220–221.

through the abolition of private property, through *communism*." Although
communism is the dynamic principle of the future and the "actual phase
necessary to the next stage of historical development...communism as such
is not the goal of human development."[29]

In a two-part essay, "Progress of Social Reform on the Continent,"
published in Robert Owen's *The New Moral World* (November 1843),
Engels had also chosen the word "socialism" rather than "communism" as
the most fitting description of his own response to the social question. He
objected to post-1836 French Communists because of their egalitarianism
aimed at leveling downward instead of upward and attributed this prejudice
to "their total ignorance of history and political economy." He objected to
the tracing of their origins to primitive Christianity, to their organization into
secret societies, and to their reliance on force to achieve their goal, though
he subsequently changed his mind on this last point. As for their German
counterparts, they made the same mistake as the French in claiming that
"Christianity is communism."[30]

German Philosophical Communism

Unlike France, Engels noted, Germany boasts of another party that
advocates communism on philosophical rather than political or religious
grounds. In contrast to German workers' communism, it is a philosophical
party among the educated classes of society "unconnected in its origins with
either French or English Communists." He included Marx among the leaders
of this new party whose major task would be to "prove that either all the
philosophical efforts of the German nation, from Kant to Hegel, have been
useless...or, that they must end in Communism."[31]

The young Engels made a special effort to convince his English audience
that Marx's philosophical communism had the support of respectable as well
as thinking people in Germany. It will appear very singular to Englishmen,
he wrote, "that a party which aims at the destruction of private property is
chiefly made up by those who have property...[and are recruited] from those
classes only which have enjoyed a pretty good education." As he added in a
subsequent essay published in the same journal in February 1844, the
"'learned Communists' of Germany" are supported not by French
Communists but by the most distinguished Socialist authors of France.

---

[29] Ibid., 3:294–296, 306.
[30] Ibid., 3:397–399, 403.
[31] Ibid., 3:403–406.

Although he traced the origins of communism and socialism to widespread misery at the time, "French and German working-class Communism are its direct [products]...and English Socialism, as well as the Communism of the German educated bourgeoisie, are its indirect products."[32]

The unique contribution of German philosophical communism and English socialism was to unite theory and practice by bringing theory to the modern proletariat. It thereby bridged the gap between a socialism that was initially philosophical but later scientific, and a communism that was markedly working class. As a result, workers' communism became socialist, in the sense of learned and theoretical, while philosophical socialism metamorphosed into "mass-type socialism and communism." Since socialism was distinguished by its theoretical response to the social question, and communism by its practical response, they evidently needed each other. Wrote Engels in 1845, "Communism is a question of humanity and not of the workers alone." Even the bourgeoisie stands to benefit from a communist solution to the "open, declared war of the poor against the rich."[33]

From having initially identified themselves as Socialists, Marx and Engels identified themselves as Communists in 1845 because in Germany "Socialism means nothing but the different vague, undefined, and undefinable imaginations of those who see that something must be done and who yet cannot make up their minds to go the whole length of the community system." Unlike the English Socialists or Chartists who had opted for communism, German Socialists were still wedded to an abstract humanism with little bearing on the labor movement. In England the terms "socialist" and "communist" were interchangeable, so that it didn't matter which term one used. That was because the "English Socialists are far more ...practical than the French," and because "their communist propositions are supported by proof based on facts." As an example of their practical outlook, Engels noted their exposition of communist principles in penny and twopenny pamphlets, their Communist Hall in Manchester that seated as many as three thousand people on Sundays, and their communist community of some eight thousand in Manchester.[34]

There were three routes to communism for Marx and Engels. Engels first pointed them out in his article "Progress of Social Reform on the Continent," in *The New Moral World* (November 1843). French Socialists became Communists on *political* grounds "by first asking for political liberty and

---

[32] Ibid., 3:407, 416; and 4:302.
[33] Ibid., 4:53, 582–583.
[34] Ibid., 4:241; and 3:385, 387.

equality; and, finding these insufficient, joining social liberty and equality to these political claims." German Socialists became Communists on *philosophical* grounds "by reasoning upon first principles," by reflecting on the nature of the human condition and human self-alienation. Meanwhile, English Socialists became Communists on *economic* grounds by examining the consequences of the Industrial Revolution and the spread of the factory system, "the rapid rise of misery, demoralization, and pauperism."[35]

In his *Economic and Philosophic Manuscripts*, Marx reaffirmed these differences between French, German, and English Communists. In France, Marx noted, "Equality is the *basis* of communism...its *political* justification." In Germany, where the principal form of estrangement takes the form of self-alienation, the basis of communism is self-awareness; it finds its *philosophical* justification in Feuerbach's "positive, humanistic, and naturalistic criticism." As for English Communists, they have an *economic* justification of communism based on "real, material, *practical* need taking only itself as its standard." That Marx's party called itself "Communist" did not mean that it traveled the same road as the English and French Communists. What distinguished it was that communism was not its goal, but a means only.[36]

What accounts for Marx and Engels' disdain for French "political" communism and their partiality for English "practical" communism? What made them "agree much more with the English Socialists than with any other party"? Although German Communists first learned about communism from their French brothers, "we soon found out that we knew more than our teachers." Meanwhile, "we shall have to learn a great deal yet from the English Socialists...[since] in everything bearing upon practice, upon the *facts* of the present state of society, we find that the English Socialists are a long way before [ahead of] us."[37]

Not only did the Chartists have a keen understanding of the social question, wrote Engels in 1845, but "most of the Chartist leaders are...already Communists." Although that was an overstatement, the Chartist left wing was led by Julian Harney and Ernest Jones, both future members of the Communist League. Not for nothing did Engels attend Chartist meetings, serve as foreign correspondent of the Chartist weekly *Northern Star* from 1843 to 1848, and describe himself as a "CHARTIST AGENT."[38]

---

[35] Ibid., 3:392–393. See also 3:429, 431, 442–443.
[36] Ibid., 3:232, 312–313.
[37] Ibid., 3:407.
[38] Ibid., 4:582; and 38:133; original emphasis.

Marx and Engels' ranking of alternative communisms should put an end to the contention by an influential school of Marxologists that from the beginning of 1844 until the end of 1850, "their revolutionary tactics were primarily influenced by the tradition of Babeuf, Buonarroti, and Blanqui"— not just a strategy but a "theory already at hand...a tradition of revolutionary socialism that was nearly fifty years old when Marx encountered it in Paris"![39] On the contrary, the Correspondence Committees constituted the only instance in Marx's political life in which he did not make concessions to rival communist, socialist, and working-class movements.

In the early 1840s, Marx and Engels defined themselves as "socialists" as well as "communists." As late as March 1845, Marx penned for future reference a "Plan of the 'Library of the Best Foreign Socialist Writers.'" It called for a series of German translations from English and French socialists and communists, Buonarroti's classic among others.[40] The "Plan" is noteworthy for using the term "socialist" so broadly that it included not only communists, but also the French materialists who had influenced them.

Marx's rationale for classifying the materialists Holbach and Helvétius as "socialists" was that "communism...derives *directly* from French *materialism*," not only French communism, but also German and English. Thus "*Bentham* based his system of *correctly understood interest* on Helvétius' morality, and *Owen* proceeded from *Bentham's* system to found English communism." As Engels noted at the time, Bentham's writings are "almost exclusively the property of the proletariat; for though Bentham has a school within the radical bourgeoisie, it is only the proletariat and the Socialists who have succeeded in developing his teachings a step forward."[41]

From Philosophical to Scientific Communism

The German Ideology marks a turning point in Marx and Engels' rethinking of "communism" as a function of what is historically consequential and not just politically desirable. This change in perspective was a logical consequence of their adoption of a new conceptual framework, the materialist-economic interpretation of history. Along the lines of their

---

[39] Stanley Moore, *Three Tactics: The Background in Marx* (New York: Monthly Review Press, 1963), 16, 22. See Draper's devastating attack with heavy artillery against this Marx-Blanquist myth, in *Karl Marx's Theory of Revolution*, 2:591–612; and 3:34–39, 120–171, 337–359.

[40] Marx and Engels, *Collected Works*, 4:667, 697 n.89, 719 n.242.

[41] Ibid., 4:131, 528.

explanation of the change from feudalism to capitalism in England, the authors predicted a transition from capitalism to socialism brought about by objective economic processes independent of the actions of political parties.[42] Here was Marx's scientific basis for redeeming the workers from their condition of social misery and distress. The Communist Correspondence Committees were launched for the purpose of disseminating this new theory.

Communism and socialism would henceforth acquire different meanings in connection with their social origins in different classes. As Engels noted in retrospect, the historical materialist outlook could now explain what hitherto had been only a difference in ideologies. Henceforth, communism "no longer meant the concoction, by means of the imagination, of an ideal society as perfect as possible, but insight into the nature, the conditions, and the consequent general aims of the struggle waged by the proletariat."[43] Communism among the French and Germans, Chartism among the English, no longer appeared as phenomena that could just as well not have happened.

For the first time in *The German Ideology* (1845–1846), Marx and Engels clearly defined themselves as communists instead of socialists. In Germany, socialism was looked upon as the most reasonable social order, as an ideal to be imposed on the rest of humanity. In their attempt to detach communist ideas from the real movement of the workers, and "to reconcile communism with the ideas prevailing at the time," socialists failed to make a radical rupture with existing society.[44] In sharp contrast, "Communism is for us not a *state of affairs* which is to be established, an *ideal* to which reality [will] have to adjust itself. We call communism the *real* movement which abolishes the present state of things." It is a movement of proletarians created by large-scale industry, and "differs from all previous movements in that it overturns the basis of all earlier relations of production."[45]

Marx and Engels no longer defined themselves as socialists, because German socialism was a philosophical doctrine blind to economic realities and lacking a sense of history. "True socialism is a perfect example of a social literary movement that has come into being without any real party interests and now, after the formation of the communist party [Communist Correspondence Committees], it intends to persist in spite of it." Consequently, "since the appearance of a real communist party in Germany,

[42] Ibid., 5:35–89.
[43] Engels, "On the History of the Communist League," *Selected Works*, 2:344–345.
[44] Marx and Engels, *Collected Works*, 5:455–457.
[45] Ibid., 5:49, 81.

the public of the true socialists will be more and more limited to the petty bourgeoisie and the sterile literati who represent it."[46]

But in defining themselves as Communists, Marx and Engels disputed the sectarian views of French workers' communism and of Weitling's "real communists." Marx and Engels believed that "each new class which puts itself in the place of the one ruling before it is compelled...to present its interests as the common interest," and that "initially its interest really is...connected with the common interest." In sharp contrast, Babeuf, Buonarroti, and their followers viewed history as a story of unrelieved theft and usurpation, and flatly denied that the interest of an exploiting class could ever correspond to the general interest. This accounts for their combined hatred of modernity, humanism, liberalism, and democracy, for their repudiation of all alliances with the "progressive" bourgeoisie, and for their unqualified rejection of modern bourgeois society. As one astute commentator sums up Marx's differences with the egalitarian communism of Weitling and the League of the Just, "Marx was an early advocate of bourgeois institutions and never discarded liberal values...Marx was considered a moderate and was suspected of bourgeois tendencies."[47]

Marx's response to this and similar accusations was that the different forms of communism "have as their real content the needs of the time in which they arose." They are to be defined by those needs, not by their ideal expression in the form of doctrine. "The assertion that all systems are dogmatic...gets us nowhere with regard to this basis and this content of the communist systems." On examination, one finds that they are expressions either of different working classes or of the same working class at different stages of its development. "Unlike the English and the French, the Germans did not encounter fully developed class relations.... It is, therefore, perfectly natural that the only existing German communist system [prior to the Correspondence Committees] should be a reproduction of French ideas in terms of a mental outlook...limited by the petty circumstances of the artisan."[48]

The earlier unscientific communism of the League of the Just was accordingly superseded by Marx and Engels' philosophical socialism and then by a communism they believed to be scientific. Even so, Marx's philosophical socialism was not so much eclipsed as it was compounded by

---

[46] Ibid., 5:457.
[47] Ibid., 5:60–61; Babeuf, "Babeuf's Defense," in Fried and Sanders, 66; and Steven Seidman, *Liberalism and the Origins of European Social Theory* (Berkeley/Los Angeles: University of California Press, 1983), 104, 328 n.13.
[48] Marx and Engels, *Collected Works*, 5:462.

new accretions. In effect, he grafted a materialist interpretation of history onto his earlier socialist humanism to constitute what Engels would subsequently label "scientific socialism." Such was the contribution of the Communist Correspondence Committees to the nascent Communist League.

3. A Marriage of Incompatibles?

At the beginning there were two independent movements. On the one hand, a pure workers' movement, deriving from French Communist workers: the utopian communism of Weitling represents a stage of its development. On the other hand, a theoretical movement, resulting from the dissolution of Hegel's philosophy: this group was dominated from the very first by Marx. The *Communist Manifesto* of January 1848 represents the unification of the two movements, a unification completed in the struggles of the [1848] revolution.

Frederick Engels, *Socialism in Germany* (1891)

Marx's task was to reconcile the irreconcilable.

Henry Collins and C. Abramsky, *Karl Marx and the
British Labour Movement* (1965)

The Manifesto was the political credo of the Communist League (1847–1852). It was the intellectual product of the fusion of the League of the Just, whose origins dated from 1836, and Karl Marx and Frederick Engels' Communist Correspondence Committees, founded in 1846. The first was the party of German workers' communism, the second of German philosophical communism. While the League of the Just provided the bulk of the members of the new organization, the Committees of Correspondence provided the ideology. It was a marriage of convenience rather than a marriage of equals.

The confluence of these two parties signified the fulfillment of Marx's youthful dream that philosophy might find its material weapons in the proletariat, and the proletariat find its intellectual weapons in philosophy. This union of mainly German émigrés in London, Paris, and Brussels had for its goal the emancipation of the proletariat, but as a condition of the emancipation of humanity. "The *head* of this emancipation is *philosophy*," wrote Marx in 1844, "its *heart* is the *proletariat*."[1] With philosophy in the driver's seat, the proletariat became the steam engine of a prospective locomotive of revolution having universal humanism, free, all-round self-development as its ultimate goal.

Marx appropriated the name "communist" from the German and French workers' movement, first, because he favored a radical rupture with traditional ideas and property relations and, second, because communists

---

[1]   Marx and Engels, *Collected Works*, 3:187.

represented the only force in society with sufficient numbers and determination to abolish the old order and replace it with a new one. In principle, if not in fact, his rupture went far beyond that of his working-class allies. What they wanted was the abolition of private property and the advent of a community of goods. He envisioned a final solution not only to the "social question" but also to the "human question"—freedom for self-cultivation and the means thereto for all.

The irony and bizarre feature of this marriage was that Marx refused to level downward, to sacrifice the high tradition of European art and science for the sake of equality. Culturally, he was a conservative; politically, a liberal and a democrat. Only on economic issues did he share common ground with socialists and communists. Although humanism was not a stranger to the communist movement, it did not enjoy pride of place. Rather than a goal, it was deemed a consequence of proletarian emancipation. For Marx it was the end and communism the means. Because Marx refused to bow before the narrow economic demands of the proletarian vanguard, his first marriage of humanism and communism lasted only five years and ended in divorce.[2] If for no other reason, it is necessary to investigate the origins of the Manifesto in order to understand his later marriages, the self-destructive potential of Marxism, and its consequences for the Soviet Union.

Birth of the Communist League

In February 1847, the League of the Just invited Marx and Engels to assist in restructuring it from a sectarian and conspiratorial organization into a broadly based proletarian party. At issue was a merger with the Correspondence Committees, which prompted the League to announce in February that in France and Belgium, where the Correspondence Committees had replaced the League as centers of communist propaganda, "we have temporarily organized ourselves on new lines." Marx then informed his associates in Germany and other countries about his arrangements with the League's governing body and "invited them not only to join the League, but also to take an active part in reorganizing it."[3]

Marx planned to change the League's orientation from conspiracies aimed at overthrowing governments to propaganda aimed at preparing workers for revolution through the spread of communist ideas. Through the

---

[2] Ibid., 10:628–629.
[3] Cited by Fedoseyev et al., *Karl Marx*, 124–125, 127.

merger of the theoretically oriented Correspondence Committees and the practically focused League of the Just, he finally achieved the goal he had set for himself in 1843, that of making theory a material force assimilated by the masses, of joining the arm of criticism and the criticism of arms, and of using the intellectual weapons of philosophy to guide the material weapons of the proletariat.[4] Thanks to the merger, the Communist League became the embodiment of Marx's social and political philosophy, and the *Communist Manifesto* became its intellectual expression.

Although existing conditions precluded the League from operating above ground, Marx did everything possible to overcome its isolation and to establish a network of open and legal fronts in the form of workers' educational societies. "The League was either to establish contact with existing educational societies or set up new ones." On Marx and Engels' initiative, a German Workers' Society comprised mainly of émigrés was organized in Brussels in August. Patterned on the German Workers' Educational Society in London, it became a recruiting center for the reconstructed League. As testimony to its effectiveness, its "initial membership of 37 rose within a few months to almost 100, with Communist League members playing the leading part."[5]

The Communist League dates from its First Congress in London in June 1847. Although financial difficulties prevented Marx from attending, Engels took an active role in the course and substance of the proceedings. The "Communist Credo," or draft program of the new League, was written by Engels, who also helped in drafting a new set of rules.[6] He further succeeded in changing the League's name to the Communist League and in replacing its old motto, "All Men are Brothers," with "Working Men of All Countries, Unite!"

In drafting the new program, Engels had to consider that the members of the League had not yet freed themselves from the influence of utopian ideas. This accounts for the form he gave to the draft program, a confession of faith, and for the concessions to sentimental and utopian "workers' communism" in the first six questions and answers of his revolutionary catechism.[7] But he withdrew most of them in a second draft in October. With the support of the Paris branches of the League, the first six points were completely revised, some omitted altogether, others substantially changed and placed in a different order.

---

[4] Marx and Engels, *Collected Works*, 3:182, 187.
[5] Fedoseyev et al., *Karl Marx*, 127.
[6] Marx and Engels, *Collected Works*, 6:96, 585.
[7] Ibid., 6:671 n.69.

Notwithstanding the concessions, the June draft imposed the fundamental goal of Marx and Engels' philosophical humanism on the reorganized League. In answer to Question 2 on the aim of the communists, Engels replies: "To organize society in such a way that every member of it can develop and use all his capabilities and powers in complete freedom." This formulation, typical of his and Marx's early writings, challenged the League of the Just's focus on economic and political emancipation. It tells us that humanism is the final goal and communism only a means.

The June draft also contains a redefinition of communism that breaks with any attempt to trace its origins back to early Christianity. In answer to Question 13 concerning the feasibility of introducing community of property, Engels replies that it became feasible only as a result of the Industrial Revolution. "Communism has only arisen since machinery and other inventions made it possible to hold out the prospect of an all-sided development...for all members of society. Communism is the theory of a liberation which was not possible for the slaves, the serfs, or the handicraftsmen, but only for the proletarians and hence it belongs of necessity to the nineteenth century."[8]

How do Communists expect to achieve this aim of all-round human development? "By the elimination of private property and its replacement by community of property." Although the goal was an integral part of Marx's philosophical humanism, the method of achieving it was a concession to workers' communism. Taken at face-value, "elimination of private property" means the abolition of private property in the means of production *and* consumption; "community of property" means common ownership of everything! But that is hardly what Engels meant—his usage being other than straightforward.

Further concessions are evident in Engels' answers to Questions 4 and 5. Engels bases the struggle for a community of property not only on the level of economic development ushered in by the Industrial Revolution, but also on the "consciousness or feeling of every individual [that] there exist certain irrefutable basic principles which...require no proof." As an example he notes that every individual strives to be happy, adding that the happiness of each is inseparable from the happiness of all.[9] What have these platitudes to do with his and Marx's materialist-economic interpretation of history? Nothing at all!

---

[8]   Ibid., 6:99, 101.
[9]   Ibid., 6:96.

The expression "emancipation of humanity" in Article One of the June 1847 draft rules is another instance of Engels' boring from within. It harkens back to the humanist conclusion of his 1845 *Condition of the Working-Class in England* that "Communism is a question of humanity and not of the workers alone." It reaffirms Marx's distinction in his first major statement on humanism in the 1844 *Critique of Hegel's Philosophy of Law: Introduction*, that the emancipation of humanity goes beyond a *"merely* political revolution and should not be confused with "emancipation of society." The immediate task of philosophy, Marx wrote, is to bring about *"general human emancipation,"* the *"complete rewinning of man,"* the *"emancipation of the human being"* as the practical outcome of the teaching or theory that "man is the highest being for man" and of the *"categorical imperative to overthrow all relations* in which man is a debased, enslaved, forsaken, despicable being." This includes a lot, everything from overcoming man's estrangement from the object of his labor and his laboring activity to overcoming self-alienation and alienation from other human beings.[10]

As a result of the ensuing discussion over several months, Article One was changed from "The League aims at the emancipation of humanity by spreading the theory of community of property" to "The aim of the League is the overthrow of the bourgeoisie, the rule of the proletariat, the abolition of the old bourgeois society...and the formation of a new society without classes and without private property."[11] Thus in the revised rules adopted in December the emancipation of humanity gave way to the emancipation of the proletariat, a victory for Schapper and a defeat for Marx and Engels.

The League Divided

The discussions of the draft program and rules resulted in an ideological struggle within the League's branches in France, Belgium, Germany, and Switzerland. From June to September four main factions contended to get their revisions adopted. From Right to Left, they consisted of workers responsive to the True Socialism of Karl Grün, the supporters of Marx and Engels' socialist humanism predicated on class struggle, the Schapperites influenced by Marx and Engels' scientific socialism minus their humanism, and the Weitlingians who claimed to be the only "real communists."[12]

---

[10] Ibid., 4:582; and 3:176, 182, 184, 186, 187.
[11] Ibid., 6:585, 633.
[12] Ibid., 6:609–610, 709–710 n.346, 711 n.355.

At issue was a contest between rival socialist humanisms, between rival versions of workers' communism, and between workers' communism and socialist humanism. Under Feuerbach's influence, the True Socialists in the League opposed Marx's emphasis on the class struggle as inhuman.[13] Meanwhile, Weitling's followers went to the opposite extreme of questioning Marx's focus on the all-round development of human capacities. The Address of the Central Authority of the Communist League dated 14 September 1847 contained a quarterly report on these factional struggles that erupted after the First Congress.

After Marx and Engels agreed in January to help the old League reform itself, the Schapperites became Marx and Engels' allies. According to Schapper's account, Weitling's followers in Paris spent most of their time discussing questions raised in his 1842 *Guarantees of Harmony and Freedom*, until those who became bored with the discussions began looking elsewhere for enlightenment. Those fed up with Weitling's dogmatism turned to Karl Grün, who had translated Proudhon's *System of Economic Contradictions* into German and used it as the basis of his lectures in Paris on True Socialism. But once his hostility toward communism became evident they turned against him. Thus they continued on the same track as the other Weitlingians in being "mainly concerned to develop further the communist principle [of community of property]."[14]

Following these divisions on the eve of the First Congress, the quarrels resumed on the basis of the same irreconcilable principles. Since Schapper and Marx had yet to split over their differences, their party of progress represented a majority of League members. Supported by the Weitlingians, they first expelled the True Socialists. "But then, when it came to the election of a delegate to the Congress, the two parties clashed," the party of progress and the Weitlingians. As a result, the branches supporting the party of progress resolved to separate from the branches on which the main strength of the Weitlingians rested. Thus when the Congress convened without the Old Guard egalitarians, it had no compunctions in expelling the dissident one-third.[15]

Paris continued to be the seat of the factional quarrels that came to a head in October. Under the continuing influence of Grün's doctrines, "One of the communities opposed the communist principles and was expelled from the League by a decision of the Central Authority."[16] That same month

---

[13] Hook, *From Hegel to Marx*, 253.
[14] Marx and Engels, *Collected Works*, 6:590, 591.
[15] Ibid., 6:591, 592, 609–610.
[16] Ibid., 6:711 n.355.

Engels completed his "Principles of Communism," an expanded but revised version of the "Communist Credo." Incorporating the results of several months of heated discussion, it renounced the Credo's humanist goal while simultaneously reintroducing it by the back door, so to speak.

In the "Principles" Engels redefined communism as the "doctrine of the conditions for the emancipation of the proletariat." But by "emancipation" he meant not only or even mainly the abolition of wage-slavery. In answer to Question 13, emancipation is conceived in humanist and not only economic terms, as a condition in which enough will be produced so that "every member of society will thereby be enabled to develop and exercise all his powers and abilities in perfect freedom." As if that were not clear and comprehensible, Engels repeated himself in answer to Question 20. Thus, communism will have as its result the "all-round development of the abilities of all members of society through doing away with the hitherto existing division of labor, through industrial education...through the participation of all in the enjoyments provided by all."[17]

Yet the same document declares that the "abolition of private ownership is indeed the most succinct and characteristic summary of the entire social system necessarily following from the development of industry, and is therefore rightly put forward by the Communists as their main demand"! This statement is misleading on two counts: first, because Engels used the ambiguous phrase "abolition of private ownership" to cover up his and Marx's project limited to common ownership of the means of production; second, because the "Principles" give priority not to the abolition of private property in land and capital, but rather to the free and universal development of human potentialities.

That this is what Engels meant is evident from his answer to Question 14. With "private ownership...abolished in its stead there will be common use of all the instruments of production and the distribution of all the products by common agreement."[18] What kind of common agreement? The answer was an agreement to distribute goods in a way that contributes to all-round human development in a postscarcity society. Meanwhile, goods will be distributed as incentives toward increased production; until there is enough for all, workers will be paid according to how much they produce rather than how much each needs.

The "Principles" and the "Credo" both support a democratic reorganization of society. According to the "Credo," the "fundamental

---

[17] Ibid., 6:341, 347, 353, 354.
[18] Ibid., 6:348.

condition for the introduction of community of property is the political
liberation of the proletariat through a democratic constitution." This
"political liberation" is referred to in the "Principles" as "the winning of
democracy and the realization of socialist measures following upon it."
Democracy will be achieved during "moments of action" thanks to a
temporary alliance of Communists and democratic Socialists who have not
entered the service of the ruling class. As for North America, where a
democratic constitution has already been introduced, "the Communists must
make common cause with the party that will turn the constitution against the
bourgeoisie and use it in the interest of the proletariat," that is, the party for
land reform and for a 10-hour working day.[19]

The June and October 1847 draft programs that preceded the Manifesto
favored a liberal humanist program and a democratic socialist strategy.
Engels appropriated the name "Communist" for his tour de force, but gave it
a novel meaning. As Schapper, the first president of the Communist League,
justified the earlier usage: "We are...distinguished...by our attack on the
existing social order and on private property, by wanting community of
property, by being Communists." Not a word about the June's draft aim to
develop and use all human capacities in complete freedom! Instead, "We
proclaim the greatest revolution ever proclaimed in the world...liberation
from the fetters of money rule, from the fetters of the bourgeoisie." Schapper
focused on communism's negative goal, not on the emancipation of
humanity as Engels understood it, but on emancipation from wage-slavery
through "struggle against the bourgeoisie."[20]

The agents of the revolution, Schapper thundered, included proletarians
in the broadest sense. "In contemporary society, the proletarians are those
who can have no capital to live on, worker and professor, artist and petty-
bourgeois alike." Like Weitling, Schapper focused on the struggle between
capitalists and the capital-less, on the perennial war between rich and poor,
whereas the Manifesto shifted the focus to the modern struggle between
"Bourgeois and Proletarians."

Is it any wonder, then, that Marx scorned Schapper's communism as
"artisan-communism" and that Engels wrote contemptuously of its
"handicraft prejudices," according to which "community of goods was
demanded as the necessary consequence of 'equality'"?[21]

---

[19] Ibid., 6:102, 356, 667 n.38.
[20] Ibid., 6:595, 600.
[21] Ryazanoff, *The Communist Manifesto*, Appendix E, 289; Draper, *Karl Marx's
Theory of Revolution*, 2:655, 714 n.6; and Engels, "On the History of the Communist
League," in *Selected Works*, 2:339, 343.

Ideological differences between Schapper's and Marx's factions were among the contributing causes of the League's foundering; the differences were paved over and reconciled in name only, as in the body of rules adopted in December—rules that contradicted the principles of Engels' "Credo."[22] The differences were further aggravated by the progressive displacement of the Schapperite majority from control over the Central Authority. During the League's first nine months (June 1847–March 1848), the Schapperites held the presidency, while members of Marx's faction held the position of secretary. Afterward the roles were reversed until in March 1850 both top positions were held by Marx and Engels. The fact that Marxists gained control of the League but were always a minority finally led to a showdown with the proletarian majority.

The League's Breakup

Michael Harrington claims that between 1848 and 1850, "Marx and Engels changed their minds about their basic political orientation no less than three times." This is an overstatement since their shifts were over matters of strategy only. Nonetheless, they shifted from a strategy of alliance with the liberal bourgeoisie in the Manifesto to a strategy of direct confrontation with the bourgeoisie in "The Bourgeoisie and the Counter-Revolution." That was their first change of mind, in December 1848. The second came in February 1849 when they devised a new strategy of alliances between the proletariat, petty bourgeoisie, and peasants—an electoral and subsequently extra-parliamentary strategy officially spelled out in their March 1850 Address of the Central Authority to the League. The Address called for a launching of both "an independent secret and public organization of the workers' party alongside the official democrats," and for a "Revolution in Permanence"—tantamount to a concerted struggle to overthrow the petty bourgeoisie on the heels of a successful democratic revolution. The third change of mind came in September 1850 when Marx and Engels challenged both the imminence of a petty-bourgeois democratic revolution and the conspiratorial strategy of making the revolution permanent.[23]

---

[22] Marx and Engels, *Collected Works*, 6:633.
[23] Harrington, "The Democratic Essence of Socialism," in Bender, 107; Karl Marx, "The Bourgeoisie and the Counter-Revolution," *Collected Works*, 8:160–163, 178; idem, "The *Kölnische Zeitung* on the Elections," *Collected Works*, 8:288–289; and Marx and Engels, *Collected Works*, 10:280–287, 626–629.

It was this last shift in strategy that led to the decisive rupture with the Schapperites, after which the latter "formed their own central authority in an attempt to influence all the League organizations and isolate the supporters of Marx and Engels, whose expulsion they announced."[24] Marx retaliated by expelling the Schapperites in November, but then scuttled his own League two years later on the grounds that it had outlived its usefulness. The division into two Leagues brought to a head the differences between the two factions that until then had been dormant.

At the meeting of the Central Authority on 15 September 1850, Marx accused the Schapperites of abandoning the international outlook of the Manifesto, of preparing to make a communist revolution in Germany without considering the circumstances in neighboring countries, and without waiting for the petty bourgeoisie to have its turn at ruling. Their proposed revolution hinged on a great "effort of *will*...[when they should have said] to the workers: You have 15, 20, 50 years of civil war to go through in order to alter the situation and to train yourselves for the exercise of power." In turn, and for indefinitely postponing the moment of action, the Schapperites "called the defenders of the Manifesto reactionaries."[25]

Why defenders of the Manifesto? Why had the Manifesto become a bone of contention? Because of its materialistic interpretation of history, its deference to reality and to the objective conditions of revolution as opposed to subjective schemes based on class interest alone.

Schapper's parting speech at the 15 September meeting is a clue to his differences with Marx going back to 1847. "Just as in France the proletariat parts company with the Montagne and *La Presse* [delegates in the 1848 Legislative Assembly representing the bloc of moderate Jacobins and democratic Socialists grouped round Louis Blanc's newspaper *La Réforme*], so it is here also: the people who represent the party in principle [Schapper's faction] part company with those who organize the proletariat [Marx's faction]...there should be two leagues, one for those who work with the pen and one for those who work in other ways." What other ways? "The question at issue is whether we ourselves chop off a few heads right at the start or whether it is our own heads that will fall. In France the workers will come to power and thereby *we* in Germany...[where] we can take such measures as are necessary to ensure the rule of the proletariat."[26]

To this outburst Marx replied that he had always defied the momentary opinions of the proletariat and, by implication, those of its natural born

---

[24] Marx and Engels, *Collected Works*, 10:708–709 n.446.
[25] Ibid., 10:626–627.
[26] Ibid., 10:627–628, 650 n.50.

leaders. Fortunately, he added, the League cannot yet come to power for, if it did, "the measures it would introduce would be petty-bourgeois and not directly proletarian." In France, "it isn't the proletariat alone that gains power but the peasants and the petty bourgeois as well, and it will have to carry out not its, but their measures."[27] In effect, one should let bourgeois republicans and petty-bourgeois democrats make their own revolutions and then proceed where they leave off.

How did the Blanquist exiles in London perceive the split? They believed it paralleled that in the German Workers' Educational Society. "In both of them the *bourgeois element* and the *proletarian party* have separated from each other under *identical* circumstances." According to August Willich (1810–1878), coleader with Schapper of the rival League, "Engels, Marx, etc. represented the *bourgeois element*."[28]

Marx disputed this account of the rupture. The breakup of the League came in response not only to his and Engels' reassessment of the political conditions for revolution—but also to their analysis of the economic prerequisites of revolution. In their "Review: May to October [1850]," they explained the outbreak of the European revolutions in 1848 as a response to the British commercial crisis of April–October 1847 and its repercussions on the Continent. "The panic which broke out in Paris after February and spread throughout the Continent," they concluded, "contributed infinitely more to the revolutions of 1848 than the revolutions to the commercial crisis." However, a new cycle of industrial development began in Great Britain and North America toward the end of 1848 that also had repercussions on the Continent, with the result that by the end of 1849, "the revival of business was general." Consequently, "With this general prosperity, in which the productive forces of bourgeois society develop as luxuriantly as is at all possible within bourgeois relationships, there can be no talk of a real revolution. *A new revolution is possible only in consequence of a new crisis.*"[29] Precisely this recognition is what made Marx and Engels' strategy realistic.

Underlying the differences in strategy were also diverging views about revolutionary development. As Engels spelled out the premises of his party's theory of revolution through clearly demarcated stages, "this party never imagined itself capable of producing, at any time...that revolution which was to carry its ideas into practice." History showed that after the aristocracy had its turn at ruling, the bourgeoisie then had its turn, "and how at the

---

[27] Ibid., 10:628–629.
[28] Ibid., 12:507–508.
[29] Ibid., 10:150, 495–497, 507, 510.

present moment two more classes claim their turn of domination, the petty
trading class, and the industrial working class." But not both together. "The
practical revolutionary experiences of 1848–49 confirmed the reasonings of
theory...the conclusion that the democracy of the petty traders must first
have its turn, before the Communist working class could hope to
permanently establish itself in power." Willich was not so sure. He
attempted to leapfrog his party into power over the backs of the petty
bourgeoisie.[30]

A few words should be said about Willich, who subsequently displaced
Schapper as the principal figure in the rival League. Retired as an officer
from the Prussian army because of his communist views, he succeeded
Schapper as president of the unified League until March 1848. During the
military uprising in Germany (May–July 1849), he commanded a volunteer
corps of eight companies numbering some 800 partisans and consisting
mostly of workers. They distinguished themselves by their bravery and were
the last to leave German soil. Engels was Willich's adjutant throughout the
campaign.[31]

While Schapper is mentioned as early as volume 6 of Marx and Engels'
Collected Works, Willich's name first appears in volume 9. As in Schapper's
case, the references are generally favorable until the split in 1850. After that
there are mostly slurs concerning Schapper's drinking bouts, his
"hippopotamus belly" and "hippopotamus clique," Willich's "strict
asceticism," his alleged comparison of himself with Jesus Christ (whom he
resembled physically), his role as leader of the lumpenproletariat, his
mission to save the world as a "crusader in the full sense of the word," his
love of "barracks communism...moral authority and the dictates of self-
sacrifice."[32]

Marx and Engels outdid themselves in ridiculing the character of
Willich, this "Great Field Marshal and social Messiah." In nothing less than
three major works, their 100-page *Great Men of the Exile* completed in 1852
but published posthumously, Marx's *Revelations Concerning the Communist
Trial in Cologne* (1853), and his *Knight of the Noble Consciousness* (1854),
they continued to hammer away on the same theme. That Schapper was
spared the most vitriolic abuse may be explained by his break with Willich

---

[30] Ibid., 11:389; and L. D. Easton, "August Willich, Marx, and Left-Hegelian
Socialism," *Cahiers de l'Institut de Science Economique Appliquée* (August 1965),
108, 119.

[31] Marx and Engels, *Collected Works*, 9:482–483, 588–589 n.404; and 10:169–170.

[32] Ibid., 38:442–442, 452; 11:312–313; and 12:504. See also Engels' lampoon in a
letter to Marx (23 September 1851), 38:460.

in the spring of 1852. (The final break occurred in October 1853, after which Schapper became reconciled with Marx and later joined the General Council of the First International.)[33]

Following the split in September 1850, Marx and Engels continued to refer to the rival League as the "Schapper-Willich party." But in retrospect they acknowledged Willich's leadership by calling it the "Willich-Schapper party" or "Willich-Schapper group."[34]

Where did this enigmatic fellow, who shed his military uniform for a carpenter's apron, stand ideologically? Having come under Feuerbach's influence, Willich became a communist on philosophical grounds. What kind of communist? In a letter to Marx's wife Jenny (25 June 1849), Engels described him as "brave, cool-headed and adroit...in battle," but otherwise "a tedious ideologist and a true socialist." It was only after the split that Engels lampooned him as the "communist Cromwell," a "crazy martial clod," a leveler of the crudest sort whose "one idea has been to conquer the communist Canaan from without, exterminating the original inhabitants"![35]

Willich's socialism was a confusing mix. "Engels was suggesting that for Willich socialism was essentially a matter of high principles and the proper mental picture of a new social order," and that Willich was "preoccupied, as both he and Marx had been earlier, with socialism as a question of the 'realization of humanity'"! Although he subscribed to the Manifesto's materialist interpretation of history, he lacked Marx's expertise when it came to applying it. Instead of adjusting his political sights to underlying changes in the economy of which he was mainly unaware, he went blindly down the path toward a new revolution. Not understanding the reasons for Marx's September 1850 repudiation of the March Address to the League, he asked in all innocence: "Why should the workers spill their blood for 'decrepit capitalist domination'?" Was not Marx's postponement of the struggle for socialism evidence of "opportunism"?[36]

Willich's differences with Marx were also of a personal nature. Willich identified himself with the proletarians he sought to liberate; Marx did not. "Beloved and trusted by his volunteers, Willich shared their poverty, took no privileges for himself, and never shirked even the hardest manual labor." While Willich disdained all luxury, Marx lived beyond his means. Willich

---

[33] Marx and Engels, *Collected Works*, 38:633–634, n.503; 39:126, 378; and 11:656–657, n.155.

[34] Ibid., 11:402–403, 445, 449; 12:497; and 38:285.

[35] Ibid., 38:204, 320, 323, 400; and Easton, "August Willich, Marx, and Left-Hegelian Socialism," in *Cahiers*, 105, 108.

[36] Easton, "August Willich, Marx, and Left-Hegelian Socialism," 109–110.

remained a bachelor, while Marx fathered no less than eight children, including an illegitimate son by a servant girl who continued in his hire! Marx arranged for private lessons in music and drama and for the private schooling of his three daughters. Considering his definition of luxuries in *Capital* as articles consumed only by capitalists and by those dependent on their largesse, his life-style can only be described as bourgeois. Besides his and his wife's inheritance, he depended on Engels' continuing patronage, on the exploitation of textile workers in the Manchester firm of Ermen & Engels where Engels rose to become a partner. According to one biographer, "in spite of being continually short of money and many times on the brink of financial collapse, the Marx family's domestic economy was always predicated on the maintenance of a middle-class life style...[and] can only be called poverty relative to his expectations."[37] The irony is that Marx's life-style befitted his peculiar brand of communism—a communism in mortal conflict with Willich's. Mortal conflict? Yes, considering that Willich once challenged Marx to a duel!

Marxists are not the least bit embarrassed by the stark contrast between their hero's *domestic* economy and his *political* economy. Marx is a prime example of what communist humanism means in practice. Taking Marx as a model, no communist is going to sacrifice his claim to self-cultivation for the promise of a classless society, much less join the wage-earning proletariat. Thus communist humanism was cause for a double bitterness that eventually would spell its doom. It bred disillusionment not only with humanism's false promises, but also with communism for encouraging its leaders to live in the style of Marx and Engels. Willich's communism may have been naïve, but at least his followers cannot be faulted for living by a double standard.

A century later, Marx's domestic economy would be replicated throughout the former Soviet Union. If deeds count for more than words, Marx's life-style may be taken as the crucible for distinguishing a phoney from a genuine communist. Once it became the fashion for the Soviet *nomenklatura*, it prefigured the coming Soviet "meltdown."

True to form, Willich cosponsored the League's circular of March 1850 exhorting German workers to join forces with—while preserving their independence of—the petty bourgeoisie in an imminent revolutionary uprising, a permanent revolution until "state power has been taken over by the proletariat." Again, it was Willich along with Marx and Engels, Julian

---

[37] Ibid., 106, 109, 114; Seigel, *Marx's Fate*, 259–260, 265, 275, 279; and Karl Marx, *Capital*, vols. 2–3, ed. Frederick Engels (Moscow: Foreign Languages Publishing House, 1961–62), 2:403.

Harney from the British Chartists, and two French partisans of Auguste Blanqui, who launched the Universal Society of Revolutionary Communists in April 1850 aimed at insurrection and a proletarian dictatorship. The first article of the new society was penned by Willich: "The aim of the Association is the overthrow of all privileged classes and their subjection to the dictatorship of the proletariat by maintaining the revolution in permanence up to the achievement of communism...the ultimate organizational form of the human family." In the end, the League split over questions of ideology and the continuing prospects for revolution.[38]

After the split, Willich's League continued to lay plans for a German insurrection. His December 1850 and January 1851 proposals for Germany called for the introduction of communism by a military uprising and for a government of community councils or soviets sponsored and safeguarded by military units. His followers also called for a workers' insurrection in France. "Early in 1851 the Paris branch of Willich's League discussed revolutionary strategy and proposed a dictatorship by a central committee which would arm the workers, confiscate property of the nobility...and furnish employment for all in industries confiscated from their capitalist owners." As one commentator notes, "Willich's attitude was 'now or never,' much like the attitude of Lenin and the Bolsheviks in Russia's October Revolution."[39] But does anyone confuse Lenin's brand of communism with humanism?

Historical analogies can be misleading, but the foregoing account of the differences between the two Leagues suggests an historical parallel. It seems that the Willich-Schapper party adopted a line subsequently developed by Lenin and the Bolshevik majority from 1905 onward, while Marx and Engels represented the outlook of the Menshevik minority.[40] Although Lenin was in somewhat less of a hurry to launch an insurrection without prior mobilization of the workers, he shared with Willich an insurrectional strategy that Marx and Engels ridiculed.

The September 1850 confrontation between Marx and Schapper suggests that their party of progress in 1847 consisted of two different parties that had momentarily coalesced. It further suggests than Marx's ambiguous formulations in the Manifesto were concessions to the Schapperites— concessions that were rejected by the latter as insufficient. In 1847 as in 1850, the Schapperites were acting in conformity with Article One of the

---

[38] Easton, "August Willich, Marx, and Left-Hegelian Socialism," 111–113, 124–125.
[39] Ibid., 115–116, 117.
[40] See V. I. Lenin, *Selected Works*, 3 vols. (New York: International Publishers, 1967), 1:487–488, 491–495.

League's draft rules, "by spreading the theory of the community of property and [ensuring] its speediest possible practical introduction."[41] Because the Blanquist exiles in London allied themselves with the Schapperites, Marx also broke off relations with them.[42]

When the Central Authority moved from London to Paris in March 1848, Marx was elected chairman, and Schapper was elected secretary. In March 1850 it moved back to London with Engels as acting secretary. A power struggle then surfaced between the Schapperites, who had the membership behind them but only token representation in the Central Authority, and the minority represented by Marx and Engels. At issue was the old division between workers' communism and the philosophical humanism of a clique of intellectuals who had infiltrated the proletarian movement. There was a strong undercurrent of anti-intellectualism among League members. This is confirmed by Schapper's insistence on two leagues, one for street-fighters and the other for pen-pushers like Marx and Engels, and by Marx's disgust with the Schapperites for wanting to exclude all writers from their midst.[43]

The frustrations experienced by Marx and Engels in having to collaborate with the Schapperites led them in retrospect to regret ever having become involved in the League's creation. They had better things to do than to waste their time trying to get their views accepted among political émigrés who ended by rejecting them. In November 1847, Engels still believed that the humanist passages in the "Principles" might be endorsed, "save for a few minor points." At the time, he prided himself on having produced a program of which he could say "there is nothing in it which conflicts with our views." But less than six months after the split with the Schapperites, both he and Marx were relieved that the "system of mutual concessions, half-measures tolerated for decency's sake, and the obligation to bear one's share of public ridicule in the party along with all these jackasses, all this is now over." To this comment by Marx in a letter dated 11 February 1851, Engels responded that "emigration is an institution which inevitably turns a man into a fool, an ass and a base rascal unless he withdraws wholly therefrom, and unless he is content to be an independent writer who doesn't give a tinker's curse for the so-called revolutionary party."[44]

---

[41] Marx and Engels, *Collected Works*, 6:585.
[42] Ibid., 10:694 n.344.
[43] Ibid., 10:628; and 38:310.
[44] Ibid., 38:149, 286, 287.

In a follow-up letter on February 13, Engels reiterated that they had no real grounds for complaining of their political isolation from the émigré rabble. For years they had been acting as though they had a party "when, in fact, we had no party, and when the people we considered as belonging to our party...didn't even understand the rudiments of our stuff." How can people like us, he asked, "fit into a 'party'...a herd of jackasses who swear by us because they think we're of the same kidney as they?" So "it is no loss if we are no longer held to be the 'right and adequate expression' of the ignorant curs with whom we have been thrown together over the past few years." Far better to preserve one's independence, to resist being dragged down again into the political whirlpool, to have "no responsibility for jackasses," and to engage in "merciless criticism of everyone." The main task, Engels concluded, is "to find some way of getting our things published...without being under the necessity of mentioning any one of these vipers."[45]

Only two weeks later Marx and Engels were outraged by a major scandal at a mass banquet and meeting in celebration of the anniversary of the February 1848 revolution in France. Sponsored by the Fraternal Society of French Social Democrats, founded in the autumn of 1850 for the purpose of providing material assistance to French political exiles in London, the banquet was attended by some 250 Germans and 200 English Chartists, in addition to some 150 Frenchmen and 100 or so Poles and Hungarians. Marx and Engels refused to attend owing to the presence of the rival League and its Blanquist allies. Julian Harney, a leader of the Chartist left wing, was the only member of Marx's League who attended in an official capacity, but there were two of Marx's comrades who bought tickets. When the émigrés began shouting about spies in their midst, the two uninvited guests were "man-handled out of the hall...kicked, stamped on, cuffed, and nearly rent to pieces." Their hats were torn off and their hair was torn out. Altogether some "200 FRATERNAL MURDERERS...discharged their revolutionary energies" upon a pair of unarmed men, while Harney stood by doing nothing.[46]

Marx was so outraged that he considered taking legal action against the assailants. In a letter to one of his supporters, Marx urged him "to brand these cowardly, calumnious, infamous assassins before the German proletariat, and wherever else this can be done."[47]

---

[45] Ibid., 38:290, 291.
[46] Ibid., 38:292–293, 297–298, 303–304; original emphasis.
[47] Ibid., 38:310–312, 380.

Although Marx's League adopted a new set of rules in January 1851, a month later he and Engels withdrew from political activity in order to return to their studies that had been interrupted since the February Revolution of 1848. Marx immersed himself in the classics of political economy in the hope of preparing the proletariat for the revolutionary struggles that lay ahead. As he reminisced in a February 1860 letter to a former League member, he had been reproached even before the split with the Schapperites for having "allowed the League's agitational work to go to sleep." There was good reason for doing so, he explained: "I am a *critic* and was really fed up with the things I experienced in 1849–52." As a result, the Communist League "ceased to exist for me eight years ago...[when] I was no longer connected with *any* association and was firmly convinced that my theoretical works were of greater benefit to the working class than participation in associations whose days on the Continent were over."[48]

Even before they scuttled their League, Marx and Engels had the satisfaction of being "rid of the entire loud-mouthed, muddle-headed, impotent émigré rabble in London, and of being at long last able to work again undisturbed." As Engels bragged in a letter (9 July 1851) to a German compatriot in Geneva, "We have always been superior to the riff-raff and, in any serious movement, have dominated them; but we have meanwhile learnt an enormous amount from our experience since 1848, and have made good use of the lull since 1850 to resume our swotting [daily literary grind]."[49] The League had never amounted to much anyway, and when the moment for action finally came with the outbreak of the German Revolution in May 1849 (trailing by more than a year the February Revolution in France), the "few hundred separate League members vanished in the enormous mass that had been suddenly hurled into the movement."[50]

Rather than a mass-based proletarian party, the Communist League before it split in 1850 was still a "tiny cadres' organization of some 200–300 members spread throughout Western Europe."[51] As the Manifesto acknowledged at the time, "The Communists do not form a separate party," but work within existing parties to promote the interests of the proletariat as a whole. In England, members of the League became Chartists, the only workers' party organized on a national scale anywhere in the world. The

---

[48] Marx and Engels, *Selected Correspondence*, 146, 147.
[49] Marx and Engels, *Collected Works*, 38:380, 382.
[50] Frederick Engels, "Marx and the *Neue Rheinische Zeitung*," in Marx and Engels, *Selected Works*, 2:330.
[51] Monty Johnstone, "Marx and Engels and the Concept of the Party," *The Socialist Register 1967*, ed. Ralph Miliband and John Saville (London: Merlin Press, 1967), 124.

leaders of its left wing, Julian Harney and Ernest Jones, were members of the League and loyal to Marx even though Harney kept up his connections with the Schapperites. In France, members of the League joined the party of Social Democrats, and in Germany the Democratic Party—the only way for Communists to get "the ear of the working class."[52]

Life After Death

The Manifesto was the ideological product not of a united League, but of a divided one even after the Old Guard Communists (Weitlingians) had been expelled. By December 1847, when Marx was commissioned to write the Manifesto, the League had been reduced to two main factions: (1) the Conspiratorial Communists (Schapper-Willich), in a hurry to establish community of property as a condition of equality; and (2) the Socialist Humanists (Marx-Engels), for whom a solution to the human question depended on a solution to the social question. In agreement with the Manifesto's materialist interpretation of history, they nonetheless disagreed over both the strategy of the revolution and its immediate and final goals.

The Manifesto reflects this ambivalence. Owing to the divisions within the League and the need for compromise, it tried to satisfy both factions. On the one hand, it affirmed the goal of the Schapperites: "Abolition of private property." On the other hand, it preserved the substance of Marx and Engels' humanism: "In place of the old bourgeois society...we shall have an association in which the free development of each is the condition for the free development of all."

The Manifesto's program is a tour de force in reconciling opposites. Consider the following sequence. First, "The distinguishing feature of Communism is not the abolition of property generally, but the abolition of bourgeois property." This sentence openly proclaims the goal of socialism, while discrediting the nursery tale of a "specter," a haunting and terrifying power that, if given a chance, would gladly blow up European society. But how is this sentence consistent with "the theory of the Communists may be summed up in the single sentence: Abolition of private property"? By calling for the expropriation of *private* property, not just *bourgeois private* property, the second sentence proclaims the goal of communism, not just socialism, as a sop to the conspiratorial current in favor of a "community of goods."

---

[52] Marx and Engels, *Selected Correspondence*, 476.

The irony is that the League split apart while the Manifesto remained intact. Soon after, the two Leagues dissolved; but the Manifesto lived on. Its service to a host of conflicting political ideologies—and not always in the name of Marxism—had just begun.

What happened to the Manifesto once the League disappeared? It took fifteen years for the European working class to recover from the defeat of the Parisian insurrection of June 1848, the "first great battle between the Proletariat and Bourgeoisie." The proletariat did not recover sufficient strength for another assault on the ruling class until the founding of the International Working Men's Association (First International) in 1864. "But this association, formed with the express aim of welding into one body the whole militant proletariat of Europe and America, could not at once proclaim the principles laid down in the Manifesto." It had to have a different, broader program to accommodate the English Chartists, the followers of Proudhon in France, Belgium, Italy, and Spain, and the school of democratic Socialists in Germany.[53]

So it was not until the International had brought home to the workers the "insufficiency of their various favorite nostrums" that the way was cleared for the Manifesto's revival. But by then the International, too, was on the verge of expiring. In breaking up in 1874, however, it "left the workers quite different men from what it had found them in 1864." Although the Manifesto had momentarily disappeared from sight, in the 1870s it was resurrected and "came to the front again"—so Engels believed.[54]

Engels exaggerated. Engels, observes Joseph Schumpeter, "claimed too much for the First International," and he "was the victim of a similar optical delusion as regards the Manifesto." As late as 1888, on the eve of the founding of the Second International, it was still the case that, *except for Germany*, "only small minorities...followed the Marxist flag." Therefore, since the position of the Manifesto in the history of socialism was tied to the acceptance of Marxism, the Manifesto could not, as of 1888, have become "the common platform acknowledged by millions of working men from Siberia to California."[55] The Manifesto had to wait for the Second or Socialist International to acquire this exalted position—but the International only began its work of proselytism in 1889!

---

[53] Frederick Engels, "Preface to the English Edition of 1888," in Bender, 47–48.
[54] Ibid.
[55] Joseph Schumpeter, "The *Communist Manifesto* in Sociology and Economics," in Bender, 178–179.

4. Making Communism Credible

> We issued a number of partly printed, partly lithographed pamphlets in which we subjected to ruthless criticism that mixture of French-English socialism or communism and German philosophy that then constituted the secret teachings of the League; in its stead we advanced the study of the economic structure of bourgeois society...and finally explained in popular form that it was not a question of carrying some utopian system into life but of consciously participating in the historic process of the revolutionary transformation of society going on before our very eyes.
>
> Karl Marx, *Herr Vogt* (1860)

Although an impersonal document, the Manifesto stands out as the single, most complete statement of Marx's revolutionary theory and practice. "Of the scattered writings...in which we put our views before the public at that time [1840s]," Marx wrote in 1859, "I recall only the 'Manifesto of the Communist Party'...and the 'Discourse on Free Trade.'"[1] The decisive points of his new worldview had been first publicized in his 1847 *The Poverty of Philosophy*, but only in polemical form. These were incorporated into the economic-historical first section of the Manifesto. As for his speech on free trade, its practical lessons reappear in the Manifesto's last section on revolutionary strategy.

It goes without saying that *Capital* is Marx's major theoretical work. But it lacks a program, a critique of alternative socialisms, and a political strategy, so it cannot compete with the Manifesto on these grounds. What is its relation to the Manifesto? In view of the citations at the end of chapter 32 of *Capital* summarizing the argument of volume 1, it is an extended addendum to the Manifesto's opening economic section. The skeletal structure of the communist worldview dates from the Manifesto, the rest of the edifice would be added later. Thus the Manifesto is the most succinct answer to the question, "What is Marxism?"

The Manifesto is not just a political tract. Earlier socialists had criticized the nascent capitalist mode of production, but could not explain its consequences or gain the mastery over them. To do so, says Engels, it was

---

[1] Karl Marx, *A Contribution to the Critique of Political Economy* (Chicago: Charles Kerr, 1904), 14.

necessary "to present the capitalistic method of production in its historical connection and its inevitableness during a particular period, and therefore, also, to present its inevitable downfall; and...to lay bare its essential character." These led to Marx's two great discoveries, "the materialistic conception of history and the revelation of the secret of capitalistic production through surplus value."[2] The first was the foundation stone of the Manifesto; the second, its theoretical capstone some two decades later. Together they contributed to making the Manifesto credible.

Thus the Manifesto marks a break with Marx's earlier *theoretical humanism* that began with a philosophy of man and the human essence instead of an economically given historical period. In a major polemic with contemporary Marxists describing themselves as Socialist Humanists after the young Marx, the French philosopher Louis Althusser extolled Marx's rupture as an epistemological shift from philosophical humanism to a *theoretical antihumanism* as the basis of Marx's practical humanism. Marx's humanist goal survived the rupture, but it would henceforth be derived from a new foundation in his materialist interpretation of history.[3]

Under Our Very Eyes

Unlike Engels' "Communist Confession of Faith" and "Principles of Communism," the Manifesto is addressed to the general public, not to Communists. Its purpose, as the brief prologue tells us, is to put an end to speculation and nursery tales about the Specter of Communism. Thus, "It is high time that Communists should openly...publish their views, their aims, their tendencies...with a Manifesto of the party itself."

The Manifesto depicts communism as "an existing class struggle...a historical movement going on under our very eyes." This definition follows a convention adopted in the *German Ideology*: "Communism is for us not a *state of affairs* which is to be established, an *ideal* to which reality [will] have to adjust itself. We call communism the *real* movement which abolishes the present state of things." As long as the proletariat is not sufficiently developed to constitute a distinct class, its theorists are only utopians who improvise systems in hope of redemption. But as the class struggle becomes more clearly defined and they have no longer need for

---

[2]   Frederick Engels, "Socialism: Utopian and Scientific," *Selected Works*, 2:135–136.
[3]   Louis Althusser et al., *Polémica sobre marxismo y humanismo*, trans. Marta Harnecker (Mexico City: Siglo XXI, 1968), 6–18, 172–176, 186–192.

faith or prescriptions, "they have only to take note of what is happening before their eyes and to become its mouthpiece."[4]

This is the context for understanding the four parts or sections of the Manifesto. Their subtitles responded to the principal issues crucial to the revolutionary enterprise. "Bourgeois and Proletarians" underscores the fundamental cleavage in modern society, the class struggle between capitalists and wage-earners. "Proletarians and Communists" focuses on the political vanguard of the proletariat, its program and line of march designed to lead the proletarians to victory through the conquest of political power. "Socialist and Communist Literature" targets the misleaders in the cultural or literary battle for the allegiance of the masses, the fake socialisms and communisms advocated by self-styled friends of the people. "Position of the Communists in Relation to the Various Existing Opposition Parties" outlines the Communists' revolutionary strategy and choice of allies in the struggle for power. In effect, the Manifesto asks: What is happening in modern society that augurs its impending doom at the hands of the working class? What does the working class want, what are its demands? Who are the workers' phoney friends and what lies behind their fakery? How can the working class acquire political power?

Communism became credible by posing and answering Marx's fundamental questions in the order in which they appear in the Manifesto. That is to say, one begins with an understanding of present social reality and the forces leading to its dissolution. Then, one adopts a program that makes use of these forces as leverage. Next, one cautions against false prophets, the adoption of alternative programs that are misguided in attempting to block the main current. Finally, it is not enough to unmask and denounce the status quo and to paint an ideal picture of a future society; one complements the program with a strategy that will bring it to fruition. Unlike all previous communist manifestos, Marx's Manifesto sets forth a new revolutionary project, namely, to identify, so as consciously to ride, the wave of the future.

Section 1 of the Manifesto presents the fundamental premises of the materialist or economic interpretation of history in application to modern bourgeois society. Rather than beginning with communist demands, Communists should start with the facts at hand, and then prune down their demands to what is feasible. They should apply what Marx called his "dialectical" (multifaceted) approach to social questions. Besides the conventional focusing on the stable elements defining a given social order,

---

[4] Marx and Engels, *Collected Works*, 5:49, 177.

they should focus on the destabilizing factors.[5] They should rely on Machiavelli's two premises basic to both the revolutionary enterprise and the science of modern politics: (1) History is made under conditions that are not freely chosen; and (2) The conscious element is continually foiled by the operation of unintended consequences, by forces operating independently of the human will.

The next section makes a brief for flesh-and-bones communism, "a historical movement" as opposed to "principles that have been invented...by this or that would-be universal reformer." Actual communism represents the interests not just of Communists but the "common interests of the entire proletariat." The Manifesto articulates what it takes to be the workers' actual demands in a program defining their immediate, transitional, and ultimate aims.

While section 1 of the Manifesto focuses on the economic struggle and section 2 covers the struggle in the political arena, section 3 goes to battle on the cultural front. To the classification of competing socialisms into reactionary, conservative, and critical-utopian, it adds a class analysis of each.

On the premise that the proletariat requires the support of the immense majority for victory, the concluding section addresses the question of the potential allies of the Communists. Although Communists fight for the immediate aims and momentary interests of the workers, "in the movement of the present, they also represent and take care of the future of that movement." But whether in France, Switzerland, Germany, or Poland, they ally themselves only with revolutionary parties, those of the working class and the bourgeoisie. Communist strategy requires that only one fundamental enemy be confronted at any given time, first with the bourgeoisie in a revolution against the nobility and then against their former ally.

The Line of March

In the Manifesto the Communists are distinguished, among other things, by their theoretical knowledge of economic forces and by their grasp of human history: "they have over the great mass of the proletariat the advantage of clearly understanding the line of march, the conditions, and the ultimate general results of the proletarian movement." Class struggle rather

---

[5]   Karl Marx, *Capital*, vol. 1, ed. Frederick Engels (New York; Modern Library, n.d.), 26.

than cooperation defines the direction events are taking, the "march of modern history." The Manifesto's program and strategy are functions of what has happened, what is happening, and what may be expected to happen in view of the operation of economic forces.

The Manifesto's first concern is to understand the history of class struggles: where the class struggle is leading, and the stages through which it develops. In its modern form the class struggle is the outcome of a proletariat that began as a class in itself and matured into a class for itself. This movement was first prefigured in Marx's *Poverty of Philosophy*: "The domination of capital has created for this mass [of proletarians] a common situation, common interests...already a class as against capital, but not yet for itself."[6]

Already in 1844 Marx characterized communism as a movement with a history of its own. Initially, it finds expression as a crude, downward-leveling tendency that "wants to destroy *everything* which is not capable of being possessed by all as *private property*." An expression of general envy hostile to talent and to individual self-cultivation, this crude communism would not do away with the category of laborer but extend it to all men. Who in the modern world would want this kind of communism, this "abstract negation of the whole world of culture and civilization," this regression to the "*unnatural* simplicity of the poor and crude man who has few needs and who has not only failed to go beyond private property, but has not yet even reached it"? Because of universal envy transformed into resentment, crude communism is contaminated by the vileness of private property, the desire to *have* riches instead of to *be* a rich man, rich in talents as a result of self-cultivation. Only with the help of philosophy does communism gradually become the "real *appropriation* of the *human* essence by and for man...the complete return of man to himself [free of alienation]...accomplished consciously and embracing the entire wealth of previous development." This mature communism, as yet only a possibility but destined to replace crude communism, is the "*positive* transcendence of *private property*" and, as such, "equals humanism."[7]

The Manifesto's point of departure is the communist movement still in its swaddling clothes—crude communism—notwithstanding its defects. As such, communism is the "dynamic principle of the immediate future, but...not the goal of human development." It takes "*actual* communist

---

6 Marx and Engels, *Collected Works*, 5:211.
7 Ibid., 3:294–295, 296.

action to abolish actual private property," but such action is only a means through "a very rough and protracted process."[8]

Unlike the *Economic and Philosophic Manuscripts*, Marx's later works give precedence to the means over the end. The only realistic consideration is *"what the proletariat is*, and what, in accordance with this *being*, it will historically be compelled to do." This line from *The Holy Family* is spelled out in *The German Ideology*. As a class, the proletariat "has to bear all the burdens of society without enjoying its advantages." Forced into the "sharpest contradiction to all other classes," from it "emanates the consciousness of the necessity of a fundamental revolution, the communist consciousness."[9] This was how Marx and Engels perceived communism in 1845–1846 and subsequently in the Manifesto.

As he noted in his afterword to volume 1 of *Capital*, Marx considered the historical movement as alone worthy of investigation, through "the confrontation and the comparison of a fact not with ideas, but with another fact."[10]

What is the line of march? It is the direct line from a bourgeois to a proletarian revolution without intermediaries, without a transitional regime under the rule of an intermediate class. It is a two-stage process in which the proletariat begins by playing second fiddle to the bourgeoisie in the struggle against the vestiges of feudalism and simple commodity production. Therefore, during the first stage of the bourgeois revolution, "the proletarians do not fight their [immediate] enemies, but the enemies of their enemies, the remnants of absolute monarchy, the landowners, the non-industrial bourgeoisie, the petty bourgeoisie."

Unable to compete with the bourgeoisie and destined to disappear with the progress of industry, the intermediate classes of petty commodity producers, peasants, and petty bourgeoisie are not a significant economic or political force. Consequently, they are not in a position to seize power, much less rule. So the line of march passes through only two revolutions separated by a respectable interval, except that in the case of Germany "the bourgeois revolution...will be but the prelude to an immediate following proletarian revolution."

The enemies of the "progressive" industrial bourgeoisie are "reactionary, for they try to roll back the wheel of history." The landowners, the petty bourgeoisie, and the financial and commercial bourgeoisie have their roots in precapitalist societies and, to that extent, precede and are independent of

---

[8]   Ibid., 3:306, 313.
[9]   Ibid., 4:37; and 5:52.
[10]   Marx, *Capital*, 1:23.

industrial capital. Whereas the industrial bourgeoisie personifies creative capital in the sphere of production, the nonindustrial bourgeoisie represents parasitic capital confined to the sphere of circulation. The panegyric in section 1 of the Manifesto is dedicated to the former, not the latter. The industrial bourgeoisie created capitalism, whereas the parasitic sectors of the bourgeoisie have no economic system they can call their own.

Since the financial and commercial bourgeoisie are enemies of the industrial capitalists, the industrial bourgeoisie must be the basic and immediate enemy of the proletariat. That the Manifesto relies on the support of its immediate enemy in the struggle against the enemies of its enemy is evident from its transitional program at the end of section 2. Thus the chief capitalists slated for expropriation are the owners of real estate and financial capital. As for the owners of commercial capital, they too will be expropriated—but only inasmuch as the "means of communication and transportation" are means of circulation required in "buying and selling" rather than in delivering raw materials and half-finished goods for further production.

As the Manifesto elaborates these complicated relationships, "The [industrial] bourgeoisie finds itself involved in a constant battle…with those portions of the bourgeoisie itself, whose interests have become antagonistic to the progress of industry." In these battles it is "compelled to appeal to the proletariat, to ask for its help, and thus, to drag it into the political arena." It thereby furnishes the weapons for its future grave-diggers. So, once the bourgeois revolution is consummated, the proletariat enters a second stage of preparations for a new struggle against its former ally.

Finally, when the class struggle between bourgeois and proletarians reaches a critical point, a "section of the ruling class cuts itself adrift, and joins the revolutionary class, the class that holds the future in its hands." Just as the proletariat becomes the principal ally of the bourgeoisie in the bourgeois revolution, so now "a portion of the bourgeoisie goes over to the proletariat, and in particular…[those] who have raised themselves to the level of comprehending theoretically the historical movement as a whole."

So much for the general outline, the overall line of march. But when it comes to particulars, there are two quite different scenarios. First, there is the scenario of violent revolution, a "more or less veiled civil war…up to the point where that war breaks out into open revolution, and where the violent overthrow of the bourgeoisie lays the foundation for the sway of the proletariat." Second, there is the scenario of peaceful revolution in which the first step of the proletariat is "to win the battle of democracy," and the second step is to use its political supremacy "to wrest, by degrees, all capital from the bourgeoisie."

The Manifesto fails to clarify the conditions in which these opposite scenarios are applicable, except to hint that the violent course is what most likely *will* happen and the peaceful course what the Communists strive to *make* happen. Not until *Capital* is there a discussion of a "pro-slavery rebellion" that might interrupt the democratic process of expropriating the bourgeoisie. As Engels recalled in his 1886 preface to the first English translation, although Marx's "study led to the conclusion that, at least in Europe, England is the only country where the inevitable social revolution might be effected by peaceful and legal means...he hardly expected the English ruling classes to submit, without a 'pro-slavery rebellion.'"[11]

As Marx presented the line of march in November 1850, the "coming historical process" is not to be understood as "an *application of systems*, which the thinkers of society...devise or have devised." He faults them not only for preferring ideals to reality, but also for subordinating "the whole movement to one of its elements."[12]

While the proletariat is the subjective agent of the social revolution, the Manifesto also makes a case for communism with the help of impersonal agencies. "For many a decade past the history of industry and commerce is but the history of the revolt of modern productive forces against modern conditions of production, against the property relations that are the conditions for the existence of the bourgeoisie and of its rule." Commercial crises put on "trial, each time more threateningly, the existence of the entire bourgeois society." Communists are not the only revolutionaries of consequence. Thus "Modern bourgeois society...a society that has conjured up such gigantic means of production and of exchange, is like the sorcerer, who is no longer able to control the powers of the nether world whom he has called up by his spells." As Marx mused in a speech on 14 April 1856, "Steam, electricity, and the self-acting mule were [even in 1848] revolutionists of a rather more dangerous character than even...Blanqui."[13]

Marx was among the few historians of the nineteenth century to underscore the self-defeating character of this movement. "In our days everything seems pregnant with its contrary." Industrial and scientific

---

[11] Ibid., 1:313, 317; and Frederick Engels, "Preface," *Capital*, 1:32. See also Marx's speech at Amsterdam (8 September 1872) in Robert C. Tucker, ed., *The Marx-Engels Reader*, 2nd ed. (New York/London: Norton, 1978), 523.
[12] Marx, "The Class Struggles in France, 1848–1850," *Collected Works*, 10:126–127.
[13] Marx and Engels, *Collected Works*, 14:655.

progress, "by some strange weird spell, are turned into sources of want."[14] The Manifesto says as much. "It is enough to mention the commercial crises...that, in all earlier epochs, would have seemed an absurdity—the epidemic of over-production...as if a famine, a universal war of devastation had cut off the supply of every means of subsistence."

Marx and Engels were not alone in defining communism as a movement rather than a position. Their principal rival for leadership of the communist movement in 1848, Auguste Blanqui, defined it as a "*tendency* rather than a concrete aim." What kind of tendency? A tendency toward equality, not a terrestrial paradise, since an equality of burdens and benefits is a condition that can only be approximated. Skeptical of human nature and insistent on taking humans as they are rather than as they should be, he wrote: "One should not attempt to make leaps, but human steps, and one should always keep on marching." Asked about his program, he replied, "I do not know what it will be; I do not know what I will do; I will act according to circumstances."[15] The propagandist of the deed does not stop on one side of the river to contemplate and discuss what might be on the opposite bank. He crosses over—and looks.

Winning the Battle of Democracy

The Manifesto tried to make communism credible by also presenting it as a logical extension of democracy. By 1848 the ideological contest between liberals and democrats, defenders respectively of restricted and universal suffrage, constitutional monarchy and republican government, was becoming the principal bone of contention in European politics. The signs of the times heralded the coming victory of democracy, so that to link communism with the wave of the future portended eventual success for it as well.

For a clue to the meaning of democracy in the Manifesto one may turn to Marx and Engels' writings during the events leading up to and shortly following its publication. As Engels pointed out in a letter to the Chartist newspaper, *The Northern Star* (4 April 1846), universal suffrage will contravene the interests of the majority unless workers have access to a free press that only money can buy. Thanks to the liberal doctrine of civil liberties, the constitutional state, due process, and equality under the law,

---

[14] Ibid., 14:655–656.
[15] Cited by Nomad, *Apostles of Revolution*, 30, 80–81.

liberalism passes for democracy until the proletariat achieves enough
independence of thought to recognize that liberalism means "nothing else
but giving *inequality* the name of equality." In all countries from 1815 to
1830, Engels noted, "the essentially democratic movement of the working
class was more or less made subservient to the liberal movement of the
bourgeoisie." As a result, one "could not yet see the total difference between
liberalism and democracy—emancipation of the middle classes and
emancipation of the working classes."[16] He was not suggesting that workers
have no use for civil liberties, but only that civil rights should not be taken
as ends in themselves. Marx agreed.[17]

The presumption underlying democratic demands is that the unfettered
will of the majority ultimately benefits the majority. In an essay on 13
November 1847, Engels cited approvingly "universal suffrage, direct
elections, paid representation...the essential conditions of political
sovereignty" as a step forward to social emancipation. He followed this with
an article on 9 January 1848 listing the six demands of the English Chartists
in their People's Charter: annual parliaments, universal suffrage, vote by
ballot, abolition of the property qualification for members of parliament,
paid representation, and equal electoral districts.[18] The Chartists had made
democracy their principal demand in the conviction that it prepared the way
for social equality and a solution to the property question.

The will of the majority also figured in Marx's accounts of democracy.
In his appeal to primary electors in Cologne in an article on 26 January
1849, he asked "And what is the will of the majority?" It is not a unified will
but a sum of contradictory wills linked to one another by certain common
interests. The will of the people, the will of the majority, is "democratic
humbug." It is "the will not of separate social estates and classes, but of a
single class, and of those other classes and sections of classes which are
subordinated to this one ruling class." This is what Marx found unacceptable
in bourgeois democracy.[19] Democracy as practiced was not capable of
curing social ills. In effect, the only acceptable democracy was one that
followed a proletarian revolution instead of leading up to it, an opinion Marx
shared with Engels but presented ambiguously in the Manifesto.

---

[16] Marx and Engels, *Collected Works*, 6:28–29.

[17] Karl Marx, "The Communism of the *Rheinischer Beobachter*," *Collected Works*,
6:221–222, 225.

[18] F. Engels, "The Manifesto of M. de Lamartine," *Collected Works*, 6:365; and idem,
"Feargus O'Connor and the Irish People," *Collected Works*, 6:449.

[19] K. Marx, "The Berlin National-Zeitung to the Primary Electors," *Collected Works*,
8:272; and 41:561–562.

As an example of postbourgeois or proletarian democracy, Marx later cited the experience of the Paris Commune. In 1871 he pinpointed what he considered essential to full democracy: the transformation of the state and its organs from masters into servants of society. To achieve this tour de force the Commune made use of two infallible means. First, "it filled all posts...by election on the basis of universal suffrage of all concerned, subject to the right of recall at any time." Second, it swept away place-hunting and careerism by ensuring that "all officials, high or low, were paid only the wages received by other workers." As a result, bureaucrats, politicians, and judges were dismissed and replaced by ordinary workers serving on a part-time and short-term basis. In place of the old bureaucratic machine, the Commune introduced "self-government of the producers...the political form at last discovered under which to work out the economic emancipation of labor."[20] There had been a preview of this situation in the Manifesto: "the public power will lose its political character...[will cease being] the organized power of one class for oppressing another."

Among the elliptical statements of the Manifesto is that concerning the first step in the revolution. It is "to raise the proletariat to the position of ruling class, to win the battle of democracy" or, in the literal translation of this last clause, "which is the struggle of democracy." Its source may be traced to Engels' "Principles of Communism," which Marx used in composing the Manifesto. Engels speaks of "the winning of democracy and the realization of the socialist measures following upon it," a clear indication that the battle of democracy is a struggle for the real rather than formal rule of the majority that would dispossess the bourgeoisie and centralize all instruments of production in the hands of the state.

How is this battle to be won? The proletariat must first win the battle *for* democracy, in order later to win the battle *of* democracy. To win the first, "the workers begin to form combinations (Trades' Unions) against the bourgeois." They club together not only to keep up the rate of wages, but also to exact political concessions. The ever-expanding union of workers is needed "to centralize the numerous local struggles...into one national struggle between classes." The organization of workers into a political party on a national scale eventually "compels legislative recognition of particular interests of the workers, by taking advantage of the divisions among the bourgeoisie." In this way the Ten Hours Bill in England became law.

---

[20] F. Engels, Introduction to Karl Marx, "The Civil War in France," *Selected Works*, 1:484; and Marx, "The Civil War in France," *Selected Works*, 1:520, 522.

Marx believed that the proletarian majority would ultimately win the battle of democracy under these conditions, that this scenario was realistic because of the sheer number of wage-earners, their combination in trade unions, their homogeneity as a class-in-itself, their political organization as a class-for-itself, and the humanist premise that man is a rational animal acting in accordance with self-interest. The Manifesto's faith in democracy is predicated on this unwarranted confusion of human potential and actuality.

Virtually all of Marx's revolutionary predecessors rejected this naïve faith on the grounds that oppressive social conditions interfere with man's rational potential and that, whatever might be the proletariat's potential, its behavior was in fact irrational. Whether because of widespread ignorance, the daily struggle for survival and other mundane preoccupations, or fear of the authorities, they believed the proletariat was incapable of liberating itself by itself. Among the bizarre features of the Manifesto is its presumption to the contrary, one that flies in the face of its materialistic and scientific interpretation of history.

Rational behavior would appear to be a monopoly of ruling classes. By "freeloading" or getting others to work for them, they are able to satisfy their needs with the least possible effort. History is rational inasmuch as it is the history of elites with the urge to get something for nothing, the "urge to exploit and to dominate." The privileged status of the lucky minority has its roots in past conquests by those "who would rather fight and rob than work and starve."[21] As Hernando Cortés, the Spanish Conquistador, reputedly said: "I came to Mexico not to till the ground like a peasant. I came for *gold!*"

"Leaving aside the ambiguities of Marx's teaching," writes Maximilien Rubel, its enduring message is to be found in the "social criticism founded upon the idea or postulate of democracy…[a postulate] common to socialism, anarchism, and communism." But is democracy in fact their common denominator? The socialist legacy following Saint-Simon was not democratic but technocratic, the communist current stemming from Babeuf had no more faith than Lenin had in workers' self-government, and the anarchism of Bakunin and his adepts relied on an invisible dictatorship to activate and guide the social revolution. One might add that democracy has not borne out Marx and Engels' expectations. As Rubel concedes, "the predictions that Marx…made about the emancipatory and creative force of

---

[21] Nomad, *Aspects of Revolt*, 14, 209.

democracy, as conquered by the workers' movement, have been thoroughly refuted."[22]

An incorrigible democrat, Marx valued above all the independent historical initiatives of the working class. As he noted in a letter to W. Bracke (5 May 1875), "Every step of real movement is worth more than a dozen programmes." Workers have an immediate stake in bread-and-butter issues out of concern not only for their well-being, but also for the inroads made on the capitalist fortress by reducing profits. As Marx stressed the importance of this ongoing class war in the form of immediate demands in a letter dated 21 February 1881, "The doctrinaire and necessarily fantastic anticipation of...a revolution in the future only diverts one from the struggle of the present."[23]

No Sectarian Principles of Their Own

Marx detested sects. "The sect," he wrote to J. B. Schweitzer (13 October 1868), "sees the justification for its existence...not in what it has in *common* with the class movement but in the *particular shibboleth* which *distinguishes* it from the movement."[24] Like the Communist League, he wrote to F. Bolte (23 November 1871), the First International was "founded in order to replace the socialist or semisocialist sects by a real organization of the working class." To survive, a class movement of the workers must already have smashed sectarianism and become alerted to its revival within the class movement. Of little consequence politically, sects are useful only when workers are not yet ready for taking initiatives on a mass scale. Otherwise, "all sects are essentially reactionary"![25]

Engels, too, hoped to put an end to sectarianism in the class struggle. In a letter to Florence Kelley Wischnewetzky (28 December 1886) he called on his German friends in America to bore from within mass parties and organizations rather than to form their own groups in opposition, "to go in for any real general working class movement...and work it gradually up to the theoretical level." And in a follow-up letter (27 January 1887) he explained that, as in 1848 when Marx joined the Democratic party in Germany to get the ear of the workers, in 1864 when he founded the

---

[22] Maximilien Rubel, "Marx's Concept of Democracy," *Democracy* (Fall 1983), 104, 105.
[23] Marx and Engels, *Selected Correspondence*, 360, 410.
[24] Ibid., 258.
[25] Ibid., 326.

International "he drew up the General Rules in such a way that *all* working-class Socialists of that period could join it."[26]

"There is nothing resembling 'sectarianism' in Marxism," wrote Lenin in March 1913, "in the sense of its being...a doctrine which arose *away from* the highroad of development of world civilization." On the contrary, the teachings incorporated in the Manifesto are the "legitimate successor to the best that was created by mankind in the nineteenth century in the shape of German philosophy, English political economy and French socialism."[27] Not just French socialism, he added in his encyclopedic article "Karl Marx" written a year later, but also "French revolutionary doctrines in general."[28]

The Manifesto's debt to this French contribution also included the "great French philosophers of the eighteenth century," according to Engels. Rousseau's *Social Contract* was the inspiration behind the first democratic constitution in the modern world, the Jacobin Constitution adopted on 24 June 1793, the word made flesh.[29] As Engels further noted, "the *Contrat Social* of Rousseau...only could come into being, as a democratic republic," adding that it also found its realization in the Reign of Terror against the wishes of the bourgeoisie. Most of the ideological baggage of the Manifesto can be traced to mainly French sources. Besides democracy (Rousseau), Engels lists technocracy (Saint-Simon), socialism (Fourier), and communism (Babeuf).[30]

"In the meantime, along with and after the French philosophy of the eighteenth century," wrote Engels, there appeared "the new German philosophy culminating in Hegel." Although Engels examines only Hegel's methodological contribution to Marxism, Hegel and his disciple Feuerbach were among the principal sources of Marx's liberalism as well as humanism. Under the influence of the French Revolution, Hegel penned his liberal theory of the constitutional state and the role of freedom in history.[31] Between 1839 and 1842 Marx also drew from the fund of ideas of the

---

[26] Ibid., 474, 476.

[27] V. I. Lenin, "The Three Sources and Three Component Parts of Marxism," in *Marx, Engels, Marxism*, 5th English ed. (Moscow: Foreign Languages Publishing House, 1953), 84.

[28] V. I. Lenin, "Karl Marx," *Selected Works*, 1:7.

[29] R. R. Palmer, *Twelve Who Ruled: The Year of Terror in the French Revolution* (Princeton: Princeton University Press, 1989; orig. pub. 1941), 34, 310, 386.

[30] Engels, "Socialism: Utopian and Scientific," *Selected Works*, 2:116–119, 121–123, 123–124.

[31] Ibid., 2:128. On Hegel's liberalism, see Andrew Hacker, *Political Theory: Philosophy, Ideology, Science* (New York: Macmillan, 1961), 433–434, 445–448, 451–452; and Carl J. Friedrich, ed., *The Philosophy of Hegel* (New York: Modern Library, 1953), 11–16, 21–23, 149–153, 272–277, 291–297, 307–319.

Young Hegelians, a typical combination of humanism and liberalism. Marx's 1843 commentary on Hegel's *Philosophy of Right* testifies to both sets of influences.

Seven Principles Rolled into One

In his campaign to rid the communist movement of its sectarian features, Marx sought to incorporate it into the ideological mainstream of Western Civilization. For this purpose he linked it up with the Renaissance ideal of the complete man, with the liberal doctrine of civil rights, and with the democratic credo of universal suffrage and majority rule. In his hands, communism became an adjunct of the secular struggle for human freedom in fulfillment of the promise of humanism, liberalism, and democracy.

Modern communism, he argued, was also tied to the Industrial Revolution, sharing its faith in the limitless progress of science, technology, and the wealth of nations. Far from negating the great achievements of bourgeois civilization, Marx's communism assimilated them. To his lasting credit, he attacked capitalism on its own grounds for failing to live up to its ideal of human progress.[32]

At the same time, he could not afford to slight the revolutionary aspirations of the original communists and their contribution to discrediting the established order.[33] This meant carrying the socialist project to its extreme conclusion by nationalizing not only the land and basic industry, but all means of production and transportation both large and small. Only independent artisans and peasants would be allowed to keep their properties in the expectation that they would soon be ruined by competition and by the economies of scale benefiting large socialist enterprises.

As the Manifesto explains, the various crafts are rendered worthless by new methods of production. There is no need to expropriate the "property of the petty artisan and of the small peasant, a form of property that preceded the bourgeois form...[because] the development of industry has to a great extent already destroyed it, and is still destroying it daily." Besides, independent artisans and small peasants have no capital of their own, and their meager property "affords no surplus wherewith to command the labor of others."

---

[32] Shlomo Avineri, *The Social and Political Thought of Karl Marx* (New York: Cambridge University Press, 1968), 37, 182–183, 204; and Seidman, *Liberalism and the Origins of European Social Theory*, 107–113, 115–117.

[33] Seidman, *Liberalism and the Origins of European Social Theory*, 117–118.

The Manifesto's brief for revolutionary extremism also meant going beyond the socialist program to the abolition of all private property, not just bourgeois property. This involved common ownership of all the forces of production, not just physical plant but also labor-power. That is the significance of the Manifesto's call for the abolition of buying and selling, for the end of commerce can only mean the creation of a sector of free goods that are there for the taking. Marx's faith in industrial progress led him to believe that eventually this sector would embrace all goods. In that event it would be pointless to pay for work performed. Although private ownership of labor-power would not have been abolished de jure, it would cease to be of any private benefit because its fruits would be common to all and it would have been nullified de facto.

The Manifesto further addresses what might be called the anarchist solution to the social question. This involves the abolition of the bureaucratic apparatus of the state and its repressive functions. Whether the state gradually becomes obsolete or is directly smashed, in either event it is done away with. So, in a sense, Marx's document is also in part an anarchist manifesto.

The Manifesto not only has a place for these competing "isms," but also raises them to the honored status of inviolable principles. Although there is a sense in which communism is a means to humanism, it was not a means in Machiavelli's sense, to be sacrificed for some other end. Like the illustrious Florentine, Marx took for granted that the end justifies the means, provided, of course, that the means are not in turn revered as universal human values. What is unique about the Manifesto is that humanism, liberalism, democracy, technocracy, socialism, anarchism, and communism were not conceived as rival but as complementary goals, each compatible with the others. Accordingly, communism is presented not only as a means to humanism, but also as an end, and as the fulfillment as well of liberalism, democracy, technocracy, socialism, and anarchism—seven principles rolled into one.

The Manifesto's tour de force was to weave together these diverse currents within the communist movement. The *Communist Journal*, the League's organ, made a special point of calling for working-class unity or solidarity. Its trial number declared: "If we are to achieve solidarity, the spokesmen of the various [workers'] parties must cease their bitter attacks upon those who hold other views.... Therefore, proletarians of all lands, unite!"[34] This slogan was not just the capstone of the Manifesto, but also

---

[34] Ryazanoff, *The Communist Manifesto*, Appendix E, 292–293, 294.

served as headpiece to the journal and to the League's statutes formalized in June 1847. Henceforth, the "key words…were no longer *love for humanity*, but *organization*; no longer *equality*, but *solidarity*."[35]

In its trial number in September 1847, the journal made a brief not only for "community of goods," but also for a society "wherein all mankind can live as free and happy creatures." Communists, we are told, "have no desire to exchange freedom for equality." Democracy is another inviolate principle. Should a majority of citizens hesitate to take the final step to communism, then "we shall have to submit to the popular will."[36]

Since these several ideologies to a lesser or greater degree had taken hold of the proletarians, concessions were made to each. But the Manifesto's focus is not evenly distributed over all of them. Some have priority of place. The extremes are barely touched upon in passing, and, except for the word "communism," the only "isms" in high relief are those occupying middle ground. Although the manifesto of a communist party, special attention is given to those ideologies with the greatest currency in working-class circles. Neither humanism and liberalism at one extreme nor anarchism and communism at the opposite pole are among them.

The preferred ideologies are democracy, technocracy, and socialism. Let me briefly pinpoint each.

"*Democracy nowadays is communism*," wrote Engels as early as 1845.[37] As the ideology most widely shared by working people, the Manifesto assigns it a preeminent role. "The proletarian movement is the self-conscious, independent movement of the immense majority, in the interests of the immense majority." How are those interests to be served? Presumably, through representative government and majority rule, another term for democracy. Universal suffrage stands at the top of the list of working-class demands. "Finally, they [Communists] labor everywhere for the union and agreement of the democratic parties of all countries." That means that these parties are the principal allies of the Communists.

The Manifesto opens with a brief for technocracy. By "technocracy" I mean the control of industry by technical experts, a planned rather than market economy, and the rapid development of science, technology, and labor-saving devices that hold forth the promise of a postscarcity economy, an expanding sector of free goods, and the full satisfaction of the multiple needs indispensable to human self-fulfillment. The encomiums to the

---

[35] Dirk Struik, *The Birth of the Communist Manifesto* (New York: International Publishers, 1971), 58.

[36] Ryazanoff, *The Communist Manifesto*, Appendix E, 289–290, 292–294.

[37] F. Engels, "The Festival of Nations in London," *Collected Works*, 6:5.

capitalist mode of production in section 1 of the Manifesto are at bottom praise for having, "during its rule of scarce one hundred years. . . created more massive and more colossal productive forces than have all previous generations together." But its past record is hardly an argument for preserving a system that can no longer deliver the goods, that is no longer able to control the gigantic means of production it has created, that is governed by the greed for profits rather than by the prospect of overcoming poverty.

On close inspection, the praise for capitalism is at bottom acclaim for the benefits of applied science or technology, the "Subjection of Nature's forces to man, machinery, application of chemistry to industry and agriculture, steam navigation, railways, electric telegraphs, clearing of whole continents for cultivation, canalization of rivers." What earlier century, Marx asks, "had even a presentiment that such productive forces slumbered in the lap of social labor?" Who could boast of such marvels, "wonders far surpassing Egyptian pyramids, Roman aqueducts, and Gothic cathedrals?" Only modern technology was capable of showing what man's activity might bring forth. The application of science to industry had made possible new wants, "a demand ever rising." So much wealth had brought about an "epidemic of over-production. . . [because the] conditions of bourgeois society are too narrow to comprise the wealth created by them."

In these passages from section 1 we have a brief for capitalism only insofar as it promoted technology and the wealth of nations, after which common instead of private ownership becomes a sine qua non of continued progress. What kind of common ownership? The answer is common ownership of the means of production, otherwise known as socialism, as distinct from a community of goods, traditionally identified with communism. To make communism credible, section 2 breaks with customary usage by equating socialism with an elementary form of communism, thereby undercutting the criticism of communism as unrealistic.

It is noteworthy that the Manifesto employs the term "socialism" in a derogatory sense. One finds it only in section 3 in connection with Marx's critique of "Christian socialism," "feudal socialism," "petty-bourgeois socialism," "'True' socialism," "reactionary socialism," and "critical-utopian socialism." Nowhere does he use the expression *communist socialism*, although that is the meaning he gives to the word "communism." The Manifesto's slogan, "Abolition of private property," is not to be taken literally, for it means only the "abolition of bourgeois private property."

Thus personal property, including labor-power, "is not thereby transformed into social property."

Such is the ideological core or centerpiece of the Manifesto. But the exposition would be incomplete without pinpointing the passages in passing that pay more than lip service to those ideologies of only marginal importance to the working class.

The Manifesto's humanism is barely visible and to be gleaned with some difficulty from two short passages. The first tells us what humanism is; the second, what it is not. At issue is what postcapitalist society promises that counts for more than overcoming human misery. The Manifesto's answer is "an association, in which the free development of each is the condition for the free development of all"—a society of universal rather than restricted or privileged humanism. The second passage depicts the opposite condition, that of "universal asceticism and social leveling in its crudest form." Instead of leveling upward, it signifies leveling downward—equality with a dose of vengeance.

Turning next to liberalism, there is a brief for it in section 3. In no uncertain terms the Manifesto supports the "fight of the German, and, especially, of the Prussian bourgeoisie against feudal aristocracy and absolute monarchy—in other words, the liberal movement." In almost the same breath it opposes the "traditional anathemas against liberalism, against representative government, against bourgeois legislation, bourgeois liberty and equality." By implication, the Manifesto defends civil rights, not just "free trade" under capitalism. Thus it disputes the nostrum that "the masses...had nothing to gain, and everything to lose, by this bourgeois movement." Absolute monarchy, the feudal squirearchy, and arbitrary rule are secondary targets of the Manifesto, but targets nonetheless.

At the opposite pole of humanism and liberalism, the Manifesto provides token support for both communism and anarchism. Section 2 of the Manifesto calls for the abolition not only of bourgeois property, but also of commerce generally. "This talk about free selling and buying, and all the other 'brave words' of our bourgeoisie about freedom in general, have a meaning, if any, only in contrast with restricted selling and buying, with the fettered traders of the Middle Ages, but have no meaning when opposed to the Communistic abolition of buying and selling." The feudal and Church authorities had no intention of abolishing money, whereas that is what the Communists propose. Thus the Manifesto opens the door to an economy of free goods in which, short of the limits imposed by rationing, each person takes from the common stores whatever may be needed. Such was the model of a higher stage of communist society barely hinted at in the Manifesto but

later spelled out in Marx's *Critique of the Gotha Programme*. In the
envisioned postscarcity economy, distribution according to work would
become superfluous, thereby making distribution according to need credible
for the first time.

To be sure, the word "communism" in the Manifesto does not always
stand for something positive. It also designates the purely negative or
destructive movement aimed at abolishing the status quo. This is the
meaning Marx attached to "political" communism in his *Economic and
Philosophic Manuscripts*. But this usage covers only the Manifesto's
political objectives: "formation of the proletariat into a class [for itself],
overthrow of the bourgeois supremacy, conquest of political power by the
proletariat." Considerably more is at stake, however—the Manifesto's
economic objectives—"the most radical rupture with traditional property
relations."

Even anarchism has a niche in the Manifesto: "The executive of the
modern State is but a committee for managing the common affairs of the
whole bourgeoisie." That alone is an argument for abolishing not only the
executive, but also the legislature for managing the *uncommon* affairs of the
bourgeoisie. "Political power, properly so-called, is merely the organized
power of one class for oppressing another," declares the Manifesto. So the
entire state apparatus must be smashed in the course of sweeping away
classes and class antagonisms.

In summary, the Manifesto's call for solidarity—"Working Men of All
Countries, Unite!"—means for workers to stop squabbling over these seven
political "isms." All have a place in the Communists' public statement of
their aims, although to call it "communist" is less accurate than to define it
by the core ideologies of democracy, technocracy, and socialism. To the
question "Is the *Communist Manifesto* a communist manifesto?" the answer
must be a qualified "yes and no." Thus the Manifesto is both something
more and something less than a communist manifesto. Paradoxically, it was
Marx's marriage of incompatibles that made communism credible.

5. Amending the Manifesto

> Thus the history of the Manifesto reflects, to a great extent, the history of the modern working-class movement....Yet, when it was written, we could not have called it a *Socialist* Manifesto.

Engels, Preface to the 1888 English edition

A quarter century after the Manifesto's appearance, Marx and Engels conceded that it needed alteration. Although "the general principles laid down in the Manifesto are, on the whole, as correct today as ever...this programme has in some details become antiquated." "But, then, the Manifesto has become a historical document which we have no longer any right to alter."[1]

It was not just the details that needed improvement and called for amendment. Found lacking or downright mistaken in the Manifesto were its theses concerning the reactionary role of the democratic petty bourgeoisie; the role of science as a dependent factor of production; the reliance on the existing state apparatus to build communism once the battle for democracy has been won; the voluntary transition to communism exclusively through centralized public ownership; the abolition of bourgeois property as the basic principle of communism; the anarchy of production as the economic dissolvent of capitalist society; and the forcible—understood as violent—overthrow of all oppressive social conditions.

As a corrective to these faults, Marx and Engels informally amended the Manifesto. Their amendments included, first, the assignment of a progressive role to the petty bourgeoisie; second, the interpretation of science as an independent factor of production distinct from labor; third, the acknowledgment that the working class cannot transform society within the framework of the bourgeois state; fourth, the assignment of an important function to cooperatives in the transition to communism; fifth, the redefinition of communism conformable to the principle, "From each according to his ability, to each according to his needs"; sixth, the recognition of the separation of management from ownership as central to

---

[1] Marx and Engels, "Preface to the German edition of 1872," in Bender, *Karl Marx. The Communist Manifesto*, 43–44.

the breakdown of the old society and the birth of the new; and seventh, the articulation of a strategy of ballots without bullets.[2]

The Democratic Petty Bourgeoisie

The Manifesto depicts the industrial bourgeoisie as the immediate enemy of the proletariat, and the petty bourgeoisie as the immediate enemy of the industrial bourgeoisie. As long as the latter must contend with "the remnants of absolute monarchy, the landowners, the non-industrial bourgeoisie, the petty bourgeoisie," the proletarians fight the same enemies. Their principal ally is the progressive bourgeoisie. "The lower middle class, the small manufacturer, the shopkeeper, the artisan, the peasant, all these fight against the bourgeoisie, to save from extinction their existence as fractions of the middle class." They are not only conservative, "they are reactionary, for they try to roll back the wheel of history." Only by chance do the petty bourgeois perform a revolutionary role when, because of their impending transfer into the proletariat, they desert their own class and defend not their present interests but their future interests as proletarians.

This depiction in section 1 of the Manifesto is reaffirmed in sections 3 and 4. Attention is drawn not only to the old petty bourgeoisie, "precursors of the modern bourgeoisie...[who] still vegetate side by side with [it]," but also to a "new class of petty bourgeoisie...ever renewing itself as a supplementary part of bourgeois society." These intermediate classes resist the forces of modern capitalism; they oppose the centralizing tendencies of the modern state; their self-styled socialism is "reactionary and utopian." Thus in Germany the Communists ally themselves with "the bourgeoisie whenever it acts in a revolutionary way, against the absolute monarchy, the feudal squirearchy, and the petty bourgeoisie."

So the petty bourgeoisie cannot be a reliable ally of the Communists. Marx would soon swallow those words. Within a month of the Manifesto's publication he would follow Engels' lead by acknowledging the democratic interests of the petty bourgeoisie and by calling for an alliance not only with it, but also with those hitherto depicted as reactionary peasants embroiled in the "idiocy of rural life." The "Demands of the Communist Party in Germany" (25 March 1848) depicts the petty bourgeoisie as a "class which, until the winning of democracy and the realization of the socialist measures following upon it, has in many respects the same interest as the proletariat."

---

[2]   See Struik, *Birth of the Communist Manifesto*, 68–72.

Thus Marx sought to reach "an understanding with these democratic Socialists."[3]

In 1850, Marx and Engels acknowledged the inconsistency between the Manifesto's strategy of fighting them and its commitment to "labor everywhere for the union and agreement of the democratic parties of all countries." Henceforth, the democratic petty bourgeois would be assigned a progressive role and would cease to be branded as "reactionary." Alliances would be formed with them as the immediate friends of the proletariat—albeit its future enemies.[4]

Engels' assessment, according to Draper, was more "up-to-date than the flat hostility that Marx wrote into the Manifesto." Increasingly, even the reactionary sectors of the petty bourgeoisie were seeing the advantages of detaching themselves from the feudal squirearchy and lining up with the bourgeoisie. Their upwardly mobile members continually crossed the threshold separating them from the bottom layer of capitalists.

But are not all petty bourgeois small capitalists? On the contrary, says Draper interpreting Marx, "The petty-bourgeoisie earn their living by dint [mainly] of their own labor and their own property; the bourgeoisie live on the earnings from the labor of others."[5]

The amended strategy toward the petty bourgeoisie received its classic formulation in Marx and Engels' March 1850 "Address of the Central Committee to the Communist League." Once the liberal bourgeoisie took possession of the state power in Germany after the March movement in 1848, it used that power to advantage by turning against its working-class allies. Deserted by the liberal bourgeoisie, the proletariat could count only on the petty bourgeoisie to prevent the liberal bourgeoisie from consolidating its power. Meanwhile, having become radicalized by defeat, the various factions of the petty bourgeoisie wanted their turn at ruling with the help of the proletariat. So they began calling themselves "republicans or reds, just as the republican petty bourgeois in France now call themselves socialists."[6]

What, then, is the relation of the Communist League to these petty-bourgeois democrats and republicans? "[I]t marches together with them against the [bourgeois] faction which it aims at overthrowing, it opposes them in everything whereby they seek to consolidate their position in their own interests." Destined to replace the bourgeoisie in power, they may be

---

[3] Marx and Engels, *Collected Works*, 6:355, 356; and 7:4.
[4] Ibid., 10:277–286.
[5] Draper, *Karl Marx's Theory of Revolution*, 2:198, 289.
[6] Marx and Engels, *Collected Works*, 10:278–279, 281.

counted on to play the same treacherous role as did the bourgeoisie before them. Although their program would curtail the bureaucracy, shift taxes onto the big landowners and capitalists, establish bourgeois property relations in the countryside through an agrarian reform, and raise wages and improve working conditions for the proletariat, wage-earners would remain in the same lowly status as before. It is not enough that the workers' position would become more tolerable for the moment. So, unlike the petty bourgeois who strive to bring the revolution to a close once they seize power, "it is our interest to make the revolution permanent." That means to "carry to the extreme the proposals of the democrats, who in any case will not act in a revolutionary but in a merely reformist manner." And that means to carry out "direct attacks upon private property" until all the possessing classes have been expropriated and forced out of their position of dominance.[7]

Paradoxically, this was the strategy that the Willich-Schapper League applied in Germany to the dismay of Marx and Engels, because it took the form of a military conspiracy and led to the trial of Marx's supporters. As Engels defended the members of Marx's League, they had not collaborated with the petty-bourgeois conspirators, they were not guilty of treason, and their only "plot...[was] against, not the existing government, but its probable successor."

Marx also defended the League's members at Cologne. "The Communists can help accelerate the dissolution of bourgeois society and yet leave the dissolution...in the hands of bourgeois society." The accused proceeded "from the outrageous assumption that the present Prussian government would collapse without their having to lift a finger." The Communists were intent on "forming not the *government party of the future* but the *opposition party of the future*." Thus the Marx party should not be on trial, but rather the "group [that] broke off from the Communist League...the Willich-Schapper group."[8]

Did these protestations against the trial at Cologne signify another change in strategy? Not at all. Marx and Engels opposed only the conspiratorial-military character of the alliance with the democratic petty bourgeoisie. Political pressure had obliged them to present to the public a face different from the one they showed to their inner circle.

---

[7] Ibid., 10:280–281, 286.
[8] Ibid., 11:390, 404, 449.

A Productive Force Distinct from Labor

In its sketch of capitalist society the Manifesto failed to underline the *independent* role of science and of scientists. Not until *Capital* (1867) and the preparatory notebooks leading up to it, the 1857–1858 *Grundrisse*, does Marx amend the Manifesto by making science a separate factor of production. In the *Grundrisse* he notes that "to the degree that large industry develops, the creation of real wealth comes to depend less on labor time and on the amount of labor employed than on the power of the agencies set in motion during labor time...[it] depends rather on the general state of science and on the progress of technology." This being the case, socialism rests on a political economy of expertise even more than on a political economy of labor—and herewith we mark a major amendment to the Manifesto.[9]

The *Grundrisse* envisions the end of the capitalist order through the agency of a scientific-technological revolution that not only precedes the proletarian revolution, but makes it possible. For Marx, the operation of exploitation, the "theft of alien labor time...appears as a miserable foundation in the face of this new one, created by large scale industry." By calling to life all the powers of science and technology, capitalism makes "the creation of wealth independent (relatively) of the labor time employed on it." Machines are *"organs of the human brain, created by the human hand*; the power of knowledge objectified." Thus the growth of machine culture testifies to the degree that "general social knowledge has become a direct force of production."[10]

In the Manifesto, the bourgeoisie were seen as the principal agent of industrial progress, a "bourgeoisie [that] cannot exist without constantly revolutionizing the instruments of production." Men of science were depicted as servants, as mere "wage-laborers" enlisted in the service of the bourgeoisie. In sharp contrast, both the *Grundrisse* and *Capital* depict the forces of science and technology—and therefore also men of science—as gradually asserting their independence. The steam engine did not come into the world sui generis. "It was, on the contrary, the invention of machines that made a revolution in the form of steam-engines necessary"[11]—and it was men of science who invented the machines. In this reversal of the Manifesto's causal order in *Capital* we have an amendment to the Manifesto that gives credit where credit is due.

---

[9] Karl Marx, "The *Grundrisse*," in Tucker (1978), 284.
[10] Ibid., 284, 285.
[11] Marx, *Capital*, 1:409–410.

Because "modern industry...makes science a productive force distinct from labor," the man of knowledge and the productive laborer find themselves at loggerheads. Marx quotes William Thompson, the radical political economist: "Knowledge, instead of remaining the handmaid of the laborer...has almost everywhere arrayed itself against labor...in order to render their [the laborers'] muscular powers entirely mechanical and obedient." Here we have another amendment to the Manifesto—an amendment within an amendment. For if science or scientifically based knowledge counts as a fourth factor of production, then its owners—men of science and knowledge workers generally—should logically constitute a separate class also destined to have its turn at ruling![12]

Ironically, that was Bakunin's theory and the main thrust of his critique of classical Marxism. Not for nothing had he detected in Marx's writings an argument for a new class, a technocracy of "higher grade" workers defined by the ownership of scientific and technical knowledge. To it belong "scientists, artists, engineers, inventors, accountants, educators, government officials, and their subordinate elites who enforce labor discipline." Underneath them is a different class of lower-grade workers, "prevented from applying creative ideas or intelligence, who blindly and mechanically carry out the orders of the intellectual-managerial elite." In this scenario, the new mode of production is "under the direct command of the State engineers who will constitute the new privileged scientific-political class." Thus, as Bakunin envisioned the outcome of a Marxist proletarian revolution, "It will be the reign of *scientific intelligence*...[of] a new bureaucracy of real and pretended scientists and scholars, and the world will be divided into a minority ruling in the name of knowledge and an immense majority."[13]

The irony is that Marx acknowledged the privileged status of scientific workers under socialism as well as capitalism. Under capitalism, their superior pay is predicated on the greater value of their labor-power. Under socialism, their pay will be based on the compounded quantity and composite quality of their work: "Universal labor is all scientific labor, all discovery and all invention," labor that depends partly on direct cooperation and partly on the utilization of the labors of those who have gone before, "on the collective labor of the dead as well as the living."[14]

---

[12] Ibid., 1:397 and 397 n.2; 3:862.

[13] Michael Bakunin, "Revolutionary Catechism," in Sam Dolgoff, ed. and trans., *Bakunin on Anarchy* (Montréal: Black Rose Books, 1990), 90; Maximoff, *The Political Philosophy of Bakunin*, 289; and Michael Bakunin, *Marxism, Freedom and the State*, ed. and trans. K. J. Kenafick (London: Freedom Press, 1950), 38.

[14] Marx, *Capital*, 3:102; and idem, "Critique of the Gotha Programme," *Selected Works*, 2:23–24.

Beginning with *Anti-Dühring* (1878), Engels began addressing this new revolutionary force. In the course of developing a new philosophical-scientific worldview to which the epigones have given the name of dialectical materialism, the scientific and technical intelligentsia had become for him the main force of socialism. In effect, he replaced the young Marx's alliance of philosophers and proletarians with a new alliance of scientists and proletarians. As he might have interpolated a statement of the young Marx, "science cannot be made a reality without the assistance of the proletariat, and the proletariat cannot be assisted without science being made a reality."[15]

Although Marx made socialism a science, it was Engels who provided the label. The more ruthlessly science advances, he declared, "the more it finds itself in harmony with the interests and aspirations of the workers." Thus scientific socialism emerged in response to two different but closely related social problems: the class antagonism between bourgeois and proletarians; and the anarchy or irrationality of the capitalist mode of production and exchange.[16] Socialism expresses the confluence of the interests of wage earners intent on overcoming exploitation and the interests of scientific workers scandalized by the planlessness of capitalist production and distribution. In their unfitness to rule, the owners of capital are condemned by the standards of modern science and technology as well as by the objective needs of the proletariat.

The technocratic cast of Engels' thought is evident in his efforts to make socialism attractive to scientists and technicians. As one commentator notes, socialism would "abolish commodity production (i.e., production for the market) and thereby liberate conscious agents from the tyranny of blind laws." It promised to bring everything under control, mainly through "the conscious steering of history on the basis of scientific knowledge," that is to say, through scientific planning and "the avoidance of unintended results."[17]

Engels' thesis—that science, technology, and economic planning will be the agents of this social transformation—is a classic statement of the technocratic credo. Although the word "technocracy" means in ordinary speech no more than economic planning and control by scientists and

---

[15] See my essay, "Engels' Contribution to Marxism," in R. Miliband and J. Saville, eds., *The Socialist Register 1965* (London: Merlin Press, 1965), 298.

[16] Frederick Engels, *Ludwig Feuerbach* (New York: International Publishers, 1941), 61; and idem, *Anti-Dühring*, 2nd ed. (Moscow: Foreign Languages Publishing House, 1959; orig. pub. 1878), 27, 379–382.

[17] Andrzej Walicki, *Marxism and the Leap to the Kingdom of Freedom* (Stanford: Stanford University Press, 1995), 195; and Engels, "Socialism: Utopian and Scientific," *Selected Works*, 2:143, 152, 154.

engineers, its implicit rationale is the overcoming not only of capitalist waste and inefficiency, but also of capitalists as the principal beneficiaries of the economic system. Scientists and engineers have little use for industrial incompetence, and also for a system that favors people of property at the expense of the producers. Thus the spectacle of economic retardation led Engels to amend the Manifesto's class struggle scenario as one not only between bourgeois and proletarians, but also between bourgeois and the scientists and technological specialists directly in charge of production—experts without property versus proprietors without expertise.

Demolition of the State Machine

Instead of a minimum program concerned with bread-and-butter issues—higher wages, social security, and improved working conditions—the Manifesto's program calls for the organization of the proletariat into a political party aimed at winning the battle of democracy, and then using its political supremacy "to wrest, by degrees, all capital from the bourgeoisie." With the publication of "The Eighteenth Brumaire of Louis Bonaparte" (1852), however, Marx was already having second thoughts about relying on the existing state machinery to expropriate the capitalists. "The centralization of the state that modern society requires arises only on the ruins of the military-bureaucratic government machinery which was forged in opposition to feudalism." But that machinery had yet to be dismantled.[18]

In 1852 Marx targeted not the bourgeois parliamentary state but its immediate precursor, the military-bureaucratic state that sprang up in the days of the absolute monarchy. It was the executive, not the legislative power, that operated as a fetter on the developing social revolution in its preliminary phase. "This executive power with its enormous bureaucratic and military organization, with its ingenious state machinery...with a host of officials numbering half a million, this appalling parasitic body...enmeshes the body of French society like a net and chokes all its pores."[19] Although it had undermined the feudal system by raising the bourgeoisie to political power, it had outlived its original usefulness.

The bourgeoisie subsequently used it to suffocate the revolution. The "parliamentary republic found itself compelled to strengthen, along with the repressive measures, the resources and centralization of governmental

---

[18] Karl Marx, "The Eighteenth Brumaire of Louis Bonaparte," in Marx and Engels, *Selected Works*, 1:340 and 340 n.1.

[19] Ibid., 1:332.

power." According to Marx, on the Continent all "revolutions perfected this machine instead of smashing it," while the "parties that contended in turn for domination regarded the possession of this huge state edifice as the principal spoils of the victor."[20]

But there was still another unanticipated act in this drama of state power. Under the second Bonaparte the state "made itself completely independent." Instead of a servant of the economically dominant bourgeoisie, it became their master. "Bonaparte represents a class, and the most numerous class of French society at that, the *small-holding peasants*." Thus the same Bonaparte, after initially submitting to the bourgeois parliament in 1849–1850, dissolved the bourgeois parliament on the eighteenth Brumaire (2 December 1851).[21]

But the peasants who hoped to preserve the remnants of petty commodity production under the new bourgeois order—were they the sole class represented by Bonaparte? At best Bonaparte represented their past, not their future, while he simultaneously represented the future, not the past, of the bourgeoisie.[22]

"Bonaparte feels it to be his mission to safeguard 'bourgeois order,'" wrote Marx, which makes him a representative of bourgeois interests. "Nevertheless, he is somebody solely due to the fact that he has broken the material power of the middle class." He must continue to keep the bourgeoisie in a condition of dependence, because "by protecting its material power, he generates its political power anew." Only in the role of broker and by playing off one class against another could he hope to maintain himself in power. He must therefore "make the lower classes of the people happy within the frame of bourgeois society...[and] appear as the patriarchal benefactor of all classes."[23]

As Marx presents it, Bonapartism is a politically unstable regime in which executive and legislative power are concentrated in a single person who tries to placate all classes, but "cannot give to one class without taking from another." Driven by the conflicting demands on his person, he survives only by "keeping the public gaze fixed on himself...[and] by springing constant surprises [to keep people off balance]." In violating everything held sacred by the 1848 Revolution, the Bonapartist leader "makes some tolerant of revolution, others desirous of revolution, and produces actual anarchy in the name of order." But in so doing, he also strips the "halo from the entire

---

[20] Ibid., 1:333.
[21] Ibid., 1: 333–334.
[22] Ibid., 1:335.
[23] Ibid., 1:340, 341, 342.

state machine, profanes it and makes it at once loathsome and ridiculous."[24]
This was not Marx's last word on Bonapartism, but it was surely another
amendment to the Manifesto.

Was the Bonapartist state a throwback to the military-bureaucratic state,
or was it a modern successor to the bourgeois-parliamentary state? Marx's
Eighteenth Brumaire (1852) did not resolve this question. It was resolved in
The Civil War in France (1871): "In reality, it [Bonapartism] was the only
form of government possible at a time when the bourgeoisie had already
lost, and the working class had not yet acquired, the faculty of ruling the
nation."[25] The basic condition of modern Bonapartism, Marx concluded, was
an equilibrium between the bourgeoisie and proletariat in which real
governmental authority had to be exercised by a third party, a special caste
of army officers and state officials. That the bourgeoisie had ceded political
power to this caste in exchange for protection and the preservation of its
economic power signified that winning the battle of democracy in a
parliamentary republic was no longer possible.

In a letter to Dr. Kugelmann (12 April 1971), Marx recalled that in the
last chapter of his *Eighteenth Brumaire* he had said that "the next attempt of
the French revolution will be no longer, as before, to transfer the
bureaucratic military machine from one hand to another, but to *smash* it."[26]
In any case, the apparatus he had in mind in 1871 was the Bonapartist state
machinery, not that of the parliamentary republic—Bonaparte had already
smashed the latter!

This machinery consisted of the standing army, police, government
bureaucracy, judiciary, and clergy representing the officially designated state
religion. Handed down by the absolute monarchy as a weapon in the nascent
bourgeois arsenal against feudalism, it was swept away by the gigantic
broom of the 1789 Revolution. Then came the turn of the parliamentary
republic "under the direct control of the propertied classes...[when] the State
power assumed more and more the character of the national power of capital
over labor."[27]

Threatened by an imminent proletarian upheaval, the bourgeoisie
invested the executive with increased powers of repression that were
bourgeois rather than feudal. Bit by bit, they divested their parliamentary
stronghold, the National Assembly, of its leading role in government.

---

[24] Ibid., 1:342, 343, 343–344.
[25] Marx, "The Civil War in France," *Selected Works*, 1:518.
[26] Karl Marx, *Letters to Dr. Kugelmann* (New York: International Publishers, 1934),
123.
[27] Marx, "The Civil War in France," *Selected Works*, 1:516–517, 517–518.

Bonapartism was the final act in this divestment, a transitional regime whose standing army, police, judiciary, and prison system continued to be used for repressing the proletariat. Precisely that is why "the working class cannot simply lay hold of the ready-made state machinery, and wield it for its own purposes." To "win the battle of democracy" would henceforth mean the "destruction of the State power."[28] It was an amendment to the Manifesto, since said destruction had become a condition of the disappearance of class distinctions.

Yet far from abolishing the state and its centralized powers, Marx proposed to use them for the benefit of the proletariat. Thus Marx defended the Commune State, the Paris Commune of 1871 that replaced the Versailles government: "It was essentially a working-class government...the political form at last discovered under which to work out the economic emancipation of labor." However, instead of adopting the liberal principle of the separation of powers, the Commune salvaged a major feature of the Bonapartist regime by establishing a "working, not a parliamentary, body, executive and legislative at the same time."[29]

For the first time, the Commune established an effective form of suffrage making it "really democratic." It was not enough to make all public offices elective. Delegates were subjected to a popular mandate that, if violated, could lead to their immediate recall. No longer shapers of the people's will, they became its servants and custodians—public servants in more than name only.

To make recall effective, indirect representation was necessary. A large and inchoate multitude cannot recall its delegates, because it lacks the organization and centralized powers to do so. So in a rough sketch of a workers' republic which the Commune had little time to implement, the rural communes "were to administer their common affairs by an assembly of delegates in the central town, and these district assemblies were again to send deputies to the National Delegation in Paris, each delegate to be at any time revocable and bound by the *mandat impératif* (formal instructions) of his constituents."[30] Centralized government would be retained, but municipal governments would be able to exert control at the national level. Contrary to democratic opinion, Marx considered the Commune's system of indirect representation to be *more* rather than *less* democratic than the system of direct representation in parliamentary regimes. There was nothing like *this* in the Manifesto!

---

[28] Ibid., 1:516, 518, 520.
[29] Ibid., 1:519, 522.
[30] Ibid., 1:520, 522.

To ensure that the delegates would be workers, the Commune decreed that "public service had to be done at workmen's wages." There was to be no more pilfering of the national treasury, taxes were no longer to be used as means of personal enrichment by the people's self-styled representatives. This check on careerism promised to put an end to professional politicians, while ensuring what Marx called "self-government of the producers."[31]

The Commune also, for the first time, made that "catchword of bourgeois revolutions, cheap government, a reality, by destroying the two greatest sources of expenditure—the standing army and State functionalism." Working men and women would no longer be taxed to support the government sinecures at extortionate salaries. "But neither cheap government nor the 'true republic' was its [the Commune's] ultimate aim." Its ultimate aim was to abolish that class-property which makes the labor of the many the wealth of the few. As Engels observed in his 1891 "Introduction" to Marx's *Civil War in France*, the Commune decreed that all factories closed down by their owners were to be transformed into cooperatives by the workers formerly employed in them. In addition, plans were made for "the organization of these cooperatives in one great union."[32]

What Marx called the self-government of the producers thus included cooperatives as well as the "shattering" of the Bonapartist state. The state would not be abolished as yet, but replaced by a new democratic one. "Truly democratic," Engels noted, because the parliamentary republic was only nominally democratic, "at best an evil inherited by the proletariat after its victorious struggle for class supremacy." Meanwhile, the proletariat "cannot avoid having to lop off at once as much as possible until such time as a generation reared in new, free social conditions is able to throw the entire lumber of the state on the scrap heap." Ultimately, that is what Marx meant by *destruction of the state power by means of the state power*. What was it like? "Look at the Paris Commune. That was the Dictatorship of the Proletariat."[33]

---

[31] Ibid., 1:519–520.
[32] Ibid., 1:522–523; and Frederick Engels, "Introduction" to Marx's "The Civil War in France," *Selected Works*, 1:479.
[33] Engels, "Introduction," 1:484–485.

A Cooperative Commonwealth?

The Paris Commune was the impetus for Marx's revived use of the word "communism" and for renewed efforts to diffuse the almost forgotten Manifesto. As Engels recalled in his preface to the English edition of 1888, after Marx's League was formally dissolved the Manifesto "seemed thenceforth to be doomed to oblivion." Although the reawakening of the European working class paved the way for the First International in 1864, "this association...could not at once proclaim the principles laid down in the Manifesto," but it did prepare the ground for their eventual discussion.[34] The Paris Commune was the turning point.

A new German edition appeared in 1872 with a preface by Marx and Engels in which they conceded that, in view of the changed historical circumstances since 1848 and the experience of the Commune, the transitional program would "be very differently worded today." As Marx explained in *The Civil War in France*, the Commune wanted to turn over all land and capital to a national union of cooperative societies, to transform them into "instruments of free and associated labor." But that is "Communism, 'impossible' Communism!" shrieked members of the ruling class. *Au contraire!* replied Marx, not "impossible," but "'possible' Communism"![35]

The Manifesto makes no mention of cooperatives and has apparently no use for them. Instead, "The proletariat will use its political supremacy...to centralize all instruments of production in the hands of the State." What does it mean "to centralize"? The Manifesto offers the following examples: "Centralization of credit in the hands of the State, by means of a national bank with State capital and an exclusive monopoly"; centralization of the means of communication and transportation in the hands of the state; centralization of factories and instruments of production in the hands of the state; and extension of the public power until "all production has been concentrated in the hands of a vast association of the whole nation." So illustrated, centralization can only mean "in the hands of the State."[36] Thus Marx's 1871 identification of a cooperative commonwealth with possible communism marked yet another major amendment to the Manifesto.

---

[34] Bender, *Karl Marx. The Communist Manifesto*, 47.
[35] Ibid., 43–44; and Marx, "The Civil War in France," *Selected Works*, 1:523.
[36] V. Sazonov, *On the "Manifesto of the Communist Party" of Marx and Engels* (Moscow: Progress Publishers, 1984), 81.

Marx's initial defense of cooperatives goes back to his 1864 "Inaugural Address." The growth of the cooperative movement, he proclaimed, was an even more significant event for the working class than the passage of the Ten Hours Bill, "a still greater victory of the political economy of labor over the political economy of property." "The cooperative factories raised by the unassisted efforts of a few bold 'hands'...cannot be over-rated." That is because they show, first, that production on a large scale "may be carried on without the existence of a class of masters employing a class of hands"; and second, that "like slave labor, like serf labor, hired labor is but a transitory and inferior form, destined to disappear." The only qualification to this sanguine assessment is that historical experience shows that "cooperative labor if kept within the narrow circle...of private workmen, will never be able to arrest the growth in geometrical progression of [capitalist] monopoly." To emancipate the working masses, cooperative labor needs to be developed to national dimensions by national means. "To conquer political power had therefore become the great duty of the working classes."[37]

With this experience in mind, Marx defended the efforts of the Paris Commune to build a cooperative commonwealth. "If cooperative production is...to supersede the Capitalist system; if united cooperative societies are to regulate national production upon a common plan, thus...putting an end to the constant anarchy and periodical convulsions which are the fatality of Capitalist production—what else, gentleman, would it be but Communism, 'possible' Communism?"[38]

Again, in his 1875 "Critique of the Gotha Programme," Marx reaffirmed his support of a cooperative commonwealth. "That the workers desire to establish the conditions for cooperative production...on a national scale in their own country, only means that they are working to revolutionize the present conditions of production." It is one thing to erect cooperatives with the aid of the bourgeois state, however, and another to erect them under a proletarian dictatorship. Consequently, "as far as the present cooperative societies are concerned, they are of some value *only* in so far as they are the independent creation of the workers and not the protégés either of the government or of the bourgeois."[39]

At the very least, a cooperative commonwealth qualifies as a lower stage of socialism. In praise of Robert Owen, the father of the cooperative movement, Engels writes: "He introduced as transition measures to the

---

[37] Marx, "Inaugural Address," *Selected Works*, 1:382–384.
[38] Marx, "The Civil War in France," *Selected Works*, 1:523.
[39] Marx, "Critique of the Gotha Programme," *Selected Works*, 2:30–31.

complete communistic organization of society...cooperative societies for retail trade and production." In such societies we have "practical proof that the merchant and the manufacturer are socially quite unnecessary"—a reaffirmation of Marx's thesis in the "Inaugural Address." Cooperation is not a "panacea for all social ills, but only a first step towards a much more radical revolution of society."[40] Yet even this transitional role for cooperatives effectively amended the Manifesto's scenario, in which cooperatives do not figure at all.

To be sure, Marx did not anticipate that, as they grew in size and earnings, cooperatives would rely predominantly on hired instead of voluntary labor. He did not anticipate that the divorce between ownership and control in the modern corporation would also come to characterize the cooperative form of organization. He did not anticipate the emergence of class antagonism within the cooperative movement in the struggle between labor and management, the unionization of co-op workers, and the periodical strikes against the enterprises supposedly owned by those workers.[41] Most significantly, Marx failed to anticipate that a new class of "masters" would make its appearance in the form of co-op managers and their professional staffs—fellow workers rather than capitalists. Such was the unforeseen outcome of the cooperatives' "'possible' Communism."

To Each According to His Needs

In 1875 the word "communism" acquired renewed currency in Marx's "Critique of the Gotha Programme." For the first time, he delineated not only a lower stage of communism "as it *emerges* from capitalist society," but also a higher stage to be "*developed* on its own foundations." What Marx called the lower stage has come to be referred to as "socialism," a society "still stamped with the birth marks of the old society from whose womb it emerges." That is as far as the Manifesto takes us. Not until the 1875 "Critique" do we learn—in a major amendment to the Manifesto—that communist society inscribes on its banner not the socialist principle, "From each according to his ability, to each according to his work," but the higher

---

[40] Engels, "Socialism: Utopian and Scientific," *Selected Works*, 2:127.
[41] Karl Kautsky, *The Labour Revolution*, trans. H. J. Stenning (New York: Dial Press, 1925), 191. See also G. N. Ostergaard and A. H. Halsey, *Power in Cooperatives: A Study of the Internal Politics of British Retail Societies* (Oxford: Basil Blackwell, 1965), xvi, 170–171, 199–200.

principle, "From each according to his ability, to each according to his needs."[42]

The "Critique of the Gotha Programme" consists of a series of marginal notes on the proposed Unity Program designed to bring together the principal German workers' organizations into a single party. Known as the Gotha Programme of the newly created Socialist Workers Party, it was a hodgepodge of the socialist objectives of Marx's followers in the old Social-Democratic Workers Party and the piecemeal liberal and democratic reforms proposed by the General Association of German Workers led by followers of Ferdinand Lassalle (1825–1864). Because Bakunin's writings had assiduously nurtured the opinion—entirely erroneous according to Marx—that he and Engels had been secretly guiding the Social-Democratic Party from London and were "responsible for everything that happened in the labor movement in Germany," he considered it urgent to clarify where they stood and to show how "our position is altogether remote from the said programme."[43]

In scrutinizing the Unity Program, Marx noted that it failed to deal with the "political transition period in which the state can be nothing but the revolutionary dictatorship of the proletariat...[and] with the future state of communist society." What remained to be done was to distinguish a "first phase of communist society...when it has just emerged after prolonged birth pangs from capitalist society," and a "higher phase...after the productive forces have also increased with the all-round development of the individual, and all the springs of cooperative wealth flow more abundantly."[44]

What the Manifesto depicted as the "abolition of buying and selling" the "Critique" associates with the lower phase of communism. The "producers do not exchange their products; just as little does the labor employed on the products appear here *as the value* of these products, as a material quality possessed by them." Because money too has been abolished, "individual labor no longer exists in an indirect fashion but directly as a component part of the total labor." This means that the market no longer determines how products are assessed and compared to one another. A new measuring rod takes the place of the old: units of standard man-hours. Accordingly, the individual producer "receives a certificate from society that he has furnished such and such an amount of labor (after deducting his labor for the common

---

[42] Marx, "Critique of the Gotha Programme," *Selected Works*, 2:23–24.

[43] Frederick Engels, "Foreword" to the 1891 edition of Marx's "Critique of the Gotha Programme," *Selected Works*, 2:14; and Karl Marx, "Letter to W. Bracke," *Selected Works*, 2:15.

[44] Marx, "Critique of the Gotha Programme," *Selected Works*, 2:23–24, 33.

funds), and with this certificate he draws from the stock of means of consumption as much as costs the same amount of labor."[45]

This may sound revolutionary, but in fact "the same principle prevails as that which regulates the exchange of commodities, as far as this is exchange of equal values." Each receives what he would otherwise have received had he been paid wages instead of labor certificates. That is to say, the right of the producers is *proportional* to the labor they supply.[46]

Capitalist exploitation would certainly be eliminated under this arrangement. But as Marx points out, "the abolition of class distinctions" does not mean "the elimination of all social and political inequality." In any case, equal right does not mean equal pay. That is because "one man is superior to another physically or mentally and so supplies more labor in the same time, or can labor for a longer time." To compound the inequalities, one worker is married and must support a wife and several children, while another is single and has only himself to feed, house, and clothe. Thus "one will in fact receive more than another, one will be richer than another."[47]

As a remedy for this "defect," Engels proposed a different scenario for the first stage of communism—an amendment to Marx's amendment. "In a society of private producers, private individuals or their families pay the cost of training the qualified worker; hence, the higher price paid for qualified labor accrues first of all to private individuals." Under socialism, however, "these costs are borne by society, and to it therefore belong the fruits." Although Engels' scenario further differed from Marx's in that neither money nor commodity-values would disappear, the qualified worker would lose all claim to the "greater *values* produced by compound labor" and society would become the beneficiary.[48]

The Invading Socialist Society

Besides the subjective proletarian movement, the "self-conscious, independent movement of the immense majority," the Manifesto acknowledges the role of objective, unconscious factors propelling societies toward socialism. As an example, the Manifesto cites the "advance of industry, whose involuntary promoter is the bourgeoisie." This nondeliberate economic advance "replaces the isolation of the laborers, due to competition,

---

[45] Ibid., 2:22–23.
[46] Ibid., 2:23–24.
[47] Ibid., 2:24.
[48] Engels, *Anti-Dühring*, 277–278.

by their involuntary combination, due to association...[and] therefore, cuts from under its feet the very foundation on which the bourgeoisie produces."

Without this dual threat to bourgeois rule, its fall and the victory of the proletariat would not be "equally inevitable." But just as the conscious movement of the proletariat required changes in its program with passing time and altered circumstances, so did the Manifesto's scenario of the economic transition to socialism.

The original scenario hinges on "the revolt of modern productive forces against modern conditions of production, against the property relations that are the conditions for the existence of the bourgeoisie and of its rule." An economic absurdity, the epidemic of overproduction leads to underproduction. Because the conditions of bourgeois production are too narrow to permit operation at full capacity and to make use of the wealth created, the Manifesto concludes that the "bourgeoisie is unfit any longer to be the ruling class." It is unfit because it is incompetent to keep the wheels of industry running at full speed, because it cannot employ the disposable work force, and because the idle worker sinks into such a state of misery that "it has to feed him, instead of being fed by him."

Marx's *Capital* offers an addendum to this indictment. It shows the bourgeois to be superfluous, not just incompetent. The giant forces created by capitalism can get along without him.

In the Manifesto the prime agent of bourgeois production is the entrepreneur, or owner-manager, "the individual bourgeois manufacturer." In stark contrast, volume 3 of *Capital* shifts the focus to the changed conditions of production some two decades later, to the prevailing role of "social capital (capital of directly associated individuals) as distinct from private capital." This transformation from the individually owned enterprise to the joint-stock company, to "social undertakings," spells what Marx calls the "abolition of capital as private property within the framework of capitalist production." It is the involuntary transition to socialism without the agency of a proletarian movement.[49] *That* is more than an addendum—it is a major amendment to the Manifesto.

Such is the economic movement that makes the capitalist redundant when the owners are marginalized and someone other than the capitalist does the work of the capitalist for him. The professional manager, a wage-earner "whose price is regulated in the labor-market like that of any other labor," replaces the owners in the driver's seat. Profit is distributed no longer as entrepreneurial profit but as interest, "compensation for owning capital

---

[49] Marx, *Capital*, 3:427.

that now is entirely divorced from the function [of profit] in the actual process of production, just as this function in the person of the manager is divorced from the ownership of capital." As Marx assessed the political implications of this new phenomenon, "the ultimate development of capitalist production is a necessary transition phase towards the reconversion of capital into...the property of associated producers."[50]

What do managers do? They orchestrate the activities of workers under their supervision. "All combined labor on a large scale requires, more or less, a directing authority, in order to secure the harmonious working of individual activities....A single violin player is his own conductor; an orchestra requires a separate one." Cooperation requires the work of directing, superintending, and adjusting. This work of supervision becomes the manager's exclusive function.[51]

The role of orchestration or organization, as it is currently called, prompted Alfred Marshall, the father of neoclassical economics, "to reckon Organization apart as a distinct agent of production." The price of organizational expertise thus became the *"net earnings of management."*[52] Marx, however, stopped short of recognizing such expertise as basic to his class analysis. His failure to do so is crucial for understanding the 150-year retreat from communism. For if organizational expertise, like scientific knowledge, is a distinct factor of production, then its owners constitute a different class from the laborers they manage.

Organizational expertise should not be confused with what Marx called the "collective laborer." Yet the latter too is a productive power in its own right, since "a dozen persons working together will, in their collective working day of 144 hours, produce far more than twelve isolated men each working 12 hours, or more than one man who works twelve days in succession." To the individual productive power of labor, collective labor adds "the social productive power of labor, or the productive power of social labor." The additional surplus from this collective labor costs the capitalist nothing.[53] That too is an amendment to the Manifesto.

The image of an orchestra, first presented in volume 1 of *Capital*, recurs in volume 3. Orchestration is work that the capitalist would—if he could— pass onto the shoulders of another. As in the ancient world, the master leaves the "honor" of this drudgery to an overseer as soon as he can afford it,

---

50 Ibid., 3:427, 428.
51 Ibid., 1:363.
52 Alfred Marshall, *Principles of Economics*, 8th ed. (New York: Macmillan, 1948; orig. pub. 1920), 139, 313.
53 Marx, *Capital*, 1:358, 361, 365–366.

thereby taking leave from his business to attend to affairs of state or study philosophy. "An orchestra conductor need not own the instruments of his orchestra, nor is it within the scope of his duties as conductor to have anything to do with the 'wages' of the other musicians." As for his own wages, they are "completely isolated from the profits of enterprise in the cooperative factories of laborers, as well as in capitalist stock companies."[54]

Like the slave in antiquity, the wage-laborer must have a "master who puts him to work and rules over him." Supervision means discipline for the purpose of exploiting him. So when the job of master is delegated to a professional manager, it is the manager who compels the wage-slave "to produce his own wages and also the wages of supervision as compensation for the labor of ruling and supervising him."[55] There is nothing comparable in the Manifesto.

Economic power passes into the hands of a curious kind of proletarian, while ownership becomes diffused through the operation of the stock market. "This is the abolition of the capitalist mode of production within the capitalist mode of production...a mere phase of transition to a new form of production." Private production without the control of private property is the antechamber to social production, to means of production that cease to be private and "can thereafter be only means of production in the hands of associated producers." Thus joint-stock companies, like the cooperative factories of workers, "represent within the old form the first sprouts of the new."[56]

This process shows how a new mode of production grows out of an old one "when the development of the material forces of production and of the corresponding forms of social production have reached a particular stage." As Marx concludes this informal amendment to the Manifesto, the "capitalist stock companies, as much as the cooperative factories, should be considered as transitional forms from the capitalist mode of production to the associated one, with the only distinction that the antagonism [between labor and capital] is resolved negatively in the one and positively in the other." Such is the involuntary economic transition preliminary to the voluntary "political transition period in which the state can be nothing but the *revolutionary dictatorship of the proletariat*."[57]

---

[54] Ibid., 3:377–378, 379, 380.
[55] Ibid., 3:376, 378.
[56] Ibid., 3:429, 430, 431.
[57] Ibid., 3:431; and idem, "Critique of the Gotha Programme," *Selected Works*, 2:32–33.

The third volume of *Capital* was published posthumously in 1894, some three decades after Marx halted work on the original unfinished manuscript. But its amendments were picked up by Engels and incorporated in part 3 of *Anti-Dühring* in 1878, and then in his popular manual, *Socialism: Utopian and Scientific* (1880). The concluding part of Engels' manual clarifies the main points. To the Manifesto's thesis that the bourgeoisie is no longer fit to be the ruling class, Engels adds that it is superfluous. Rather than a merely political struggle between bourgeois and proletarians, the growth of social capital signifies a struggle between competing economic systems, "a new mode of production [that] naturally grows out of an old one." With the emergence of economies of scale and modern corporations dependent on social capital, writes Engels, "the production without any definite plan of capitalistic society capitulates to the production upon a definite plan of the invading socialistic society." Thus Marx's amendments became grounds for the thesis of "creeping socialism" along with the related scenarios of "managerial revolution," "managerial capitalism," and "managerial socialism."[58]

Ballots Instead of Bullets

Unlike socialists of the day, communists were inclined to violence. "They openly declare that their ends can be attained only by the forcible overthrow of all existing social conditions." Although forcible overthrow does not imply violence, the Manifesto's scenario of a "more or less veiled civil war" and the "violent overthrow of the bourgeoisie" surely does. Repeated use of such terms as "fight," "battle," and the image of society as more and more splitting up into two "hostile camps," suggests a violent struggle for power. As in the class struggles of the past, the proletariat is determined to wage "an uninterrupted, now hidden, now open fight that...[is bound to end] either in a revolutionary reconstitution of society at large, or in the common ruin of the contending classes."

In this perspective, to win the battle of democracy the proletariat would first have to win the ballot and then back up the ballot with bullets. How did it hope to win the ballot? Would bullets also be necessary? That communists took for their allies the democratic parties in all countries indicates that they were still struggling for an extension of the suffrage. But the Manifesto

---

[58] Marx, *Capital*, 3:431; Engels, "Socialism: Utopian and Scientific," *Selected Works*, 2:147; and Avineri, *The Social and Political Thought of Karl Marx*, 174–182.

leaves one guessing whether legal or illegal, peaceful or violent means might be used for this purpose.

This uncertainty called for an amendment, or at least an addendum. As Marx noted in a speech on the heels of the Amsterdam Congress of the First International (8 September 1872), the workers' struggle for political power and the means thereto are not everywhere the same. Thus "there are countries—such as America, England, and...I would perhaps also say Holland—where the workers can attain their goal by peaceful means." In those countries the parliamentary system is sufficiently advanced and civil liberties so well established that an incremental extension of the suffrage through a series of reform bills, as in England, remains possible. But such an extension is unlikely where the persistence of unconstitutional monarchies and military-bureaucratic regimes excludes legislative reform. Thus "we must also recognize the fact that in most countries on the Continent the lever of our revolution must be force."[59]

Two decades later this modest addendum was transformed by Engels into a major amendment. In what came to be regarded as his final political will or testament, his 1895 "Introduction" to Marx's *Class Struggles in France, 1848–1850,* questioned whether violence might be useful anywhere, even in countries without an established tradition of civil liberties and parliamentary representation.

"The mode of struggle of 1848 is today obsolete in every respect," he proclaimed. "History has proved us, and all who thought like us, wrong"— wrong in believing that the proletariat had any reasonable prospect of making a revolution with bullets. The level of economic development on the Continent in 1848 was far from ripe for overthrowing the bourgeoisie. Capitalism had yet to mature, much less become senile. That it still had considerable capacity for expansion became evident after big industry took root and transformed backward Germany into an industrial power of the first rank. Ergo, bullets could not have achieved their purpose, "a violent outbreak...offered no prospect of a final solution."[60]

In Germany the intelligent use of universal suffrage since 1866 enabled Social-Democratic votes to mushroom from some 100,000 in 1871 to about five times that number only six years later. Then came the first setback in the form of the Anti-Socialist Law. The party was momentarily dissolved and the number of votes fell to some 300,000 in 1881. But that situation was quickly remedied. Without a legal organization, without the right of

---

[59] Karl Marx, "The Possibility of Non-Violent Revolution," in Tucker (1978), 523.

[60] Frederick Engels, "Introduction" to Marx, *The Class Struggles in France, 1848 to 1850,* in *Selected Works,* 1:123, 125, 126.

association, without a press, the party's influence soared from more than half a million voters in 1884 to almost a million and a half in 1890. "The ruling classes had exhausted all their expedients—uselessly, purposelessly, unsuccessfully."[61] Thus the Anti-Socialist Law disappeared, while Socialist votes climbed to a record-breaking quarter of all the votes cast.

Thanks to a change in strategy from bullets to ballots, German Socialists supplied their comrades elsewhere with a "new weapon...when they showed them how to make use of universal suffrage." They transformed the franchise from an instrument of deception into a means of emancipation. It became their most effective propaganda, while accurately informing them of their comparative strength and that of the enemy. It also provided a means of getting in touch with the mass of people who still stood aloof from the socialist contagion. "It was found that the state institutions, in which the rule of the bourgeoisie is organized, offer the working class still further opportunities to fight these very state institutions." As a result, "the bourgeoisie and the government came to be much more afraid of the legal than of the illegal action of the workers' party."[62]

That was a major turning point in the class struggle, according to Engels. Since its conditions had radically changed, "Rebellion in the old style, street fighting with barricades, which defined the issue everywhere up to 1848, was to a considerable extent obsolete."[63]

But had street fighting ever been the chief factor in victory? For the insurgents it was merely a tactic for making the government and its troops yield to moral influences. The military had at its disposal artillery and war material that the insurgents almost entirely lacked. "No wonder, then, that even the barricade fighting conducted with the greatest heroism—Paris, June 1848; Vienna, October 1848; Dresden, May 1849—ended in the defeat of the insurrection." All that was required to quash those uprisings was for soldiers to remain obedient and their commanders firm. In the rare cases when the insurgents won, it was "because the troops failed to respond, because the commanding officers lost the faculty to decide or because their hands were tied." At best, the barricades undermined morale and the steadfastness of the soldiers.[64]

Since then, several important changes had further altered the balance of forces in favor of the regular army. The spell of the barricade was first broken militarily when the army, too, became versed in street fighting.

---

[61] Ibid., 1:128.
[62] Ibid., 1:128–129, 130.
[63] Ibid., 1:130.
[64] Ibid., 1:130, 131.

Soldiers "no longer marched straight ahead and without cover against the improvised breastwork, but went round it through garden yards and houses." Although Paris and Berlin had grown almost fourfold since 1848, their garrisons had grown even more and, by means of the railways, could in twenty-four hours be more than doubled. In 1848 army artillery was completely ineffective in dismantling barricades, whereas a half century later a single percussion shell might do the job. And, finally, since 1848, city planning had made a difference. The new quarters of the big cities were "laid out in long, straight, broad streets, as though made to give full effect to the new cannon and rifles" that shot four times as far, ten times as fast, and as many times as accurately as the old guns and ammunition.[65]

Pursuing their new strategy, German socialists in 1895 further boosted their votes to over two million. Together, those who voted and the youth who stood behind them constituted "the most numerous, most compact mass, the decisive 'shock force' of the international proletarian army." The party's growth had proceeded steadily; all government interventions against it had failed to harness it. "If it continues in this fashion," wrote Engels, "by the end of the century we shall conquer the greater part of the middle strata of society...and grow into the decisive power." To keep the party intact until the hour of decision was essential, to avoid the bloodletting associated with the Paris Commune, to avoid frittering away the party's shock forces in vanguard skirmishes.[66]

The irony of the situation was not lost on Engels. While "revolutionaries" were thriving on legal methods, the self-styled "parties of order" were champing at the bit under the legal conditions they had created. Their objective was to provoke, to lure the Socialists into street fighting as the only way of getting back at the workers. "Breach of the constitution, dictatorship, return to absolutism" had become their salvation. The law had changed colors by supporting the cause of the party of overthrow. As Engels observed, "The irony of world history turns everything upside down." But to "shoot a party which numbers millions...is too much even for all the magazine rifles of Europe."[67]

Engels' political testament constituted, in effect, a repudiation of both Marx's 1871 *The Civil War in France* and his own 1891 "Introduction" to it. For the substance of his argument was that the working class *can* lay hold of the ready-made state machinery and wield it for its own purposes. Thus Engels amended his and Marx's earlier amendment.

---

[65] Ibid., 1:132, 133.
[66] Ibid., 1:135–136.
[67] Ibid., 1:136, 137.

PART II. A CONSEQUENTIAL DOCUMENT

Nothing could be more wrong than to brand the whole *Communist Manifesto* as a historical document. On the contrary: the *principles* it develops, the *method* to which it introduces us, and the *characterization* of the contemporary *mode of production* that it presents in broad strokes are more valid today than ever before.

Karl Kautsky, "The *Communist Manifesto*
after Six Decades" (1906)

In the *Communist Manifesto*...Marx and Engels wrote: "A specter haunts Europe, the specter of communism...." The specter of communism has begun to clothe itself in flesh and blood.

Nikolai Bukharin and Eugen Preobrazhensky,
The ABC of Communism (1919)

6. An Anarchist Manifesto: Bakunin

[Bakunin] could never have approved of the Manifesto's programme of State Communism...but it is also evident that the Manifesto's criticism of bourgeois society had seemed to him so valuable that he had felt it essential to popularize it in Russia, even though there were to be found in it some ideas of which he did not personally approve.

K. J. Kenafick, *Michael Bakunin and Karl Marx* (1948)

Among Marx's disciples were not only self-professed Marxists but also anarchists who accepted his theories but rejected his politics as "authoritarian." Preceding Marx to the grave in 1876, Bakunin was the first anarcho-Marxist.[1] This was his peculiar heresy that drew fire from Marxists and anarchists alike.

For Bakunin, the Manifesto served as an anarchist tract except for its mistaken strategy: first, that of winning the battle of democracy, capturing the state instead of smashing it; second, that of centralizing all instruments of production in the hands of the state instead of turning them over to the associated workers. Bakunin championed a substitute for the state, "a dictatorship without badge, without title, without official power, and all the more powerful as it was devoid of all appearance of power."[2] Yet it had more than a superficial resemblance to the ideas set forth in the Manifesto.

The Main Evil

Bakunin's was hardly a farfetched reading of the Manifesto's claims: "The executive of the modern State is but a committee for managing the common affairs of the whole bourgeoisie"; and "Political power, properly so called, is merely the organized power of one class for oppressing another." In such terms, the Manifesto points to the state and to political power as fundamental props of the workers' immediate enemy—the industrial

---

[1] See Donald C. Hodges, ed. and trans., *Philosophy of the Urban Guerrilla: The Revolutionary Writings of Abraham Guillén* (New York: William Morrow, 1973), 34–40, 72–78.

[2] Max Nomad, *Rebels and Renegades* (Freeport, NY: Books for Libraries, 1968; orig. pub. 1932),16–17.

bourgeoisie. It follows that both props have to be destroyed in the course of emancipating the workers—a conclusion shared by anarchists and Marxists alike.

In a letter to Theodor Cuno (24 January 1872), Engels characterizes anarchism as the doctrine that identifies "the *state* as the main evil to be abolished" and that demands "complete abstention from all politics."[3] But this amounts to a caricature, especially when such a doctrine is imputed to Bakunin.

As in the Manifesto, Bakunin identified capital as the "main evil to be abolished." He would have agreed with Engels that "the abolition of capital *is* precisely the social revolution."[4] Consider how Bakunin described his main objective in articles on the First International published in *L'Égalité* (7–28 August 1869): "Do you understand that the principal source of all the evils the workers must now endure is poverty, and that this poverty...is the necessary consequence of the existing economic order of society, and primarily of the submission of labor to the yoke of capital, i.e., to the bourgeoisie?" The "economic struggle of the workers against capitalist exploitation" was Bakunin's number one concern, what he called the "basic principle" of the International. Rather than freedom from state authority and political power, "economic freedom is the basis for all his [the worker's] other freedoms."[5]

Bakunin was not apolitical. In agreement with the Manifesto, he believed that "every class struggle is a political struggle." By "social liquidation" he did not mean mainly the abolition of the state, but rather "economic emancipation." He meant *"economic equality, i.e., restitution of capital to labor* or *social liquidation"*![6]

In "The Paris Commune and the Idea of the State," the preamble to the second part of *The Knouto-Germanic Empire and the Social Revolution* (1871), Bakunin reaffirmed the struggle for economic equality, or economic emancipation, as his principal objective. The "ultimate aim" of both libertarian and authoritarian socialists is "identical." "Both equally desire to create a new social order based first on the organization of collective labor...and second, on the collective ownership of the tools of production." The difference is over matters of strategy. The Marxists mistakenly believe that they can achieve this goal through the political power of the working classes in a struggle for democracy in alliance with bourgeois democrats.

---

[3]   Marx and Engels, *Selected Correspondence*, 334–335.
[4]   Ibid., 335.
[5]   Dolgoff, *Bakunin on Anarchy*, 161, 164, 167, 169.
[6]   Ibid., 164, 169, 170.

"The divergence leads to a difference in tactics. The [authoritarian] communists believe it is necessary to organize the workers' forces in order to seize the political power of the State. The revolutionary socialists organize for the purpose of...liquidating the State."[7]

However, he also made clear that social liquidation is a means, not an end, an incomplete means at that. For the abolition of authoritarian exploitative institutions targets other institutions besides the state. There are three such institutions: the fundamental institution—Capital—and the State and the Church as its principal props. The goal, "the economic transformation of society," hinges on the overthrow of these two props. "The abolition of the Church and the State should be the first and indispensable condition for the real enfranchisement of society." However, this social liquidation should be attempted "not...by a national assembly elected through universal suffrage," but by direct action and mass intervention.[8]

By implication, Bakunin's main criticism of the Marxists is that they did not base their political strategy on the economic analysis in section 1 of the Manifesto. Section 1 makes abundantly clear that, as long as the workers remain unorganized for the purpose of the economic class struggle, "the proletarians do not fight their enemies, but the enemies of their enemies, the remnants of absolute monarchy, the landowners, the non-industrial bourgeoisie, the petty bourgeoisie." Their enemies are the capitalists at the heart of the capitalist system. In agreement with section 1, Bakunin concludes that "the violent overthrow of the bourgeoisie lays the foundation for the sway of the proletariat." That is a far cry from the Manifesto's alternative strategy outlined in section 2—that of organizing a political party and "winning the battle of democracy."

A Taste for Communism

A Russian nobleman and hero of the revolutionary uprisings throughout Europe in 1848–1849 and later in the early 1870s, Bakunin got his first taste of communism from Wilhelm Weitling. His friendship with Weitling during Bakunin's sojourn in Switzerland in 1843 was "one of the capital events of his life, and completed his transformation into a practical revolutionary." Although Bakunin's anarchism is usually tied to the influence of Pierre-Joseph Proudhon, it was Weitling who first pushed him in that direction. An

---

[7] Ibid., 262–263.
[8] Ibid., 168, 269–270.

omnivorous reader, he called Weitling's *Guarantees of Harmony and Freedom* (1842) a "really remarkable book," and in a letter to Arnold Ruge cited the following passage indicative of Weitling's libertarianism: "The perfect society has no government, but only an administration, no laws, but only obligations, no punishments, but means of correction."[9]

Weitling's communism was shaped by a reading of Buonarroti's manual, and the same book also made a profound impression on Bakunin. Although Babeuf's conspiracy failed, "his ideal of a Socialist republic did not die with him." Babeuf's friend Buonarroti, wrote Bakunin, transmitted this ideal as a "sacred trust to new generations, and, owing to the secret societies which he founded in Belgium and France, Communist ideas blossomed forth." Thus Bakunin adopted Babeuf's ideal of "allotting to everyone in equal shares: education, instruction, the means of existence, and pleasures, and compelling all, without exception, in the measure of each one's capacity, to do physical or mental labor."[10]

From Buonarroti, whom he admired as the "greatest conspirator of this century," Bakunin derived not only his communist ideas, but also his conspiratorial and insurrectional strategies. In writings and speeches, he repeatedly referred to Buonarroti's manual and recommended it to his followers.[11] Although he had second thoughts about Babeuf's authoritarian brand of communism, he had no problem with Maréchal's libertarian version.

"Disappear at last, revolting distinctions between...masters and servants, governors and governed," wrote Maréchal in his "Manifesto of the Equals." Could this have been a source of Bakunin's anarchism? "It is necessary to abolish," wrote Bakunin, "all that which is called political power; for, so long as political power exists, there will be rulers and ruled."[12]

Throughout most of the 1840s Bakunin had "friendly relations with German Communists [Weitling's and Buonarroti's followers] in Switzerland and in Paris, and occasionally called himself a communist."[13] Why, then, didn't he join the Communist League as he would afterward join the First International? As he confided to his lifelong friend, the German poet Georg Herwegh, he could never join it because of the perfidiousness and

---

[9] Cited by Eugene Pyziur, *The Doctrine of Anarchism of Michael A. Bakunin* (Milwaukee, WI: Marquette University Press, 1955), 29–30.

[10] Maximoff, *The Political Philosophy of Bakunin*, 277.

[11] Pyziur, *The Doctrine of Anarchism*, 42.

[12] Maréchal, "Manifesto of the Equals," in Fried and Sanders, 51; and Maximoff, *The Political Philosophy of Bakunin*, 297.

[13] Marx Nettlau, "Mikhail Bakunin: A Biographical Sketch," in Maximoff, *The Political Philosophy of Bakunin*, 35.

pretentiousness of Marx's circle. "Dissertations about life, action, and feeling—and complete absence of life, action, feeling.... Disgusting flattery of the more advanced workers...by people who are from head to foot more bourgeois than anyone in a provincial city—in short, foolishness and lies"—and "boasting in theory and cowardice in practice."[14]

In 1844 Bakunin moved to Paris, where he became acquainted with Marx and Engels. Despite his distrust of Marx's communism, "the rivalry between Marx and Bakunin was no impediment to the fact that the greatest influence on Bakunin was his chief antagonist." Surprising as this may be, there are grounds for believing that "Bakunin's doctrine of anarchism...was largely constructed upon the basis of Marxism...[and that it] was due to Marxism that Bakunin became the founder of the communistic or collectivistic current of anarchism."[15]

Bakunin was especially impressed by the Manifesto's opening section, with the formulation of the materialist thesis and its application to modern society. The materialist interpretation of history, he wrote, "constitutes...the essential basis of scientific Socialism...[and] forms the dominating thought of the celebrated 'Communist Manifesto.'" Qualified only by his recognition that the political structure of society and ruling ideology react upon the economic foundation, Bakunin agreed with the Manifesto that the "whole history of humanity, intellectual and moral, political and social, is but the reflection of its economic history." The materialist interpretation of history determined his ranking of the main enemies of the people, his sinister trinity of Capital, State, and Church—in that order.[16]

To be sure, he arrived at this trinity by a different route. He became an atheist first under Feuerbach's auspices. Next, he became a communist under the combined influences of Weitling, Buonarroti, and Marx. Only afterward did he flaunt a fully developed anarchism through his association and friendship with Proudhon.[17]

Despite his differences with Marx, Bakunin held the Manifesto in high esteem and also had lavish praise for *Capital*. It is a remarkable commentary on his broad-mindedness that, notwithstanding Marx's efforts to blacken his character, he became the first to translate both works into Russian—a

---

[14] Bakunin, *Marxism, Freedom and the State*, 9–10; and Dolgoff, *Bakunin on Anarchy*, 27, 115.

[15] Pyziur, *The Doctrine of Anarchism*, 34–35, 41.

[16] Bakunin, *Marxism, Freedom, and the State*, 20–21, 48–49; and Maximoff, *The Political Philosophy of Bakunin*, 65, 134, 179.

[17] Pyziur, *The Doctrine of Anarchism*, 27, 29–35, 37–39; and Bakunin, "To the Comrades of the International Workingmen's Association of Locle and Chaux-de-Fonds," in Fried and Sanders, 336–337.

prodigious enterprise. His translation of the Manifesto was first published in Geneva in 1869. Although he would become Marx's bitter enemy in the struggle for control of the First International, to the end of his life he remained a self-confessed disciple in matters of theory.[18]

In Paris he also found a teacher in Proudhon. As Bakunin confided to an Italian comrade some two decades later, when reading Proudhon's book it had suddenly flashed upon him: "This [book] is the right thing." Which book? It could only have been Prouhon's masterpiece, his first work on political theory that made him famous almost overnight. In *What Is Property?* (1840), he takes Babeuf as a whipping boy and attacks communism as a system of downward leveling that would place mediocrity on a par with excellence and obstruct the free expression of our faculties. Nonetheless, he agrees with Babeuf's "principle of equalization." So Proudhon too was a communist, but under another name—the system of "Liberty," otherwise known as "anarchism."[19]

Like Proudhon, Bakunin boldly attacked property, the state, and organized religion, and called for remaking society from the bottom up. But while he occasionally called himself an "anarchist," he also called himself a "libertarian communist." That he was an anarcho-communist was also the opinion of his alter ego James Guillaume. So it is not surprising that Moses Hess (1812–1875), a former "True Socialist," then a Willich collaborator, and later a supporter of Marx in the International, described Bakunin and his followers as "Russian communists," albeit of the violent sort.[20]

On almost all other issues he disagreed with Proudhon. Whereas the importance of Marx's influence on Bakunin has been usually underestimated, that of Proudhon has been exaggerated. "In spite of all his efforts to remain on firm ground," wrote Bakunin, "Proudhon has remained an idealist." From the idea of right he proceeds to economic facts, unlike Marx, who "has spoken out and proved...that economic fact has always preceded juridical and political right." The most he could say in support of Proudhon is that "Proudhon understood and felt liberty better than he [Marx]."[21]

---

[18] K. J. Kenafick, *Michael Bakunin and Karl Marx* (Melbourne: A. Maller, 1948), 116–117; and Paul Thomas, *Karl Marx and the Anarchists* (London/Boston: Routledge & Kegan Paul, 1980), 305.

[19] Maximoff, *The Political Philosophy of Bakunin*, 37; and P. J. Proudhon, *What Is Property?* trans. Benjamin R. Tucker (London: William Reeves, n.d.; orig. pub. 1840), 249–256, 267–274.

[20] Cited by Thomas, *Karl Marx and the Anarchists*, 301, 310.

[21] Dolgoff, *Bakunin on Anarchy*, 157-159; and Pyziur, *The Doctrine of Anarchism*, 37–39, 40, 41.

In effect, Bakunin derived his communist ideas and revolutionary strategy from Weitling and Buonarroti, his materialist interpretation of history from Marx and the Manifesto, and the libertarian features of his political program from Proudhon. "Bakunin has a peculiar theory of his own, a medley of Proudhonism and communism," wrote Engels in his letter to Theodore Cuno.[22]

Bakunin made a claim to the revolutionary legacy of the Manifesto, whereas the German Social Democrats espoused its legacy of reforms. The grandfather and precursor of Bolshevism, he belongs with Lenin and Trotsky among the foremost champions of the Manifesto. How, then, did he make it serve his revolutionary purposes, and how did his amendments to it differ from those of Marx and Engels?

Redefining the "Proletariat"

By the class struggle in modern society the Manifesto meant the struggle between "Bourgeois and Proletarians." But the Manifesto's use of the term "proletariat," like the term "Third Estate" during the French Revolution, does not refer to a homogeneous entity. Neither Schapper nor Willich possessed the theoretical training required to put into words what they dimly perceived to be Marx's double-dealing of the proletarian deck. It remained for Bakunin to expose Marx's sleight-of-hand.

It is noteworthy that the Manifesto's first concrete reference to proletarians is not to the mass of ordinary laborers exploited by the bourgeoisie—Schapper and Willich's principal concern—but to the upper-crust proletariat of white hands. "The bourgeoisie has stripped of its halo every occupation hitherto honored and looked up to with reverent awe. It has converted the physician, the lawyer, the priest, the poet, the man of science, into its paid wage-laborers."[23] Included are the pen pushers reviled by Schapper and Willich, a passage that speaks volumes concerning the Manifesto's paradigm of class struggle.

Bakunin asked for clarification concerning the Manifesto's definition of the proletariat as "a class of laborers, who live only so long as they find work, and who find work only so long as their labor increases capital." The physician, the lawyer, the priest, the poet, the man of science fit the first half of the definition, but not the second half. Were the boundaries of the wage-

---

[22] Marx and Engels, *Selected Correspondence*, 334.
[23] Marx and Engels, *Collected Works*, 6:487.

earning class the same as the boundaries of the class whose labor increases capital? If not, then how should one interpret the class struggle between "Bourgeois and Proletarians"?[24]

As Bakunin read the Manifesto, Marx made the mistake of including in the proletariat several different and antagonistic classes whose only element in common is that they are wage earners. Besides those who do muscular work, there is the labor aristocracy and a class of white-collar workers who both exploit the "drudge people" and are in turn exploited. Only the first, Bakunin believed, consisted of proletarians who are exploited without exploiting anybody. Unlike the work of the labor aristocracy and "white-collar type," its work is the force required to pull a load a given distance. Those who perform this kind of work constitute the *"flower of the proletariat,"* a proletariat in the strict sense of the word.[25]

Having dissected the so-called working class into these diverse components, Bakunin redefined the class struggle as not only between proletarians and bourgeois, but also between both classes and a middle class of skilled, technical, and professional workers. At the same time, he accepted the Manifesto's thesis of the increasing polarization of society into two hostile blocs diametrically opposed to each other: "the *privileged classes*, comprising all those who are privileged with respect to possession of land, capital, and even only of bourgeois education ['What is education, if not mental capital?' he asked], and the *working classes*, disinherited with respect to land as well as capital, and deprived of all education."[26]

By redefining the proletariat as those whose labor increases capital or, if unproductive, as those who are exploited by having to work, say, ten hours daily while being paid for only eight, Bakunin took issue with Marx's sequence of historical stages. Although socialism was next in line to replace capitalism, he argued, the defeat of the bourgeoisie might or might not mean the triumph of the proletariat.

Without questioning the fundamentals of the materialist interpretation of history, Bakunin disputed the Manifesto's application of it to modern society. Contrary to the Manifesto, he envisioned postcapitalist society as under the heel of a *"fourth governing class,"* a "new class" of highly educated, professional, and scientific workers. "The State has always been the patrimony of some privileged class or other; a priestly class [first estate], an aristocratic class [second estate], a bourgeois class [third estate], and finally a bureaucratic class [fourth estate]." Therefore, only with the

---

[24] Maximoff, *The Political Philosophy of Bakunin*, 189–192, 199–201, 355, 362.
[25] Ibid., 198–201, 362.
[26] Ibid., 189, 355.

abolition of the state through a mass uprising of the proletariat—not to be mistaken for a fifth estate—is the end of class domination foreseeable.[27] These were major revisions of the Manifesto.

Not even the cooperatives of workers, Bakunin argued, are exempt from criticism. Initially, workers' self-management assured that the principle of equal pay—with no special privileges for managers, intellectual workers, and specialists—would prevail in the burgeoning cooperative movement in Europe. "The cooperative workers' associations," wrote Bakunin in "The Slumberers" (1869), "have demonstrated that the workers themselves, choosing administrators from their own ranks, receiving the same pay, can effectively control and operate industry." Therefore "managers are not at all entitled to more pay...[and] intellectuals are not entitled to more pay than are ordinary workers, nor to special privileges."[28] But it soon became apparent that the better educated workers were bent on managing the others. So it was not long before they began assigning a special value to professional expertise.

Cooperatives, Bakunin noted, contain the seeds of a new class despotism. In the course of expanding production to meet demand and increased sales, "producer cooperatives hired outside wage-workers...[and] created a new class of workers who exploit and profit from the labor of their employees."[29] So the cooperative principle of equal burdens and equal benefits passed into oblivion, to be superseded by the principle of payment according to the quality and quantity of work. Nor would it be long before cooperatives began copying the organizational structure of the modern corporation with its board of directors elected by shareholders. The directors in turn appoint a general manager, who has despotic powers over the slumbering workers. Thus it was Bakunin's great merit to have discovered that capitalism is not the proletarian's only enemy. In the case of cooperatives, management is the enemy.

The Democratic Swindle

Marx's amendments to section 2 of the Manifesto did little to soften Bakunin's criticism. Notwithstanding his admiration for the document as a whole, Bakunin tried to block acceptance of its political program by the First

---

[27] Bakunin, *Marxism, Freedom and the State*, 32, 38, 47.
[28] Michael Bakunin, "On Workers' Self-Management of Industry and Equal Remuneration," in Dolgoff, *Bakunin on Anarchy*, 423n., and 424, 425.
[29] Michael Bakunin, "On the Cooperative Movement," in Dolgoff, 399.

International. "The Marxian thought is explicitly developed in the famous Manifesto," he acknowledged. But concerning the Communists' immediate aims, he asked: "How is the proletariat to capture the State?" "What does it mean: 'the proletariat raised into a ruling class'?"[30]

There are but two means available for the conquest of the state: "a political revolution or a lawful agitation on behalf of a peaceful reform." In either case the result is the establishment of a democratic republic or so-called People's State based on universal suffrage. Such was the Manifesto's aim—to win the battle of democracy. But the "State connotes domination, and domination connotes exploitation," declared Bakunin. The democratic republic is one in which the people, lacking knowledge and political experience, only nominally rule. Democracy means a compromise with bourgeois parties that remain free to pursue their own interests politically. It sets up checks to a social revolution and "can only be instrumental in bringing about bourgeois Socialism...a new, more hypocritical and more skillful, but no less oppressive exploitation of the proletariat."[31]

As for raising the proletariat to the position of ruling class, Bakunin asked: "Will the proletariat as a whole...govern, and will there be no one to be governed?" Not at all. The Marxists have in mind an educated stratum of the proletariat, learned socialists "who, once they become rulers or representatives of the people, cease to be workers...represent not the people but themselves." The outcome, Bakunin warns, can only be a new form of despotic rule. Proudhon was right: *"Universal suffrage is counter-revolution."*[32]

Marx was not insensitive to this kind of criticism. In his "Address of the Central Council of the International Working Men's Association on the Civil War in France" (1871), he effectively rewrote the ten-point program presented in the Manifesto. In stark contrast to the highly centralized measures of state capitalism and creeping socialism proposed in 1848, the address extols the decentralized measures of the Paris Commune, pointing toward a national system of producers' cooperatives coordinated according to a common plan—*nothing less than Bakunin's proposals*!

Marx's amended transitional program aimed at the virtual destruction of the state power, so that only a few functions would remain for a central government at minimum public expense. There would be no more democratic swindle, since elected representatives would be bound by a popular mandate. Subject to immediate recall for acting on their own instead

---

[30] Maximoff, *The Political Philosophy of Bakunin*, 285, 287.
[31] Ibid., 210–217, 285–290, 293.
[32] Ibid., 214, 287.

of the electors' initiatives, they would become public servants instead of masters of society. So the Manifesto's program, Marx conceded, had in some details become antiquated.

Details? Antiquated "in some details"! As Bakunin noted in a posthumously published letter to a Belgian newspaper on the proceedings at the Hague Congress of the International in 1872, "Engels, frightened by the detestable impression which the reading of some pages of...[the Manifesto] had produced, hastened to declare that...it was an antiquated document, a theory [program] abandoned by themselves." Sheer hypocrisy, declared Bakunin, for on the eve of the Congress, "the Marxians endeavored to spread this document in all countries."[33]

In response to the Paris Commune, Marx made important concessions to local government, while retaining his overall commitment to centralization. But as Bakunin commented on Marx's revision of the Manifesto, its program of state capitalism was completely upset by French events. Marx's followers lied when they proclaimed that the Commune's program was their own. "They had to do it under pain of seeing themselves left behind and forsaken by all, so powerful was the passion that this revolution evoked in everybody."[34]

In amending the Manifesto, Bakunin disclaimed that the proletariat will use its political supremacy "to centralize all instruments of production in the hands of the State." On the contrary, "I want the organization of society and collective or social property from the bottom up, by way of free association, and not from the top down!" That was the sense in which he preferred workers' self-management to Marx's brand of political democracy. As he was the first to admit, he differed with Marx and the Manifesto mainly over matters of strategy.[35]

Leveling Downward

Bakunin expressed further reservations about the Manifesto's third section and the sentence leading into it on the ultimate goal of communism, "an association in which the free development of each is the condition for the free development of all." This was the raison d'être of the Manifesto's abolition of capital qua exploitation. For Bakunin, however, the abolition of

---

[33] Kenafick, *Michael Bakunin and Karl Marx*, 276 n.
[34] Cited by Kenafick, 210.
[35] Thomas, *Karl Marx and the Anarchists*, 303–304; and Dolgoff, *Bakunin on Anarchy*, 159, 262–263.

capital is only a necessary, not a sufficient, condition of human self-realization. "Only under conditions of full equality can individual freedom...and the real capacities of individuals obtain their complete development." From this he concluded that "in order that individual capacities prosper in full...it is necessary to do away with all individual privileges...it is necessary to attain the economic, political, and social triumph of equality." Thus Bakunin called for an association in which "all will become equally complete and integral individuals," in which all workers *equally* will "acquire knowledge, prosperity, leisure."[36]

The qualifying adjective "equally" was in line with his belief that "the real goal of history...is the humanization and emancipation, the real liberty, the prosperity and happiness of each individual." That suggests a dual rather than a single goal, except for Bakunin's admonition that workers "should above all concentrate their efforts upon the solving of this great problem of *economic emancipation*...the source of all other emancipations."[37] Thus, Bakunin followed in Babeuf's footsteps in giving precedence not to Marx and Engels' patrician ideal of self-cultivation, but to the plebeian ideal of equal and integral education.

Having dethroned and abolished God, Bakunin was left with man as the lord of creation. But he was not a humanist as Marx understood the meaning of humanism. His overriding concern was neither the disalienation of humanity nor the perfection of man's several faculties, but rather the economic emancipation of drudge-people and the overcoming of human ignorance and brutality. Although "every man should have the material and moral means to develop his whole humanity," this objective had as a condition the "most perfect equality for all."[38]

Section 3 of the Manifesto reaffirms the concluding humanism of section 2 by denouncing "universal asceticism and social leveling in its crudest form." In the 1844 manuscripts, Marx claimed that this interpretation of equality signifies a reduction rather than multiplication of human needs; ergo, it is a step backward to a more primitive state. As Engels summarized his and Marx's position in 1878, "the real content of the proletarian demand for equality is the demand for the *abolition of classes*. Any demand for equality that goes beyond that, of necessity passes into absurdity."[39] Bakunin thought otherwise.

---

[36] Maximoff, *The Political Philosophy of Bakunin*, 330, 331–332, 337.
[37] Ibid., 174, 337.
[38] Ibid., 155, 156.
[39] Engels, *Anti-Dühring*, 147–148.

There is more to communism, Bakunin protested, than the Marxists would have us believe. "Knowledge is power, ignorance is the cause of social impotence." To this he adds his preference for leveling downward instead of upward: "The situation would not be so bad if all sank to the same level of ignorance"! That is because education is "mental capital, the sum of the mental labor of all past generations." Intelligent though a person may be by nature, how can he "hold out in a struggle against collective mental power produced by centuries of development?" Thus the demand for equality implies a leveling of individual knowledge, if not of natural capacities.[40]

Leveling downward means that inequalities "will become more and more minimized under the influence of...an egalitarian social organization, and, above all, when the right of inheritance no longer burdens the coming generations." The irony is that the abolition of *all* right of inheritance is part of the Manifesto's transitional program. Within a single generation, the application of this plank would level virtually every newborn child to the same propertyless condition of "equal means of subsistence, support, education, and opportunity...until maturity"; its application would make each person's well-being dependent on his or her labor. That it got into the Manifesto at all may be attributed to Marx's effort to placate the Babouvist elements in the Communist League. Marx intended to abolish only the right to inherit bourgeois property—the transitional program could not afford to be too revolutionary. Thus both he and Engels made a point of revising the Manifesto on this sensitive issue: first, by curtailing instead of abolishing the right of inheritance; and afterward, by ridiculing any effort to abolish it until after a successful social revolution.[41]

How did Marx and Engels' scenarios of communist society compare with Bakunin's? Speaking for Bakunin, Guillaume described the first phase of communism as one in which all items produced by collective labor will belong to the community, and each member will be paid for his labor either in commodities or in currency. But there will be no general law determining how much or in accordance with what method each will get. "In some communities remuneration will be in proportion to hours worked; in others payment will be measured by both the hours of work and the kind of work performed; still other systems will be experimented with to see how they work out." Everything will depend on the consent of the workers. Nonetheless, and from the very beginning, "We should to the greatest

---

[40] Maximoff, *The Political Philosophy of Bakunin*, 355.
[41] Dolgoff, *Bakunin on Anarchy*, 88–89, 91, 97; and Thomas, *Karl Marx and the Anarchists*, 306, 310.

possible extent institute and be guided by the principle *From each according to his ability, to each according to his need.*[42] Nominally, this was Marx's principle in the "Critique of the Gotha Programme." But for Marx it meant leveling upward; for Bakunin it meant leveling downward.

Political Dissolution

This brings us to Bakunin's criticism of the Manifesto's final section. Why should the proletariat enter into *any* alliance with the bourgeoisie? Revolutionaries have no use for a policy that "draws and enmeshes its partisans, under the pretext of political tactics, into ceaseless compromises with governments and political parties." Under no circumstances could Bakunin agree that a political revolution must precede an economic revolution, that "workers must ally themselves with the more or less radical bourgeois in order to carry out a political revolution together with the bourgeoisie, and then wage an economic revolution against the latter." Such a strategy, as Marx and Engels recognized in response to the Paris Commune, failed to consider whether workers can really make use of the state for their own purposes, "whether it will actually be in their possession, or whether, as has been the case until now, their *political liberty* will prove to be only a deceitful appearance."[43]

Correctly applied, according to Bakunin, the materialist interpretation of history gives priority to the "prime question for the people...its economic emancipation." The alternative is to become caught up in the political projects of the bourgeoisie and petty bourgeoisie, "the well-known program of bourgeois democracy—universal suffrage, with direct legislation by the people; abolition of all political privileges; arming of the nation; separation of the Church from the State, and the School from the Church; free and compulsory education; freedom of the press, association, assembly. . . [and] a single, direct and progressive income tax." But is such a program a step toward collectivism? Or is its aim that of "making use of the working masses as a blind tool for attaining the political objectives of...bourgeois democracy"?[44]

By economic revolution Bakunin did not mean what Marx understood by it in volume 3 of *Capital*, the emergence of producers' cooperatives and

---

[42] James Guillaume, "On Building the New Social Order," in Dolgoff, *Bakunin on Anarchy*, 361–362.
[43] Maximoff, *The Political Philosophy of Bakunin*, 288, 300; and 293–294.
[44] Ibid., 289, 292, 382.

the abolition of the capitalist mode of production within the framework of capitalism. He meant the organization of workers into trade unions for the purpose of directly expropriating the bourgeoisie and replacing professional managers with workers' self-management, "an organization from below upwards [with] full restitution to workers...and the land to those who cultivate it." Working class solidarity in all trades, Bakunin concluded, "*is the surest guarantee of their impending deliverance.*" The key strategy can be summed up as "a general strike...[that] can only lead to a great cataclysm, which will regenerate society."[45]

Economic strikes galvanize and train workers for the ultimate seizure of the means of production. That was Bakunin's amendment to section 4 of the Manifesto. "Strikes spell war, and the masses...become organized only during and by means of war." Strikes compel isolated workers to band together with their fellow workers; they awaken what Bakunin called the "social-revolutionary instincts which reside deeply in the heart of every worker...weighed down by slavish habits and a general spirit of resignation." Strikes broaden and deepen the gulf separating workers from the bourgeois class. Strikes "destroy in the minds of the now exploited and enslaved masses of people the possibility of any compromises or deals with the enemy...they create, organize, and form a workers' army."[46]

What does section 4 of the Manifesto mean by "proletarian revolution"? It means what it says, the "forcible overthrow of all existing social conditions." Taken literally, it means "social dissolution," "liquidating the State." States do not crumble by themselves; they must be overthrown by the creation of anarchy, by the momentary victory of barbarism over civilization, by the simultaneous uprising of the proletariat and peasantry under the leadership of the proletariat.[47] That was not how Marx interpreted "forcible overthrow," but it came close to how Willich and Schapper read the Manifesto. By then the Manifesto had acquired a life of its own, so that Marx's reading of it was no more privileged than was Bakunin's.

But Marx was right—revolutions cannot be improvised. "They are not made at will by individuals, and not even by the most powerful [political] associations...[but] come about through force of circumstances," wrote Bakunin. Although they can be foreseen, they cannot be accelerated. "Universal public and private bankruptcy is the first condition for a social-

---

[45] Ibid., 298, 380, 383.
[46] Ibid., 384–385.
[47] Ibid., 204, 300, 378. See also Dolgoff, *Bakunin on Anarchy*, 66–67.

economic revolution."[48] But it is not the only condition: willful political dissolution by a revolutionary vanguard also plays a prominent role.

A Bible of the Destructive Passions

The Manifesto has been scorned by anarchists as the "Bible of legal revolutionary democracy."[49] But it may also be read as giving free rein to the destructive passions. Thus the "violent overthrow of the bourgeoisie lays the foundation for the sway of the proletariat"; "Communism abolishes...all religion and all morality instead of constituting them on a new basis"; the "Communist revolution is the most radical rupture with traditional property relations"; the "Communists everywhere support every revolutionary movement against the existing social and political order"; and "their ends can be obtained only by the forcible overthrow of all existing social conditions." These passages imply a complete break with the past. What is *that*, if not "nihilism"—a qualified version of "anarchism"?

Nor are these the only passages favoring an anarchist reading of the Manifesto. Section 1 asserts that "every class struggle is a political struggle," that the "proletarian movement is the self-conscious, independent movement of the immense majority." Section 2 demands the abolition of bourgeois property, the abolition of buying and selling, and the abolition of all right of inheritance. Except for its disguised misrepresentation of the Babouvist legacy as "reactionary," section 3 is a veritable mine of anarchist gems against bourgeois and petty-bourgeois socialism. As for section 4, Bakunin wholeheartedly agreed that "the leading question [is]...the property question," and that "proletarians have nothing to lose but their chains."

Marx's impassioned rhetoric must also have endeared the Manifesto to Bakunin. Its repeated invocations to violence and destruction, to "class struggles," "veiled civil war," "violent overthrow," "open revolution," "grave-diggers," "abolition of bourgeois property," "abolition of bourgeois individuality, bourgeois independence, and bourgeois freedom," "the most radical rupture with traditional property relations," and "the most radical rupture with traditional ideas" are worthy of an anarchist tract. The Manifesto's recurring theme of "abolition" reminds one of the declamations of the celebrated Ranter Abiezer Coppe (1619–1672) during the English

---

[48] Maximoff, *The Political Philosophy of Bakunin*, 372, 374–375.
[49] Cited by Davidson, "Reform versus Revolution," in Bender, 94.

Civil War. "Thus saith the Lord," wrote Coppe in *A Fiery Flying Roll* (1649): *"overturn, overturn, overturn."*[50]

Bear in mind that it was the original Manifesto, not Marx and Engels' 1871 concession to arming the workers and smashing the state, that Bakunin adopted with reservations. He translated it into Russian before they made this important amendment. It sufficed for Bakunin that communism in the Manifesto is a destructive movement directed against the status quo. "Let us have confidence in the eternal spirit which destroys and annihilates," he wrote in 1842. Because it gives birth to new worlds, the passion for destruction is a creative passion.[51]

How consequential was Bakunin's translation of the Manifesto and its dissemination of anarcho-Marxism in Russian anarchist circles? The term nihilism (from the Latin *nihil*, "nothing") was coined by Ivan Turgenev in his novel *Fathers and Sons* (1862) and applied to Russian Populism—a movement in the second half of the nineteenth century whose extreme wing took for its goal the total annihilation of the inherited economic and political order. Inspired by Bakunin's promotion of the destructive passions, nihilism shaped not only the original anarchist movement in Russia, but also the extremist elements that later made common cause with the Bolsheviks in 1917.[52]

Lenin's "April Theses" marked the turning point in the relations between Russian anarchists and self-styled Marxists. The rapprochement that followed Lenin's startling theses led to what one prominent anarchist called "a perfect parallelism" between the program of Bakunin's followers and the Bolshevik's new program. "Lenin's appeal for a 'break-up and a revolution a thousand times more powerful than that of February [which toppled the Czar in 1917]' had a distinctly Bakuninist ring and was precisely what most anarchists wanted to hear." In common with Bakunin's followers, Lenin called for the transformation of the imperialist war into a revolutionary civil war against the capitalist order, for the replacement of parliamentary government by Soviets patterned on the Paris Commune, for the abolition of the police, the army, and the bureaucracy, and for the leveling of incomes from the top down. Lenin's critique of the "labor aristocracy" and of the reformist tendencies within the trade unions had its origin in Bakunin's arsenal against the Marxists, as did Lenin's slogan, "All power to the Soviets." Bakunin's distrust of liberalism and democracy also rubbed off on

---

[50] Quoted in Cohn, *The Pursuit of the Millennium*, Appendix, 366.

[51] Nettlau, "Mikhail Bakunin: A Biographical Sketch," in Maximoff, 34.

[52] Paul Avrich, ed., *The Anarchists in the Russian Revolution* (Ithaca, NY: Cornell University Press, 1973), 16.

Lenin and the Bolsheviks. Thus George Plekhanov—the "father of Russian Marxism" and Lenin's early mentor—concluded that the "tactics of the Bolsheviks are the tactics of Bakunin"! [53]

---

[53] Ibid., 14, 16; Volodymy Varlamov, "Bakunin and the Russian Jacobins and Blanquists," in C. E. Black, ed., *Rewriting Russian History* (New York: Praeger, 1956), 305, 308; amd Dmitri Volkogonov, *Lenin: A New Biography*, ed. and trans. Harold Shukman (New York and London: Free Press, 1994), 22. Traceable to his reading of the Manifesto under the influence of Buonarroti and ultimately of Weishaupt's Illuminati, Bakunin's anarcho-Marxism played an important but as yet unrecognized role also in the Mexican, Spanish, and Chinese revolutions. See Hodges, *Philosophy of the Urban Guerilla*, 34–40; idem, *Sandino's Communism: Spiritual Politics for the Twenty-First Century* (Austin: University of Texas Press, 1992), 41–67.

7. A Social Democratic Manifesto: Bernstein

> The adherents of this theory of a catastrophe base it especially on the conclusions of the *Communist Manifesto*. This is a mistake in every respect...social democracy would flourish far better by lawful than by unlawful means.

Eduard Bernstein, Evolutionary Socialism (1899)

Unlike Bakunin, Eduard Bernstein (1850–1932) was appalled by the Manifesto's rhetoric of forcible overthrow. In a chapter unexplainably omitted from the English version of his 1899 masterpiece *Evolutionary Socialism*, he characterized the violent seizure of power by the proletariat as Blanquism. "The revolutionary program of action of the Manifesto is Blanquist through and through," he wrote.[1] But the Manifesto also made claim to another legal and democratic program, the basis of Bernstein's amendments.

Following the prolongation of the Anti-Socialist Law by Bismarck in 1881, Bernstein became a political exile, first in Zurich for seven years and then in London as a correspondent of German Socialist newspapers. England was the source of his revisionism. Besides being impressed by the strength of its trade unions and by the vigor of its capitalism, he was strongly influenced by the demoliberal ideology and ethical current within British socialism.

In England, Bernstein became a Fabian. Although he never joined the Fabian Society, founded in 1884 only a few years before his arrival in London, he was unquestionably influenced by *Fabian Essays in Socialism* (1889), especially by Sidney Webb's essay linking the progress of the Socialist movement with the development of the democratic ideal. Its central theme was the virtual identification of socialism with economic or industrial democracy, the logical complement of political democracy.

"The main stream which has borne European society towards Socialism during the past 100 years," wrote Webb, "is the irresistible progress of Democracy." As he summed up the Fabian program of transition to a new social order, all students of society who are abreast of their times realize that

---

[1]   Cited by Draper, *Karl Marx's Theory of Revolution*, 3:342.

major social changes can only be democratic, gradual, moral, and finally, legal and pacific.[2] Bernstein made these guidelines his own, guidelines that had no use for the Utopian and Blanquist legacies surviving within the classics of Continental socialism.

The Manifesto's Damaging Dualisms

There is a damaging dualism, Bernstein noted, an impassable gulf in the Manifesto between the passages indebted to Blanqui's revolutionary legacy and those transmitting Marx's democratic credo. As instances of the latter, section 1 defines the proletarian movement as the "self-conscious, independent movement of the immense majority"; section 2 says the first step in the revolution is "to win the battle of democracy"; section 3 ridicules the sectarian doctrine that "inculcated universal asceticism and social leveling"; and section 4 includes among the favored allies of the proletariat the respectable bourgeois parties in France and Switzerland—a democratic consensus with concessions to nonproletarian interests.

It was the Blanquist content of the Manifesto that Bernstein deliberately excised. Is the conquest of the state and its utilization by the proletariat "exclusively against the whole nonproletarian world?" he asked. Marx and Engels' 1872 preface to the New German edition of the Manifesto, he reminded his readers, asserts that the "working classes cannot simply take possession of the ready-made State machine and set it in motion for their own aims." But instead of interpreting this passage as an argument for smashing the parliamentary state, he saw it as an argument for sharing power with other political parties. In the same context he agreed with Engels that conditions were no longer propitious for revolutions by small militant minorities, that a collision with the military would check the steady growth of democracy, and that the task of the Social Democratic party is "to organize the working classes politically."[3] Such was the democratic credo he believed was implicit in the Manifesto despite its Blanquist residues.

"Democracy," declared Bernstein, signifies both the "absence" and the "suppression of class government." It is the "high school of compromise," the "political form of liberalism."[4] Therefore, it is incompatible with the

---

[2] Sidney Webb, "The Basis of Socialism: Historic," in *Fabian Essays*, ed. George Bernard Shaw (London: George Allen & Unwin, 1948; orig. pub. 1889), 31, 32.

[3] Bernstein, *Evolutionary Socialism*, xxvi–xxvii.

[4] Ibid., 142, 143–144, 150.

Manifesto's program of despotic inroads on the rights of property, not to mention a dictatorship of the proletariat.

But was the program preeminently Blanquist as Bernstein believed? On the contrary, the Manifesto was "soft on bourgeois democracy." It opposed the formation of a separate Communist party with interests apart from those of workers as a whole. "Basing himself upon the experience of the French Revolution with its long, drawn-out movement to the Left," writes one critic, "Marx wanted the workers to fight as a part of the bourgeois democratic forces." One of the basic premises of the Manifesto is that the achievement of bourgeois democracy, not socialism, was on the historical agenda in 1848. Indeed, the anarchist critics of the Manifesto were not altogether amiss in characterizing it as the "Bible of legal revolutionary democracy."[5]

Bernstein underestimated the democratic essence of the Manifesto. A scrutiny of its ten-clause program belies a strong Blanquist influence. Except for the expropriation of the means of transportation and communication, there would be no despotic inroads on the property of industrial capitalists. The program does not call for the total socialization of the means of production nor even for the abolition of hired labor. It is directed against money-dealing capital, not productive capital. The presumption is that it would be supported by the industrial bourgeoisie and count on the cooperation of other social elements besides the proletariat.[6]

The Manifesto's damaging dualism is to be found elsewhere—in the incompatibility of its materialist interpretation of history and its vision of a classless society. On this score, Bernstein was on target in criticizing the "dualism which runs through the whole monumental work of Marx." In *Capital* and in section 1 of the Manifesto this dualism consists of a "scientific theory and also...a theory laid down before its drafting." The return to the *Communist Manifesto* in the penultimate chapter of volume 1 "points...to a real residue of Utopianism in the Marxist system." The Manifesto accepted the Utopians' final solution to the social question, but "recognized their means and proofs as inadequate." As long as the final aim of socialism remained unquestioned, Marx stuck to the facts. "But as Marx approaches a point when that final aim enters seriously into the question, he becomes uncertain and unreliable...a slave to a doctrine."[7]

---

[5] Harrington, "The Democratic Essence of Socialism," in Bender, 108. See Davidson, "Reform versus Revolution," in Bender, 94.

[6] See Y. Wagner and M. Strauss, "The Theoretical Foundations of the *Communist Manifesto's* Economic Program," in Bender, *Karl Marx. The Communist Manifesto*, 153, 157–158, 160.

[7] Bernstein, *Evolutionary Socialism*, 209, 210.

If the Manifesto's theory had been fully scientific, Bernstein concludes, it would have adopted a different goal. One has to take wage-slaves as they are and not as they should be, and "they are neither so universally pauperized as was set out in the *Communist Manifesto*, nor so free from prejudices and weaknesses as their courtiers wish to make us believe."[8] They are unprepared for the task the Manifesto assigns them; therefore its goal, the abolition of classes, borders on fantasy. Such is the basis of Bernstein's maxim, "the ultimate aim of socialism is nothing...the movement is everything." That the proletariat has an ideal or ultimate goal is of secondary importance, as long as "it pursues with energy its proximate aims."[9]

Falsified by Facts

Bernstein begins his discussion of the Manifesto with the observation that it was correct in characterizing the most general tendencies in modern society, but mistaken in "several special deductions, above all in the estimate of the *time* the evolution would take." Engels had made the same point in his political testament, his 1895 preface to Marx's *Class Struggles in France*. But he failed to observe the extent to which modern capitalist development had radically departed from the Manifesto's forecasts.

"Social conditions," wrote Bernstein, "have not developed to such an acute opposition of...classes as is depicted in the Manifesto." Social evolution raised serious doubts concerning even the final collapse of capitalism. The number of capitalists was becoming greater instead of smaller, the middle classes were not disappearing, and the privileges of capitalists were yielding to democratic pressures.[10] The workers were not becoming progressively poorer, unemployment was not increasing, economic crises were becoming less severe, and exploitation was becoming less onerous owing to government protection and welfare legislation. Proletarians were becoming citizens with political rights and the right to vote, and it was no longer true that they had no country. Ergo, any expectation of the collapse of capitalism, any talk of a coming catastrophe was unrealistic and irresponsible. Although socialism was desirable, according to Bernstein, it was not inevitable.

Bernstein's maxim turned out to be prophetic. In due course the Social Democratic party in Germany adopted it, as did Social Democrats

---

[8]   Ibid., 219.
[9]   Ibid., 202, 222.
[10]   Ibid., xxiv–xxv, xxvi.

elsewhere. Even Karl Kautsky (1854–1938), the would-be champion of orthodox Marxism, made increasing concessions to Bernstein's "revisionism."

"The proletarians and also the bourgeois," wrote Kautsky in 1906, "are today no longer quite the same as they were six decades ago." The proletariat is "learning how to overcome the degrading effects of capitalism." Its situation had improved relative to that of artisans and peasants with their own means of production. "One can therefore no longer say with the *Communist Manifesto*: 'The worker is becoming a pauper, he is sinking ever deeper below the conditions of his own class.'" As for the capitalists, the revolution of 1848 "forced the industrial bourgeoisie and its adjuncts increasingly out of the camp of democracy and into the camp of reaction." Consequently, "not only are the bourgeoisie and the proletariat…differently constituted from the time of the *Communist Manifesto*, but also…political developments have gone in another direction than could have been foreseen."[11]

But what is one to make of Kautsky's conclusion? "There is no historical document that has through the decades following its composition been more brilliantly validated than the *Communist Manifesto*."[12] Validated in what respect? As a matter of history both Bakunin and Bernstein thought otherwise and had strong reasons for disputing the Manifesto's sequence of economic stages and ruling classes. And as a matter of practice the Manifesto would soon become a cultural artifact and less and less a guide to action.

Branded as an "opportunist" and lambasted for his "sham Marxism," Bernstein had only one champion on the Socialist Left, a disciple of Bakunin and the intellectual father of anarcho-syndicalism, the Frenchman Georges Sorel (1847–1922). As Sorel read Bernstein's amendments, they were confirmed by events in England on which they were predicated, much like Marx's earlier observations in *Capital*. "But during the thirty years following its publication many great changes took place in English industry, politics, and in English life generally." So the most effective way of rejuvenating Marxism was to resume the inquiry and to complete *Capital* and the Manifesto where Marx left off.[13]

---

[11] Karl Kautsky, "The *Communist Manifesto* after Six Decades," in Bender, *Karl Marx. The Communist Manifesto*, 127–131.

[12] Ibid., 131.

[13] Georges Sorel, "The Decomposition of Marxism," trans. Irving Louis Horowitz, appended to Irving Louis Horowitz, *Radicalism and the Revolt Against Reason* (London: Routledge and Kegan Paul, 1961), 215–216.

Bernstein, according to Sorel, considered himself and was in fact faithful to Marx's historical method, and therefore to the spirit of scientific socialism. Since England was the home of trade unionism whose objective is "to settle amicably the conflicts between employers and workers," it was flying in the face of facts for Marxists to keep insisting that "the mechanism of capitalist production aggravates industrial conflicts to the point of transforming them into class struggle."[14] Thus Bernstein was led not only to ask in what respects the Manifesto's scenario in section 1 had become obsolete, but also to explain why its theses were so sharply at variance with historical developments.

Like Bernstein, Sorel found the explanation in the persistence of Blanquist and Utopian residues in the Manifesto that contradicted an unfettered application of its method and that obstructed its view of reality.[15] Together, from opposite ends of the political spectrum, they purged the Manifesto of all that was not specifically Marxist, while endeavoring to preserve its realistic kernel.

As Bernstein described his amendments to section 1 of the Manifesto, they questioned the scaffolding of the monument Marx later erected in *Capital*. "To express it figuratively, he [Marx] has raised a mighty building within the framework of a scaffolding he found existing, and in its erection he kept strictly to the laws of scientific architecture as long as they did not collide with the conditions which the construction of the scaffolding prescribed." But where the scaffolding imposed limits on the building's construction, "instead of destroying the scaffolding, he changed the building." The scaffolding represents Marx's residue of utopianism, his fixed idea of the goal of socialism. The building represents his scientific conclusions based on his observations of modern capitalist development. Therefore the "scaffolding must fall if the building is to grow in its right proportions."[16]

It was not just the higher stage of communism, as sketched in the "Critique of the Gotha Programme," that Bernstein believed had been falsified. Most of his criticism of the Manifesto targets not it, but the lower stage of socialism. As Kautsky retorted when Bernstein observed that the number of capitalists had not decreased, but increased: "If it were true, then...we are going ever further from our goal the more evolution progresses, then capitalism grows stronger, not socialism."[17]

---

[14] Ibid., 216.
[15] Ibid., 229–232.
[16] Bernstein, *Evolutionary Socialism*, 210–211.
[17] Ibid., 212; Cited by Bernstein.

Reform versus Revolution

The alternative, according to Bernstein, was not to give up the socialist struggle. That Marx's goal had proved illusory had little bearing on the workers' movement. "Neither the struggle of the workers for democracy in politics nor their struggle for democracy in industry is touched by it." For the prospects of these struggles do not depend on the goal, but on the steps thereto. Rather than a betrayal of socialism, Bernstein concluded, his amendments to the Manifesto constituted "a rejection of certain remains of Utopianism which adhere to Marxism." For as long as the proletariat lags behind other classes in education and organizational clout, "the dictatorship of the proletariat means the dictatorship of club orators and writers"—a conclusion shared with Bakunin.[18]

In this light, Bernstein cobbled up a more credible version of the Manifesto than his critics, who stuck by its dead letter or went no further than Marx and Engels' amendments to it. Purged of its revolutionary foolishness, the Manifesto was given a new lease on life in Western Europe.

It was a tremendous achievement, a tour de force by which Bernstein sought to salvage the Manifesto by ridding it of its fantastic features.[19] If history is no guarantee of socialism, the socialist movement should look elsewhere for guidance. "A class which is aspiring needs a sound morale," he wrote, "a definite principle which expresses a higher...view of morals." Instead of a utopia, it needs an ideal; instead of historical cant, a cant in the spirit of Immanuel Kant![20] The Bolshevik Revolution that first established socialism in the Soviet Union, however, shows that the Manifesto's goal was not utopian. Thus Bernstein beat a retreat that turned out to be unnecessary.

"The conquest of political power by the working classes, the expropriation of the capitalists, are no end in themselves," he proclaimed. Instead, the "aim of all socialist measures...is the development and the securing of a free personality."[21] The Manifesto says as much: the expropriation of the capitalists is not the ultimate end but a means only.

Bernstein's amendments to the Manifesto were even more consequential than Bakunin's amendments to the Manifesto. In the West, strategies of reform have proven far more consequential than have strategies for revolution. Germany's Social Democracy was Bernstein's principal heir—

---

[18] Ibid., 212, 213, 219.
[19] Sorel, "The Decomposition of Marxism," in Horowitz, 216–217, 224–232.
[20] Bernstein, *Evolutionary Socialism*, 222.
[21] Ibid., xxix, 149.

the largest Socialist party on the Continent and decidedly the most influential.

Bernstein was fully aware of how the Manifesto lent itself to Blanquist, Bakuninist, and later Bolshevik interpretations. As Sidney Hook, his leading American disciple, comments in the introduction to the English translation of Bernstein's major work, "he [Bernstein] saw in Bolshevik-Leninism...a reversion to the extreme ideas of Blanqui and Bakunin which glorified force and violence under misleading formulas about historical necessity and the laws of the class struggle."[22]

It was precisely in the first section of the Manifesto that Bernstein identified the chief source of these alternative readings, in the theory of imminent economic catastrophe as the basis for a strategy of violent revolution. As he wrote in the preface to *Evolutionary Socialism*: "I set myself against the notion...that social democracy should be induced by the prospect of such an imminent, great, social catastrophe to adapt its tactics to that assumption." For scriptural support, he appealed to Engels' 1895 introduction to Marx's *Class Struggles in France, 1848–1850*.[23]

Before World War I, Bernstein's reading based on Engels' final amendments had the merit of demythologizing the Manifesto's catastrophic revolution and of legitimizing policies of gradual reform. The German trade unions became its principal supporters. Meanwhile, the party's office holders in parliament tried to expel Bernstein as a betrayer of Marx's legacy—because he threatened their Machiavellian "combination designed to keep the masses within the party and the leaders out of jail"![24] Even so, despite the party's threat of expulsion and its reaffirmation of the Manifesto's revolutionary rhetoric, in daily practice it followed in Bernstein's footsteps.

Only after World War I and the November 1918 Revolution, which won the battle of democracy for Germany, did the Social Democratic party abandon all pretence at being revolutionary. "After the War his [Bernstein's] prestige soared and...his point of view, even doctrinally, was acceptable." The presence of a Communist party drained off the revolutionary elements, leaving the Social Democratic party in the hands of reformists. When the party was reconstituted after Hitler's fall, Bernstein's ideas again became the reigning orthodoxy. Indeed, they became "the working beliefs of democratic socialist movements in the [entire] Western world."[25]

---

[22] Sidney Hook, "Introduction" to Bernstein, *Evolutionary Socialism*, xv–xvi.
[23] Bernstein, *Evolutionary Socialism*, xxiv, xxvi–xxviii.
[24] Nomad, *Rebels and Renegades*, 93.
[25] Hook, "Introduction," in Bernstein, xiv–xv.

Freedom and democracy come first, Bernstein believed. Consequently, the chief issue of our time is not that between socialism and capitalism, but rather the struggle between democracy and totalitarianism, Such was Bernstein's reading of the Manifesto that raised Social Democracy to the position of an ideological vanguard in the struggle against world communism during the Cold War—a doctrine that ultimately infiltrated the walls of the Kremlin and brought the Soviet Union to its knees.

What an anomaly—the Manifesto as the principal document legitimizing both Germanys during the threatened holocaust—with the Berlin Wall in between!

8. A Communist Manifesto: Lenin and Trotsky

> Thus arose the famous Manifesto...to this day its spirit inspires and motivates the organized and fighting proletariat of the entire civilized world.
>
> V. I. Lenin, "Frederick Engels" (1895)

> We Communists...feel and consider ourselves to be the heirs and consummators of the cause whose program was affirmed 72 years ago.
>
> Leon Trotsky, *Manifesto of the Communist International to the Workers of the World* (1919)

Lenin's informal amendments to the Manifesto are the substance of his major writings. In his narrowly polemical but influential *What Is To Be Done?* (1902) and *Two Tactics of Social-Democracy in the Democratic Revolution* (1905), he called for a revival of conspiracy and for the organization of a vanguard party of professional revolutionaries to replace the Manifesto-based mass political parties of European Social Democracy. In his later works, notably in *Imperialism, the Highest Stage of Capitalism* (1916) and *State and Revolution* (1917), he further amended the Manifesto by questioning its model of competitive capitalism and its program based on obsolete historical premises.

The Manifesto was the only Marxist classic that Lenin translated in full. As he remarked on its political importance in 1895, "This little booklet is worth whole volumes." In 1913, on the thirtieth anniversary of Marx's death, he wrote three essays hammering away at this theme. The Manifesto was a handbook for every class-conscious worker, the "main thing in the doctrine of Marx," the "best exposition to this day" of Marx's revolutionary theory and practice, a "work which has traveled all over the world," a political statement "true in all its fundamentals [if not details] and as actual and topical as though it were written yesterday."[1] That it was the manifesto of Marx's Communist party signified for Lenin that it was a communist manifesto.

---

[1] V.I. Lenin, "Frederick Engels," in *Marx, Engels, Marxism*, 67; and in the same volume, idem, "The Marx-Engels Correspondence," 81; idem, "The Three Sources and Three Component Parts of Marxism," 86; idem, "The Historical Destiny of the Doctrine of Karl Marx," 92.

Lenin's communist reading of the Manifesto reached a climax on the eve of the Revolution when he penned his *State and Revolution*. But faced with the insurmountable problems of implementing communism, he felt compelled to retreat from his earlier "foolishness." His own toughest critic, he acknowledged that the Communist ideology that had inspired the Bolsheviks in 1917 and during the years of "War Communism" (1918– 1920) was unworkable. As he reflected during his 1921 struggle against the Workers' Opposition whose program called for a return to the postulates of *State and Revolution*: "It was a fantastic idea for a Communist to dream that in three years you could drastically change the economic structure of society." But he had no regrets. For, "how can you begin a Socialist revolution...without fantasy-makers?"[2]

The Vanguard Party

Lenin's favorite author was the Russian Jacobin Nikolai Chernyshevsky whose novel *What Is To Be Done*? (1864) inspired an entire generation of Russian youth to adopt an austere revolutionary morality and to free Russia's workers and peasants from the double yoke of feudal servitude and capitalist exploitation. Its hero, Rakhmetov, is the archetype of a "new man" totally dedicated to the people's cause. That Lenin borrowed both the novel's title and its ideal of the revolutionary for his first major work on party building indicates his high regard for Chernyshevsky's work. Thus N. V. Volskii (Valentinov), a fellow Bolshevik, reported Lenin as saying, "I became acquainted with the works of Marx, Engels, and Plekhanov, but it was only Chernyshevsky who had an overwhelming influence on me...[who] showed that every right-thinking and really decent person must be a revolutionary...what his principles ought to be, how he should aim for his goal, what means and methods he should employ." The means and methods consisted of organization, discipline, and the "wise selfishness" of subordination to a collective will—the vanguard party.[3]

Lenin's *What Is To Be Done*? called for a party of professional revolutionaries steeled in self-sacrifice. It questioned the Manifesto's reliance on a party of trade unionists and the Manifesto's dictum that workers can emancipate themselves by their own efforts without help from

---

[2] Cited by Adam B. Ulam, *The Bolsheviks: The Intellectual and Political History of the Triumph of Communism in Russia* (New York: Collier, 1965), 458, 475.

[3] Cited by Volkogonov, *Lenin*, 20. For Chernyshevsky's defense of a revolutionary "collective will" see Ulam, *The Bolsheviks*, 54–55, 58–60.

outside, through the "self-conscious, independent movement of the immense majority." The Bolshevik party's hierarchical and quasi-military organization had no precedent in the Manifesto.

What Is To Be Done? further amends the Manifesto's conception of the party as a broker, mediator, and unifier of the proletarian movement, as an agent of solidarity in the face of divergent proletarian aims and tendencies. In matters of party organization, Lenin took his cues from section 3 rather than section 2 of the Manifesto. Its critique of false prophets became grounds for purges and expulsions for any divergence from Lenin's revolutionary line. However, the Manifesto is not a brief for ideological purity nor is there the least suggestion that Communists should suppress internal criticism in order to defend a monolithic doctrine.

Under conditions of Czarist oppression, it is understandable that Lenin placed a premium on secrecy and on conspiratorial organization. Although he instructed his followers in techniques of mass agitation, he also demanded that they infiltrate the enemy's ranks. They were to go among all classes in order to assess the balance of social forces at a given time. They were to learn the enemy's weak points and to take advantage of them. There is not a hint of such tactics in the Manifesto.

Lenin's broadsides against European Marxists amounted to an implicit rejection of the Manifesto's demoliberalism. His barbs against freedom of expression, reliance on economic development, trade-unionist politics, piecemeal reforms, and amateurism in matters of revolution had no parallel in the Manifesto.[4] But were these his last words on the party or did his conception of the vanguard evolve in response to changing circumstances?

In response to the eruption of the masses in the 1905 Revolution, Lenin amended his original model of party organization. Instead of co-opting the party's leaders, he called for their election. Instead of a highly centralized command structure, he encouraged independent action and initiative. Instead of a party restricted to professional cadres, he advocated a loosening of the requirements for membership. Instead of an exclusive underground organization, he created new legal and semilegal support groups.

While working underground, Lenin observed, the party had suffocated and stagnated. His initial pessimism concerning the independent role and the revolutionary possibilities of the masses had been shown to be unjustified. The popular uprisings in 1905 forced him to reconsider the problems of revolutionary strategy and to "go beyond the generalities he had until then

---

[4]   V. I. Lenin, "What Is To Be Done?" *Selected Works*, 1:102–106, 115–117, 120–122, 125–127, 141–142, 154–156, 163–169, 182–190, 200–201.

considered sufficient." As a result, the "Leninist organization shaped by the 1905 Revolution was different from its original form."[5]

Such was the origin of Lenin's celebrated democratic centralism combining the elective principle with enforced discipline by a leadership with limited instead of absolute powers. Democratic centralism meant freedom to criticize the decisions of higher bodies, freedom to organize factions preliminary to the formulation of party policy. Who, then, had the right to determine policy? The annual Party Congress, not the Central Committee entrusted with implementing its decisions.

Convinced by the failure of the liberal bourgeoisie to make its own revolution in 1905, Lenin concluded that the Bolsheviks at the head of a mass political party might do the job for them. For his party to become a real factor in Russian politics there were two prerequisites: it had to overcome its numerical weakness by accepting virtually every newcomer; and it had to seek allies from other classes. "This was the origin of the formula of the 'democratic dictatorship of the proletariat and the peasantry'...Lenin's first revolt, as it were, against Leninism."[6]

That the party was *not* to be a labor party in the narrow sense meant that it would have to become a mass-based organization and enter into an alliance with other oppressed or unenfranchised classes. It might establish a temporary alliance with the liberal bourgeoisie and its party, the Constitutional Democratic party (Kadets), or with the vast numbers of landless peasants led by the Socialist-Revolutionary party (SR). But it could not realistically have both for allies, since the SRs opposed the Kadets' liberal ideology and policy of capitalist development.

The split in the Social-Democratic party hinged on the choice of allies. In line with the Manifesto and the practice of European Marxists, the Mensheviks (Bernsteinians) formulated a two-stage strategy of revolution partial during the first stage to an alliance with the Kadets. Contrariwise, Lenin called for an alliance with the discontented peasant masses. In practice, this could only mean an alliance with the adopted party of the peasants, the SRs.

At the time, the SR party was the most radical in Russia, while the Bolsheviks adopted an intermediate position between it and the Mensheviks.

---

5   Marcel Liebman, "Lenin in 1905: A Revolution that Shook a Doctrine," in Paul M. Sweezy and Harry Magdoff, eds., *Lenin Today: Eight Essays on the Hundredth Anniversary of Lenin's Birth* (New York/London: Monthly Review Press, 1970), 58, 66. On Lenin's "pragmatism," see ibid., 59–64 and Neil Harding, *Lenin's Political Thought: Theory and Practice in the Democratic and Socialist Revolutions*, 2 vols. (Atlantic Highlands, NJ: Humanities Press, 1983), 1:102–106.
6   Liebman, "Lenin in 1905," in Sweezy and Magdoff, 67, 73.

It traced its origins to Chernyshevsky and to People's Will, the latter under the influence of the Russian Blanquists. Having adopted Bakunin's strategy of a proletarian-peasant armed struggle against autocracy, it also showed a penchant for other forms of direct action. Its theory of a noncapitalist path to socialism signified skipping the stage of bourgeois rule, another of Bakunin's nostrums. Although Lenin believed that capitalism was both progressive and inevitable, he agreed with the SRs that a democratic revolution could be made independently of the bourgeoisie.

In effect, Lenin advocated a joint party dictatorship of the Bolsheviks and the SRs, the essence of his proposed dictatorship of the proletariat and the peasantry. Prior to World War I, he disputed mainly the SRs' disregard for capitalist development and their reliance on individual terrorism against the Czar and prominent government officials. Unlike the Manifesto, he did not look upon the liberal bourgeoisie as "revolutionary," and upon the peasants as "reactionary." Instead, he castigated the Bernsteinians, the supporters of the liberal bourgeoisie, as the "Girondists of contemporary Russian Social-Democracy"—in opposition to his own "Jacobins."[7]

The SRs were mistaken rather than treacherous. They "do not know the ABC of the laws of development of commodity and capitalist production; they fail to see that...even the redistribution of the whole land in favor of the peasants...will not destroy capitalism at all, but will, on the contrary, give an impetus to its development." Failure to grasp Marx's theory of capitalist development makes the SRs "unconscious ideologists of the petty bourgeoisie," whereas the Mensheviks were witting partners of the bourgeoisie. The proletariat is not the only class that has a stake in a democratic revolution; so have the peasants and the petty bourgeoisie. Only later would a split become inevitable. "The revolutionary-democratic dictatorship of the proletariat and the peasantry is unquestionably only a transient temporary socialist aim, but to ignore this aim in the period of a democratic revolution would be downright reactionary."[8]

This was a startling amendment to the Manifesto. That a vanguard party might take the reactionary peasants as a partner in a joint revolutionary dictatorship also went beyond Marx and Engels' 1850 concession that the petty bourgeoisie might play the leading role in a democratic revolution. That role would have to be shared with the proletariat's own vanguard party. Lenin's revision of Marx and Engels' amendment was not, however,

---

[7] V. I. Lenin, "Two Tactics of Social-Democracy in the Democratic Revolution," *Selected Works*, 1:494–495, 515–518. For the preceding discussion of the SRs see Richard Pipes, *The Russian Revolution* (New York: Vintage, 1991), 146–149.

[8] Lenin, "Two Tactics," *Selected Works*, 1:484–487, 511, 516–518.

original. Bakunin had anticipated it in his own amendments to the Manifesto.

Imperialism and War

Lenin's *Imperialism* amended the Manifesto's model of competitive capitalism in several crucial respects. Section 2 of the Manifesto states that "National differences and antagonisms between peoples are daily more and more vanishing, owing to the development of the bourgeoisie, to freedom of commerce, to the world market." At the dawn of capitalism when dynastic rivalries faced increasing resistance from businessmen for being wasteful, the lords of capital had more to gain from international trade than from expensive and destructive national wars. But times had changed with the merger of bank and industrial capital. The export of capital to backward regions, the monopoly of world trade, the territorial division of the world among the great powers, the scramble for superprofits and for an ever greater share of the world market would ultimately pit the big European capitalists against one another.

There could be little peace under the new conditions. With no more free land for the taking, Lenin concluded, "*only* redivision is possible." Because the rule of big corporations accentuates the "unevenness and contradictions inherent in the world economy," wars of repartition are *inevitable*. Therefore, it is unrealistic "to talk 'seriously' about peace under imperialism," by which Lenin meant contemporary imperialism corresponding to the monopoly stage of capitalism.[9]

At the time of the Manifesto there were no movements of national liberation outside of Europe and Latin America. That the struggles of non-European peoples against the civilized powers might have a "progressive character" and take the form of "progressive wars" never entered the head of Marx or Engels. But some sixty years after the Manifesto the tables were turned when, in response to the Chinese Revolution of 1911, Lenin made a credible case for "Backward Europe and Advanced Asia"! By then capitalists in Europe had turned their backs on democracy in an effort to preserve their newly won privileges, while the Asian bourgeoisie were just beginning to fight for democracy against the remnants of landlord rule. The European bourgeoisie, wrote Lenin, "supports everything backward,

---

[9]   V. I. Lenin, "Imperialism, the Highest Stage of Capitalism," in Robert C. Tucker, ed., *The Lenin Anthology* (New York: Norton, 1975), 234, 243–244, 248, 261, 267–268.

moribund and medieval" as a means of keeping the European proletariat at bay, and in Asia from fear of losing its colonies.[10] Thus support for movements of national liberation in the East was another amendment to the Manifesto, a strategic alliance between the European proletariat and the colonial and dependent peoples, a struggle on two fronts against imperialism with the prospect of becoming a world revolution.

By World War I, according to Lenin, capitalism had grown into a system of "financial strangulation of the overwhelming majority of the population of the world by a handful of 'advanced' countries...who are drawing the whole world into *their* war over the division of *their* booty." Unlike the Manifesto, he focused on "universal ruin" from wars of redivision as the principal condition of a revolutionary situation. "The tens of millions of dead and maimed left by the...war to decide whether the British or the German group of financial plunderers is to receive the most booty...are with unprecedented rapidity opening the eyes of the millions and tens of millions of people who are downtrodden, oppressed, deceived and duped by the bourgeoisie." Thus "a world-wide revolutionary crisis is arising which...cannot end otherwise than in a proletarian revolution and in its victory."[11] Prophetic words that became history even before the war ended!

World War I provided the conditions and the opportunity to transform a war among nations into a springboard to revolution. "From a liberator of nations, which it was in the struggle against feudalism, capitalism in its imperialist stage had turned into the greatest oppressor of nations," wrote Lenin at the war's outbreak in 1914. Since defense of one's country had become a reactionary slogan, he replaced it with a different expression of national pride. "We say that the Great Russians cannot 'defend the fatherland' otherwise than by desiring the defeat of tsarism in any war"! In this spirit, Lenin appealed for support to the Socialist International's Manifesto adopted at Basel in 1912, urging socialists to take advantage of their respective governments' wartime difficulties to "hasten the downfall of capitalism." As he interpreted the Basel Manifesto, it called for the defeat of one's government and for the "conversion of a war between governments into a civil war."[12]

---

[10] V. I. Lenin, "Socialism and War," in Tucker (1975), 184, 186; and "Backward Europe and Advanced Asia," in V. I. Lenin, *The National-Liberation Movement in the East* (Moscow: Foreign Languages Publishing House, 1962), 61–62.

[11] Lenin, "Imperialism," in Tucker (1975), 207.

[12] V. I. Lenin, "On the National Pride of the Great Russians," in Tucker (1975), 198; and idem, "Socialism and War," in Tucker (1975), 191, 195.

The Labor Aristocracy

In *Imperialism* Lenin showed that under monopoly capitalism another basic tenet of the Manifesto had also lost credibility. According to the Manifesto, "with development of industry the...various interests and conditions of life within the ranks of the proletariat are more and more equalized, in proportion as machinery obliterates all distinctions of labor, and nearly everywhere reduces wages to the same low level." This may have been the case at mid-century, when a privileged stratum of workers had yet to emerge from the ranks of the proletariat. It had ceased to be true at the turn of the century.

Lenin's theory of an emergent "labor aristocracy" constituted an amendment to the Manifesto's scenario of labor degradation. As he defined it, the labor aristocracy consisted of privileged groups of higher paid wage-earners extracting "crumbs from the profits of their own national capital" and cake from the superprofits of their "'great nation' situation." These nonproletarian elements included "officials of the legal labor unions, the parliamentarians and the other intellectuals who...built themselves berths in the legal mass movements." In more general terms he characterized them as "office employees," as the "upper strata of the proletariat and the petty bourgeoisie," a "thin layer of labor bureaucracy," and the "'top' of the labor movement...[allied to] *its* national bourgeoisie against the *class* that is exploited by the bourgeoisie."

Lenin's enumeration of these higher-paid workers made use of several contradictory headings. Besides nonproletarian, proletarian, and near-proletarian strata, he included within the labor aristocracy both "semi petty-bourgeois" and "petty-bourgeois" elements. If not exclusively "non-proletarian," they were "near proletarian elements," these so-called coupon clippers of the working class. As Eric Hobsbawm explains the meaning of "petty bourgeois" in these references to the labor aristocracy, "a purely 'economist' labor movement must tend to fragment the working class into 'selfish' ('petty bourgeois') segments each pursuing its interests, if necessary in alliance with its own employers, at the expense of the rest."[13]

---

[13] V. I. Lenin, "And Now What?" in *Collected Works*, vols. 1–18 (New York: International Publishers, 1930), 18:106; idem, "The Collapse of the Second International," *Collected Works*, 18: 306–308, 319; and "Opportunism and the Collapse of the Second International," *Collected Works*, 18:388–390. See Eric Hobsbawm, "Lenin and the 'Aristocracy of Labor,'" in Sweezy and Magdoff, *Lenin Today*, 49–50.

There is a crucial distinction, according to Lenin, between "the *'upper stratum'* of the workers and the *'lower stratum of the proletariat proper.'*" A *"minority* of the proletariat," the upper stratum furnishes the "bulk of the membership of cooperatives" and "sporting clubs" as also of the trade unions. In Great Britain it had access to the electoral system, unlike the lower layer of the proletariat that had yet to win the right to vote. Lenin cites a letter from Engels to Marx (7 October 1857) describing the English proletariat as a "bourgeois proletariat *alongside* the bourgeoisie." While it is unclear what Engels meant by a "bourgeois proletariat," Lenin took it to mean the "stratum of workers-turned bourgeois...who are quite philistine in their mode of life, in the size of their earnings and in their entire outlook...the real *agents of the bourgeoisie in the working-class* movement, the labor lieutenants of the capitalist class, real vehicles of reformism and chauvinism."[14]

As he noted in his 1920 preface to *Imperialism*, "out of such enormous superprofits (since they are obtained over and above the profits which capitalists can squeeze out of the workers of their 'own' country) it is possible to *bribe* the labor leaders and the upper strata of the labor aristocracy...in a thousand different ways, direct and indirect, overt and covert."[15]

Underlying these diverse accounts of the labor aristocracy was Lenin's distinction between a top stratum comparable to the bourgeoisie—a *nonproletarian* stratum whose wages conceal an extortionate share in the surplus exceeding by several times the value of labor-power—and a *near proletarian* or bottom stratum comparable to the petty bourgeoisie. So there is reason to believe that he was on the verge of decomposing the proletariat into two fundamentally different and antagonistic classes: a *proletariat proper* in the strict sense of exploited wage-earners; and a *proletariat improper* or new class of exploiters.

What was this if not Bakunin's decomposition of Marx's vaunted working class into exploited "drudge people" and an exploiting "labor aristocracy"? Certainly, this was not Engels' understanding of the labor aristocracy any more than it was Marx's understanding of the modern proletariat. It was an amendment to the Manifesto that threatened to turn it into a communist manifesto.

---

[14] Cited by A. J. Polan, *Lenin and the End of Politics* (Berkeley/Los Angeles: University of California Press, 1984), 167; and Lenin, "Imperialism," in Tucker (1975), 209–210, 256, 257–258.
[15] Lenin, "Imperialism," in Tucker (1975), 209.

In the Manifesto the various classes—landowning aristocracy, bourgeoisie, proletariat, petty bourgeoisie, artisans, and peasants—have as their common denominator the possession of one or more of Marx's three major factors of production: land, labor, and capital. But in "A Great Beginning" (June 1919), Lenin takes a different tack. In answer to the question what the Manifesto means by the "abolition of classes," he notes that classes are defined not only by a relation to the means of production, but also "by their role in the social organization of labor, and, consequently, by the...share of social wealth of which they dispose." So, in order to abolish classes completely, it is not enough to expropriate the landowners and capitalists: "it is necessary to abolish...the distinction between manual workers and brain workers," the privileges and higher pay of the labor aristocracy.[16]

"What is a Communist?" he asked in "The Tasks of the Youth Leagues" (October 1920). "*Communis* is the Latin for 'common.' Communist society is a society in which all things...are owned in common and the people work in common."[17] That was Babeuf and Buonarroti's definition, Blanqui and Weitling's definition, Schapper and Willich's definition of communism— not the definition given by Marx in the Manifesto or in Marx and Engels' subsequent amendments to it.

Communist Socialism

In response to Bernstein, who had decommunized socialism, Lenin recommunized it. In doing so, he went far beyond the Manifesto's synthesis of revolution and reform. So radical were Lenin's amendments to the Manifesto that they bridged the gulf between a lower and higher stage of communism as sketched by Marx in the "Critique of the Gotha Programme."

Parodied as an anarchist tract, Lenin's *State and Revolution* revived the communist legacy he read into the Manifesto. Lenin's communism was two-pronged: its goal was economic leveling from the top down leading to equality of incomes; its strategy, a violent seizure of power by a conspiratorial vanguard that would smash the old state machine and replace it with a commune state or republic of equals. Such was the program of Babeuf and Buonarroti with its Machiavellian and Jesuitical practice of revolution by any means. As he might have interpolated a passage from

---

[16] V. I. Lenin, "A Great Beginning," *Selected Works*, 3:213–214.
[17] V. I. Lenin, "The Tasks of the Youth Leagues," in Tucker (1975), 669, 671.

Buonarroti, "one cannot find...regeneration save in a secret corps [vanguard party]...what the Jesuits did to mislead and enslave men, the Monde [Bolshevism] has attempted to do in order to enlighten and deliver them."[18]

The Manifesto is the single most frequently cited work in Lenin's *State and Revolution*. He refers to it no less than sixteen times, mainly in chapters 2 and 3 on the experience of the 1848 Revolution and the 1871 Paris Commune. Besides an explication of ambiguous passages in the Manifesto, Lenin's citations underscore the Manifesto's priorities in view of Marx and Engels' later amendments.[19]

However, Lenin also introduced a novel amendment of his own, an amendment to Marx's 1875 amendment to the Manifesto. In his "Critique of the Gotha Programme," Marx spelled out the Manifesto's implicit principle governing what he called the first or lower stage of communism, otherwise known as socialism. The right of the producers is proportional to the labor they supply, or in Lenin's formulation, "An equal amount of products for an equal amount of labor."[20] Like Marx, he acknowledged a defect in this principle, namely, its perpetuation of economic inequality owing to different amounts of labor. His contribution was to show how a communized socialism might overcome this inequality.

All that is required, he argued, is that people be obliged to work the same amount, to perform equal work through evening the burdens assigned to each within the social division of labor. If all persons were obliged to render to society an equal amount of labor, the foundations would be laid for an equal distribution of wealth. Thus in "the *first phase* of communist society...[all] citizens are transformed into hired employees....All that is required is that they should work equally, do their proper share of work, and get equal pay."[21]

To this important amendment Lenin added in 1919 a second major amendment. In the "Critique of the Gotha Programme" Marx defined the period of the dictatorship of the proletariat as covering the transition from capitalism to communism. But what did he mean by "communism," its lower or higher stage? As Marx originally presented it, the dictatorship covers only the "transition to the *abolition of classes* and to *a classless society*," the transition to the lower stage of communism. But is that how Lenin understood it? On the contrary, classes and class struggles persist

---

[18] Eisenstein, *The First Professional Revolutionist*, 40.
[19] V. I. Lenin, "The State and Revolution," in Tucker (1975), 329, 330, 331, 333, 334–336, 355–356.
[20] Ibid., 378.
[21] Ibid., 383.

during this lower stage—unless equal pay for all becomes the rule. However, this expedient had become unworkable even after the capitalists and landowners had been expropriated. Consequently, the dictatorship of the proletariat had to cover the further period of transition from the lower to the higher stage of communism.[22]

Traceable to the egalitarian current in modern communism, these amendments to the Manifesto stamped the Bolsheviks' new 1919 program as a departure from Marxism, thus giving sustenance to Plekhanov's criticism of Lenin's Bakuninist aberrations. There is no doubt that Lenin was distressed by the inequalities of pay that remained after the Bolsheviks' first experiment with nationalization and collectivization. That accounts for what he called his "egalitarian line," and for wage equalization being built into the party's new program. That is why under Lenin's instigation the party's Central Committee in November 1920 adopted a resolution "to effect...the gradual but steady *transition* to equalization."[23]

During its formative years, the Soviet Union fell under the sway of Lenin's egalitarian interpretation of the Manifesto and its principal amendments. Lenin's "egalitarian line" was enthusiastically endorsed by Bukharin and E. Preobrazhensky in their 1919 manual, *The ABC of Communism.* According to one commentator, their updated "bible" of latter-day communism was the "most complete and systematic compendium of Marxist-Leninist theory produced at that time," until in the 1930s its fate was sealed by the purge and execution of its authors. To quote from the manual: "The aim of communism is to secure equal pay for all...our fundamental policy [is] to work for a system of equal pay for all."[24]

In the wake of the October 1917 Revolution, "there was strong pressure from Party members to introduce full equality as soon as possible, and to make such equality include equality of pay." They also set a practical example in this matter. Thus "the income of Party members, particularly senior Party members, was often very much less than a non-Communist would be getting for doing a similar job." But how long could this

---

[22] V. I. Lenin, "A Great Beginning," *Selected Works,* 3:213–214.

[23] Eden and Cedar Paul, trans., "Program of the Communist Party of Russia" (1919), in N. Bukharin and E. Preobrazhensky, *The ABC of Communism* (Ann Arbor: University of Michigan Press, 1962), 393; and V. I. Lenin, "Once Again on the Trade Unions, the Current Situation and the Mistakes of Trotsky and Bukharin," *Selected Works,* 3:545, 546.

[24] Stephen F. Cohen, *Bukharin and the Bolshevik Revolution: A Political Biography 1888–1938* (New York: Vintage, 1975), 74–75; and Sidney Heitman, "New Introduction" to Bukharin and Preobrazhensky, *The ABC of Communism,* vii, xi–xii. See also 290.

arrangement last before Party careerists began demanding the same treatment as non-Communists? Within a short time material incentives were restored as a means of promoting economic reconstruction. However, "the 'Puritans' among the Bolsheviks did not cease to imagine...that at the end of, at the most, a year or two, equality of pay could be introduced."[25]

Making the Revolution Permanent

Trotsky, too, read the Manifesto as if it were a communist manifesto. In 1897, at the age of eighteen, he used it as the centerpiece of his propaganda at the Nikaleyev factories in the Ukraine. Throughout his life he continued to regard it as the basis of his communist worldview.[26]

In 1906 Trotsky published his reflections on the aborted 1905 revolution in Russia. The bourgeoisie, he concluded, had become a partner of the landowning aristocracy on the one hand and of foreign capitalists on the other. Consequently, it was unwilling to lead workers in a thoroughgoing struggle for land reform and political democracy. How can the revolution succeed? Who will lead it in default of the bourgeoisie? It is remarkable how much his answers agreed with Lenin's.

Since the bourgeoisie cannot make its own revolution, Trotsky concluded, the proletariat with peasant support will have to make it—an alternative scenario to that in the Manifesto. Lenin called his amendment a "continuing revolution" leading to a revolutionary-democratic dictatorship of the proletariat and peasantry. Trotsky called his amendment a "permanent revolution" leading to a full-blown dictatorship of the proletariat. As he later summed up this change in strategy, "The democratic revolution grows over directly into the socialist revolution and thereby becomes a *permanent* revolution."[27]

This was not how Marx and Engels understood the "Revolution in Permanence." Their "Address of the Central Council to the Communist

[25] P. H. Vigor, *A Guide to Marxism and its Effects on Soviet Development* (New York: Humanities Press, 1966), 161.

[26] Leon Trotsky, *My Life* (New York: Charles Scribner's Sons, 1931), 109; see also his "Manifesto of the Communist International to the Workers of the World," in *The First Five Years of the Communist International*, 2 vols. (New York: Pioneer, 1945), 1:19; and "Ninety Years of the *Communist Manifesto*," in Isaac Deutscher, ed., *The Age of Permanent Revolution: A Trotsky Anthology* (New York: Dell, 1964), 285–286.

[27] Leon Trotsky, *Results and Prospects*, in *The Permanent Revolution* and *Results and Prospects* (New York: Pathfinder, 1974), 71–73; idem, *The Permanent Revolution*, 278.

League" (March 1850) envisioned a petty-bourgeois leadership of the democratic revolution, and proletarian opposition to the petty-bourgeois democrats once they replaced the liberal bourgeoisie and had their turn at ruling. The proletariat would then compel its former ally to propose more or less socialistic measures. It would drive the proposals of the democrats to the extreme and "transform them into direct attacks upon private property."[28]

In formulating his theory of permanent revolution, Trotsky placed himself in the direct line of revolutionary Jacobinism and its adaptations by Buonarroti, Blanqui, and the League of the Just. "In 1848 the bourgeoisie was already unable to play a comparable role [to that in 1789]," he wrote, and the same was true of the petty bourgeoisie on which Marx and Engels relied to take the lead. Only the proletariat could have made the 1848 revolution succeed, but it was too weak and disorganized to play the leading part. Conditions were different in the twentieth century, with the prospect of the "political domination of the proletariat" as more than a "passing episode." In Trotsky's amendment to the Manifesto the bourgeois revolution would become the "prelude to an immediately following proletarian revolution," but in more than one country. Thus, because "capitalism has created a world market, a world division of labor...it has also prepared world economy as a whole for socialist transformation."[29]

The Socialist Swindle

We have seen that Lenin's egalitarianism had a Bakuninist caste. Had Trotsky assimilated some of the same heritage? During his first Siberian exile in 1900 he spent several weeks discussing the work of Waclaw Machajski, a Polish disciple of Bakunin who was winning converts among the community of exiles. Besides a trenchant critique of Social Democratic reformism, Machajski had developed the germs of Bakunin's critique of Marxism into a full-fledged theory of the educated proletariat as a new exploiting class. Although Trotsky rejected it out of hand, traces of Machajski's theory would reappear in *The Revolution Betrayed* (1937).[30]

What kind of measures did Trotsky advocate? A socialist program did not suffice—he also demanded "equal distribution based upon planned

---

[28] Marx and Engels, "Address of the Central Council to the Communist League," *Collected Works*, 10:286.

[29] Trotsky, *Results and Prospects*, 55–56, 57, 67, 69; and *The Permanent Revolution*, 279.

[30] Trotsky, *My Life*, 129, 143.

production." Trotsky's insistence on "equal distribution" was not made in passing. It is a recurring theme in *The Revolution Betrayed* and a further amendment to the Manifesto.[31]

Whatever the source of his "egalitarian line," Trotsky concluded that the Bolshevik party had betrayed the communist heritage traceable to Babeuf. In defense of the party's ruling prohibiting Communist functionaries from receiving more than an average worker's pay, he cites Christian Rakovsky: "In the mind of Lenin, and in all our minds, the task of the party leadership was to protect both the party and the working class from the corrupting action of privilege, place and patronage." In the context of Trotsky's references to Babeuf, this meant the party's betrayal of its communist heritage. Thus Trotsky concludes that the extraordinary incomes of the party bureaucracy, "devouring a very considerable part of the surplus value," had created the "political premises for the birth of a new possessing class."[32]

In opposition to the tendency of Marxists to equate state and socialist property, Trotsky claims that state property becomes socialist property only to the degree that social privilege and differentiation disappear. Among "survivals of the old inequality," he cites the "concealment of the income of the bureaucracy under the honorable title of 'intellectual' labor." The party's cadres "demand an almost divine veneration and a continually rising salary...accompanied by a rebirth of bourgeois inequality" in consumption and material possessions. Considering Marx's aversion to discussing the distribution question under socialism, the Manifesto was not immune from this kind of criticism.[33]

Trotsky likened Stalin's nationalization of bourgeois property and forcible collectivization of the peasantry to a ship in which the passengers continued to be divided into first, second, and third classes. "If the property belonged to all the people, that would presume an equal distribution of 'shares,' and consequently a right to the same dividend for all 'shareholders.'" But under Stalin, payments were still being made according to bourgeois norms. "The theoretical income of each citizen is...composed of two parts, a + b—that is, dividend plus wages"—but "the dividend as well as the wage payment is unequal." The shares are determined not just by differences in individual productivity and skill, but also by a "masked appropriation of the products of the labor of others." As a result, a new

---

[31] Trotsky, *Results and Prospects*, 88–89; and Leon Trotsky, *The Revolution Betrayed* (New York: Merit, 1965; orig. pub. 1937), 88, 100, 102.

[32] Trotsky, *The Revolution Betrayed*, 101, 272.

[33] Ibid., 237–238.

group of exploiters, a "privileged minority of shareholders is living at the expense of the deprived majority."[34]

"When the new [1936] constitution announces that in the Soviet Union 'abolition of the exploitation of man by man' [Article 4] has been attained, it is not telling the truth," says Trotsky. For the new *caste* of exploiters is "in the full sense of the word the sole privileged and commanding *stratum* in the Soviet society." Since the workers would have to overthrow the bureaucracy to get rid of exploitation, he concluded that the Soviet Union was a "contradictory society halfway between capitalism and socialism."[35]

The basic principle of the new Soviet Constitution, Trotsky notes, is *"From each according to his abilities, to each according to his work."* Lenin had taken this principle for granted, but had interpreted it according to his "equalitarian line." Trotsky rejects it outright as a misreading of Marx's "Critique of the Gotha Programme." "From each according to his abilities" contradicts the principle of distribution according to work, because it means that work has become an individual need—people no longer have to be compelled to work. The "Critique" recognized only one principle of communism: "From each according to his abilities, to each according to his needs." This principle assumes not only economic abundance and an all-round development of personality, but also "equality"[36]—an addendum to Marx's amendment to the Manifesto that went a long way toward reconceptualizing it as a communist manifesto.

Trotsky's objection to payment according to work was that it constitutes "in reality, payment to the advantage of 'intellectual' *at the expense* of physical, and especially unskilled work," therefore a form of exploitation inimical to the lower as well as higher stage of communism. It is *not* a "principle of socialism." The first task of socialism is to guarantee the basic necessities and comforts of life to all. In the Soviet Union, however, "personal property still wears a petty bourgeois and not a communist aspect."[37] Thus Trotsky's scenario of socialism approximated his one and only principle of communism that also defined its higher stage.

The Stalin Constitution was tantamount to "juridically liquidating the dictatorship of the proletariat." On the premise that exploitation had been abolished, the proletarian as well as the capitalist had disappeared. Since

---

[34] Ibid., 239–240. See Marx, "Critique of the Gotha Programme," *Selected Works*, 531.
[35] Trotsky, *The Revolution Betrayed*, 244, 249, 255. For the full text of the Soviet Constitution, see Anna Louise Strong, trans., "The New Constitution of 1936," appended to Sidney and Beatrice Webb, *The Truth About Soviet Russia* (New York/London: Longmans, Green, 1942), 87.
[36] Trotsky, *The Revolution Betrayed*, 258.
[37] Ibid., 259, 260.

there was no longer a class enemy to be suppressed, the dictatorship of the proletariat had lost its raison d'être. But the "Soviet proletariat still exists," Trotsky claimed, so that it was a mistake to substitute a people's dictatorship for the dictatorship of a class. In effect, the dictatorship of the proletariat was replaced by the dictatorship of the party (Article 26), the party of the labor aristocracy and political bureaucracy.[38]

Bakunin had already smelled a rat hiding behind the façade of state socialism. But it was Trotsky who actually confronted, trapped, and dissected the animal. To be sure, he refused to accept the name "socialism" for the reality. Nonetheless, he was the first to unearth beneath the new economic order a socialist swindle.

In retrospect, Trotsky's political heirs were in a position to say, "We told you so." In 1991, as in 1937 when *The Revolution Betrayed* first appeared, his followers knew only of two options for the inwardly contradictory Soviet regime: *either* the overthrow of the bureaucracy by the proletariat led by a new revolutionary party "having all the attributes of the old Bolshevism"; *or* the seizure of power by a new counterrevolutionary party with the support of large numbers of "bureaucrats, administrators, technicians, directors, party secretaries, and privileged upper circles."[39] Supposedly, the latter option prevailed when, on the heels of a planned coup by party stalwarts in August 1991, Boris Yeltsin launched a countercoup that spelled the end not only of Communist rule but also of the Soviet Union.

However, Trotsky's followers chose not to pursue his last word on the subject. In response to the Nazi-Soviet Nonaggression Pact in August 1939, he raised the prospect of a third scenario. Suppose, he argued, that World War II results not in further revolutions but in increased repression on a world scale. Then the "inability of the proletariat to take into its hands the leadership of society could actually lead…to the growth of a new exploiting class." Should the proletariat seize power but prove incapable of holding it as in the USSR, then "we would be compelled to acknowledge that the reason for the bureaucratic relapse is rooted…in the congenital incapability of the proletariat to become a ruling class." Thus Trotsky concluded that "either the Stalin regime is an abhorrent relapse in the process of transforming bourgeois society into a socialist society, or the Stalin regime is the first stage of a new exploiting society."[40]

---

[38] Ibid., 261, 263, 269. See also Strong, "The New Constitution of 1936," in Webb, 117.

[39] Trotsky, *The Revolution Betrayed*, 252–253.

[40] Leon Trotsky, "The USSR in War," in *In Defense of Marxism* (New York: Pioneer, 1942), 9.

This concession to Bruno Rizzi's *Bureaucratization of the World* (1939) signified a revival of Bakunin's and Machajski's theory of a new class of educated workers slated to become the new slave-masters. It was an amendment to the Manifesto in favor of a new balance sheet of historical evolution and the social forces that had emerged subsequent to 1848. In effect, Trotsky called attention to the need for a drastic rehaul of the Manifesto that would take into consideration the struggle against the "new class."[41]

Except for this final amendment, Trotsky summed up his revisions of the Manifesto in a 1937 preface to its translation into Africaans. Entitled "Ninety Years of the *Communist Manifesto*," the preface distinguished what he believed was still viable in the document from what had become antiquated. In view of its "irreplaceable directives upon the most important and burning questions of the struggle for emancipation," he wrote, the Manifesto needed to be corrected, revised, and amplified. Besides its errors of timing, it was mistaken in crediting the bourgeoisie with the capacity everywhere to make its own revolution. That explains why the prospect of the proletariat leading the bourgeois-democratic revolution is not even raised in the Manifesto. The Manifesto is likewise silent concerning the role of national liberation struggles and the capacity of colonial and semicolonial peoples to liberate themselves—another error underscored by Trotsky. But despite these errors, he concluded, "What other book could even distantly be compared with the *Communist Manifesto*?"[42]

---

[41] See Bruno Rizzi, *The Bureaucratization of the World*, trans. Adam Westoby (New York: Free Press, 1985; orig. pub. 1939), 58–65; and Lucien Laurat, "If One Were to Rewrite the *Communist Manifesto* Today," in Bender, 146–149. For an anatomy of postcapitalist exploitation by the "new class," see Donald C. Hodges, *America's New Economic Order* (Aldershot UK/Brookfield USA: Avebury-Ashgate, 1996), 25–28, 39–49, 64–80.

[42] Trotsky, "Ninety Years of the *Communist Manifesto*," in Deutscher (1964), 290.

9. A Socialist Manifesto: Stalin

It is obvious that if these Leftist views were to triumph in the party, the party would cease to be a Marxist party.

Joseph Stalin, "Report to the
17th Party Congress" (1934)

Stalin's theoretical works had a practical cast. As he confessed to the German author Emil Ludwig in an interview in December 1931, the "purpose of the October Revolution...is to abolish capitalism in order to establish socialism." By socialism he understood a system not "under which everybody would get the same pay," but under which "people will be paid for their labor according to the work performed...the Marxist formula of socialism, i.e., the formula of the first stage of communism." Marxist socialism has nothing in common with "equalitarianism," with the mistaken idea that the "Bolsheviks want to pool all wealth and then share it out equally." As for the higher stage of communism, that would have to wait "until classes have been finally abolished and until labor has been transformed from a means of subsistence into the prime want of man, into voluntary labor for society."[1] Meanwhile, only socialism was on the historical agenda. But this was not his last word. On the eve of his death he would also place communism on the agenda.

"By equality," according to Stalin, Marxism means the "equal duty of all to work according to their ability." People would have the right to be paid according to their work under socialism and according to their needs under communism. Although he closed the door on equal incomes in communist society, that is because of the different costs of satisfying different needs, and because "we cannot expect all people to have the same requirements and tastes...to live their individual lives on the same model."[2] But the fundamental point is that in a postscarcity economy nobody cares about personal expenses. The question of equal pay becomes irrelevant!

---

[1] Joseph V. Stalin, "Talk With the German Author Emil Ludwig" (13 December 1931), in *Works*, 16 vols. (Moscow: Foreign Languages Publishing House, 1954–1955), 13:120–121, 125.

[2] Joseph V. Stalin, "Report on the Work of the Central Committee to the Seventeenth Congress of the Communist Party of the Soviet Union," in *Leninism: Selected Writings* (New York: International Publishers, 1942), 344.

The Minimum and Maximum Programs

Stalin first characterized the Manifesto as the "Bible" of socialism in his 1906–1907 polemic against the anarchists in his native Georgia. Fueled by the works of the Russian anarchist W. Tcherkesoff in *Pages of Socialist History: Teaching and Acts of Social Democracy* (1902), the leader of the Georgian anarchists, V. Cherkezishvili, depicted the Manifesto as the "Bible" not of socialism, but of "legal revolutionary democracy." So the point of Stalin's rebuttal was to document the differences between the 1848 Manifesto and its alleged source in Victor Considérant's 1843 *Democratic Manifesto*. Whereas Considérant's Manifesto stood for the conciliation of classes, Marx's Manifesto placed its hopes in "uncompromising class struggle...the weapon by which the proletariat will capture political power and then expropriate the bourgeoisie."[3]

The Georgian anarchists, Stalin noted, simply echo Kropotkin. Basing themselves on the Manifesto, wrote the Russian anarchist Peter Kropotkin (1842–1921), the German Socialists were guilty of a twofold error. "They want to abolish the capitalist system, but they preserve the two institutions which constitute the foundation of this system: representative government and wage labor." The Manifesto makes a brief for democracy, and it would preserve the system of wage labor. First, the workers' representatives in government will "retain the right to utilize...the surplus value obtained from production." Second, "the labor of the common-laborer and that of the skilled" would not be rewarded equally; professional workers would "perform what Marx calls *complex* labor and have the right to higher wages." Thus, from the arguments of the Georgians it follows that "socialist society is impossible without a government which, in the capacity of principal master, will hire workers."[4]

In defense of the Manifesto, Stalin replied that section 2 would "substitute for the old bourgeois society an *association* [in] which...there will be *no more political power properly so-called*." Therefore, the Manifesto is committed to the same goal held by the anarchists, for "when classes are abolished, when socialism becomes firmly established, there will be no need for any political power."[5] The state will become superfluous and

---

[3]   Joseph V. Stalin, *Anarchism or Socialism?* (New York: International Publishers, 1953; orig. pub. 1906–1907), 45, 46–47. See also Davidson, "Reform versus Revolution," in Bender, 94.

[4]   Cited by Stalin, *Anarchism or Socialism?*, 49, 50.

[5]   Ibid., 50, 51.

wither away. The factor of timing alone distinguishes socialists from anarchists. In the long run, there can be no differences between them.

Stalin concedes that wages will be unequal during the initial stage of communism. But that is because "the application of the principle, 'to each according to his needs,' will undoubtedly be greatly hindered [by enemies of the people] and, as a consequence, society will be obliged *temporarily* to take...a middle path." That means compromise. So the anarchist critique concerning wages under socialism boils down to the accusation that the Manifesto is not a communist manifesto. Understandably not, for its final aim is socialism, not communism.[6] Communism would come later.

The Georgian anarchists also questioned the Manifesto's commitment to social revolution. How is its commitment to democracy, they asked, consistent with the revolutionary's reliance on bullets instead of ballots, on direct action instead of parliamentary majorities? In reply, Stalin cited section 4 of the Manifesto: "Communists...openly declare that their *ends can be obtained only by the forcible overthrow* of all existing social conditions."[7] So the question is *when*, under *what* conditions. For Stalin, what can be done *before* must be distinguished from what can be done *after* the establishment of democracy—first bullets and then ballots.

Is the Manifesto a document of bureaucrats whose plan for a dictatorship of the proletariat "spells death to the revolution?" According to the Georgian anarchists, it would be a "dictatorship over the proletariat." On the contrary, Stalin replied, the Manifesto envisions "the dictatorship of the entire proletariat as a class." How else should one construe the passage in section 2 concerning "the proletariat organized as the ruling class"? The Manifesto's despotic inroads against the rights of property would be the actions of "a class over the bourgeoisie and not the dominion of a few individuals over the proletariat."[8]

To back up his argument, Stalin cites Engels' 1891 introduction to Marx's *Civil War in France*. Do you want to know what the words "Dictatorship of the Proletariat" mean in practice? "Look at the Paris Commune," Engels said. So what was it like? Citing another source, Stalin says it was "an anonymous government consisting almost exclusively of common workers and minor office employees, the names of three-fourths of

---

6   Ibid., 35–36. See Joseph V. Stalin, "Briefly About the Disagreements in the Party" (May 1905), *Works*, 1:99–102, 104, 107.
7   Cited by Stalin, *Anarchism or Socialism?*, 52.
8   Ibid., 53–54, 54, 55.

whom were unknown outside their streets or offices." It was "not represented by a single *lawyer, deputy, journalist,* or *general*."[9]

Besides Considérant, according to Stalin, the Georgian anarchists mistakenly took Bernstein (1899) instead of Lenin as representative of what the Manifesto stood for. While Bernstein shelved socialism as a remote goal along with revolution as a means of achieving it, Lenin insisted on both. Contrary to the anarchists, therefore, the Manifesto is the "Bible" of legal democracy only if one ignores its final aim.

The achievement of socialism, Stalin concluded, depends on the prior establishment of political freedom. By political freedom he meant "freedom of speech, press, strikes, and association—in short, freedom to wage the class struggle...in a democratic republic"—"the best type of 'bridge' to socialism." As he summed up the Manifesto's program, it consisted of two parts: "the *maximum program,* the goal of which is socialism, and the *minimum program,* the object of which is to lay the road to socialism through the democratic republic." So, as Stalin read the *Communist Manifesto,* its maximum program was socialist, not communist.[10] The Manifesto was not a communist manifesto.

Everything for the Masses

In his polemic with the anarchists, Stalin identified the "cornerstone" of anarchism with the *"individual,* whose emancipation...is the principal condition for the emancipation of the masses." In sharp contrast, the cornerstone of proletarian socialism is the *"masses,* whose emancipation...is the principal condition for the emancipation of the individual." For the anarchists' principle of "Everything for the individual," Stalin substituted the slogan "Everything for the masses."[11]

What is significant about this substitution? It meant giving priority to a *"broad* socialist life as the *principal* goal."[12] It meant "we should serve the proletariat" and sacrifice our private interests for the sake of collective interests. And it meant that those who refused to do so might have to be sacrificed for the sake of the revolution!

---

[9] Ibid., 55, 56.
[10] Ibid., 40. On the Manifesto's socialist alternative to communism on grounds of practicability, see Stanley Moore, *Marx on the Choice between Socialism and Communism* (Cambridge: Harvard University Press, 1980) 77, 83, 89.
[11] Stalin, *Anarchism or Socialism?,* 8.
[12] Ibid., 31–32.

That this was Stalin's meaning was brought out on the eve of the 1936 purges. The French Revolution collapsed, he explained to his nephew Budu Svanidze, "because of the degeneration of the morals of its leaders." To safeguard the Bolshevik Revolution, he was determined to "bear down with a white-hot iron to burn in the bud the loosening of morals." By this he meant the preference assigned to personal interests over the collective interest by some of the top Bolsheviks. He had been accused of preparing another Thermidor—the month in the French revolutionary calendar when Robespierre and the Committee of Public Safety were overthrown. "That's a stupid slander," he told his nephew. "It's the others who would have brought on a Thermidor if they had been allowed to stay in power." They had already been removed from high positions in the party, but had yet to be physically eliminated, "the vermin which revolutions, unfortunately, bear with them on their crests—vermin which have to be destroyed without mercy."[13]

When his nephew protested that Trotsky was anything but corrupt, Stalin agreed. "But he carries with himself another danger that a popular revolution can't tolerate: He's an individualist to his finger tips, a hater of the masses, a revolutionary Narcissus...he thought himself the most intelligent and the most brilliant of us all for the sole reason that he knew how to wield his pen and his tongue cleverly." He was only nominally a Bolshevik. "He represented...that dying civilization which we are charged with replacing by another." His nephew stared at him in disbelief. "Yes," Stalin continued. "There's not going to be any longer a civilization of individualists, of superiors who will try to rule the 'tailless monkeys' according to their wills....What is the way out? To proceed like Hitler, to affirm flatly that the era of supermen has come and to demand all the power for them? Or to make our civilization a civilization of the masses and to send all the intellectual individualists to the devil?"[14]

"Everything for the masses" signified, in other words, that Stalin should rid the party and the country of the Old Bolsheviks whose dedication to themselves had pre-empted their former fealty to the Revolution. He considered it an easy matter to eliminate them individually. The thorny problem was that they had friends and connections almost everywhere, while their influence extended across the length and breadth of the Soviet Union. Even party stalwarts hesitated before the prospect of a purge, "because they don't want to understand the necessity for combat and destruction." Although some were in the front ranks of the revolution, "we have to get rid

---

[13] Budu Svanidze, *My Uncle Joseph Stalin*, trans. Waverly Root (New York: Putnam's Sons, 1953), 128–129.
[14] Ibid., 130–131.

of them too." The guilty by association must perish along with the truly guilty. "We can't help it. As the wisdom of the people puts it, we must hew to the line, let the chips fall where they may."[15] As in wars among nations, in class wars the bulk of the casualties are innocent. They don't deserve to die, but die they must!

With good reason, Stalin was reputedly a "monster," as were the other members of his inner circle. Khrushchev denounced him at the Twentieth Congress of the Communist Party in 1956 for repeated violations of socialist legality. But in his memoirs he also reminded his readers of Stalin's exceptional merit and intransigent "revolutionary spirit." Stalin's "pretensions to a very special role in our history were well founded, for he really was a man of outstanding skill and intelligence...[and] truly did tower over everyone around him." He was persuasive as well as forceful, and "didn't simply come with a sword and conquer our minds and bodies." Khrushchev also lauded him for being "incorruptible and irreconcilable in class questions...[and] greatly respected for it."[16]

Stalin's principle, "Everything for the masses," constituted a major amendment to the Manifesto. Committed to leveling upward rather than downward, he was opposed to doing so on an individual basis. Collective cultivation of mass aptitudes and abilities, not self-cultivation, was his goal. It mattered little that the living would have to be sacrificed for the sake of future generations.

The basic economic law of socialism, wrote Stalin in 1952, is the "maximum satisfaction of the constantly rising material and cultural requirements of the whole of society through the continuous expansion and perfection of socialist production." What is meant by raising the level of the *whole of society* if not "Everything for the masses?" As he reported to the Eighteenth Party Congress in March 1939, "Only if we outstrip the principal capitalist countries economically can we reckon upon our country being fully saturated with consumers' goods...and on being able to make the transition from the first phase of communism to its second phase." For that purpose, "we require the earnest and indomitable desire to move ahead and the readiness to make sacrifices."[17] So communism as well as socialism will

---

[15] Ibid., 131.

[16] Nikita Khrushchev, *Khrushchev Remembers*, 2 vols., ed. and trans. Strobe Talbott (Boston: Little Brown, 1970, 1974), 1:4–6, 222.

[17] Joseph V. Stalin, *Economic Problems of Socialism in the USSR* (New York: International Publishers, 1952), 33; idem "Report on the Work of the Central Committee to the Eighteenth Congress of the Communist Party of the Soviet Union," in *Leninism: Selected Writings*, 448.

have to be built at the expense of those concerned with self-cultivation, those unwilling to make personal sacrifices.

Far from shelving *communism* for an indefinite future, he proposed to begin building it as soon as the foundations of socialism had been laid. Three preliminary conditions had to be satisfied: first, continuing and unrelenting industrialization; second, the replacement of collective-farm property by nationalized property to end all buying and selling; third, cultural advancement such as will secure for ordinary members of society the development of their physical and mental abilities—a scenario for "tailless monkeys" instead of Trotsky and Co., a scenario for "the stage of humanism...through a civilization of the masses."[18]

Unrelenting Class War

As Stalin interpreted the Manifesto, its essence consisted of the theory and practice of class struggle. This "essence" inspired his several amendments to the Manifesto. Besides his principle of "Everything for the masses," these included his theory of the "weakest link" in the chain of world imperialism, of "socialism in one country," of the "intensification of repression" instead of its relaxation under socialism, of the "dictatorship of the party" as the sine qua non of proletarian dictatorship, of the "general crisis of world capitalism," and of the "real, and not declaratory, transition to communism."

Let us briefly consider each.

Building on Lenin's *Imperialism* and its theory of "moribund capitalism," Stalin formulated his own theory of proletarian revolution. The revolution will occur *"not necessarily where industry is most developed...*[but] where the chain of imperialism is weakest." Consequently, the country that begins the revolution and "makes a breach in the capitalist front, may prove to be less developed in a capitalist sense than others which are more developed." He thereby questioned a basic tenet of the Manifesto: "United action, at least of the leading civilized countries, is one of the first conditions for the emancipation of the proletariat." Marx and Engels had analyzed the conditions of the proletarian revolution in individual countries, "as the consequence of an exclusively internal development...where the proletariat forms [or is about to form] the majority, where the culture is more

---

[18] Stalin, *Economic Problems of Socialism in the USSR*, 51–53; and Svanidze, *My Uncle Joseph Stalin*, 131.

advanced, where there is more democracy." But as Lenin foresaw, the chain of imperialism "will be broken...at its weakest link"—as in Russia and possibly in even less developed countries like India.[19]

"Formerly," Stalin noted, "the victory of the revolution in a single country was considered impossible, on the assumption that the combined action of proletarians of all, or at least of the majority, of the advanced countries was necessary." But the Manifesto's premise had become refuted by events. Thus Stalin concluded that the uneven and spasmodic development of capitalism "leading inevitably to wars, the growth of the revolutionary movement in all countries of the world," had made possible and even necessary the triumph of the proletariat in one country—Russia. His sole qualification when he first formulated this theory was that a victorious revolution does not suffice for the complete and final consolidation of socialism. "That requires victory for the revolution in at least several countries."[20]

In 1926, he amended this theory not by softening it, but by making it more controversial. The "*possibility* of completely constructing socialism by the efforts of a single country," he argued, "must be answered in the affirmative." Only that does not *guarantee* that socialism will survive in the event of foreign intervention. For its victory to be guaranteed, it would require support from revolutions elsewhere.[21] Such was the heresy of a narrowly national socialism that Trotsky equated with the essence of Stalinism.

Would Stalin's national socialism be appreciably different from the Manifesto's international socialism based on conditions in the economically advanced countries? Indeed, it would. In the Manifesto, everything would be socialized and there would no longer be buying and selling. But as Stalin notes, Marx and Engels took as their model the most advanced country—England. There the concentration of production in agriculture made it possible "to convert *all* the country's means of production into public property and to put an end to commodity production."[22] In backward Russia that was impossible.

It followed that in a backward country like Russia special incentives would be necessary to prod people to produce, to catch up with and outstrip

---

[19] Joseph V. Stalin, *Foundations of Leninism*, Tenth Anniversary Edition (New York: International Publishers, 1934), 33–35.

[20] Ibid., 43–44.

[21] Joseph V. Stalin, *Problems of Leninism* (New York: International Publishers, 1926; trans. 1934), 60–62. See Marx and Engels, "The German Ideology," *Collected Works*, 5:49.

[22] Stalin, *Economic Problems of Socialism in the USSR*, 13–15.

the major capitalist powers. Any talk of wage leveling under such conditions played into the enemy's hands. "Practice has shown that the communes [which practiced leveling] would certainly have been doomed had they not abandoned equalization." Citing the Manifesto as authority, Stalin concluded that "equality in the sphere of requirements...is a piece of reactionary petty-bourgeois absurdity worthy of a primitive sect of ascetics, but not of a socialist society organized on Marxian lines."[23]

For Stalin, "there would have been no use overthrowing capitalism...if we were not going to secure a life of plenty for our people." Socialism does not rest with the abolition of exploitation, but goes beyond to the "abolition of poverty and privation; it means the organization of a prosperous and cultured life for all members of society." Who wants socialism in poverty? he asked. "Marxian socialism means, not cutting down individual requirements, but developing them to the utmost, to full bloom...[it means] the full and all-round satisfaction of all the requirements of culturally developed working people."[24] And who might they be? Everybody, the masses, was his answer.

Taking his cue from Lenin's Machiavellian treatise, "'Left-Wing' Communism: An Infantile Disorder," Stalin spelled out the implications of its thesis that the resistance of the bourgeoisie is "increased *tenfold* by their overthrow (even if only in a single country)." The persistence of capitalism in the "minds of the people" and the effect of capitalist encirclement in sustaining bourgeois modes of thought, he argued, called for an amendment to the Manifesto's scenario of the obsolescence of political power and the state under socialism. A classless society can be achieved not by relaxing, but only by "strengthening the organs of the dictatorship of the proletariat, by intensifying the class struggle." But as Trotsky was among the first to perceive, Stalin's strengthening of the state and its organs of repression threatened to become a double-edged sword that might also be used against the party.[25]

In line with the Manifesto's "despotic inroads on the rights of property," Stalin acknowledged the need for a dictatorship of the proletariat. But going beyond the Manifesto, he insisted that the substance of this dictatorship is

---

[23] Stalin, "Report on the Work of the Central Committee to the Seventeenth Congress of the Communist Party of the Soviet Union," in *Leninism*, 344, 345, 346.

[24] Ibid., 346–347.

[25] Ibid., 341–342, 348; and Lenin, "'Left-Wing' Communism: An Infantile Disorder," in Tucker (1975), 552–553. See also Trotsky, *The Revolution Betrayed*, 277–278.

the dictatorship of its vanguard and that Lenin, too, believed in the dictatorship of the Communist party.[26]

Stalin further argued that the party's dictatorship was indispensable during the transition to the higher as well as lower stage of communism, the "transition to a society without classes, to a society without a state."[27] The thorny question is over whom it would be exercised. Stalin's answer was clear and unambiguous: over those sectors resistant to the new order. Foremost among them were former landowners, capitalists, and the millions of peasants and petty bourgeois deprived of their property and means of livelihood after being forced to become workers.

Against the Manifesto's claim that the abolition of exploitation means the abolition of classes, Stalin equated the "complete victory of the socialist system" with the abolition of antagonistic classes only. There were still two friendly classes after the landowners and capitalists had been expropriated, two "new classes" of workers and peasants. "There remains...an entirely new working class" of joint owners of the nationalized means of production. "There remains the peasant class...based not on private property, but on collective property...an entirely new peasantry." Thus in the new 1936 Soviet Constitution, Article 126 acknowledges that the Communist party is the "vanguard" and "leading nucleus" no longer of the proletariat, which has ceased to exist, but of the entire "working people."[28]

Stalin is also remembered for his theory of the "general crisis of capitalism"—an addendum to Marx's theory of the economic breakdown of capitalism in the opening section of the Manifesto. Its elements go back to Stalin's *Foundations of Leninism* in 1924. Imperialism, Stalin noted, "carries the contradictions of capitalism to their last bounds, to the extreme limits, beyond which revolution begins." It compounds the antagonisms. To the antagonism between labor and capital it adds that between rival imperialist powers and "between the handful of ruling, 'civilized' nations and the hundreds of millions of colonial and dependent peoples."[29]

A general crisis unfolded when capitalism no longer had, nor could have, "either in the major countries or in the colonial and dependent countries, the strength and stability it had before the war and the October Revolution." By the "*general crisis* of capitalism" Stalin understood "the chronic undercapacity operation of industry; chronic mass unemployment; the

---

[26] Stalin, *Problems of Leninism*, 26–27, 29, 34–40, 55–56.
[27] Ibid., 55–56.
[28] Joseph V. Stalin, "On the Draft Constitution of the USSR," *Leninism: Selected Writings*, 382–384; and Strong, "The New Constitution of 1936," in Webb, 117.
[29] Stalin, *Foundations of Leninism*, 11–12.

interweaving of the industrial crisis with an agricultural crisis; [and] the absence of a tendency toward a more or less serious renewal of fixed capital." Consequently, monopoly capitalism is no longer able to find a way out of the present situation...[it] is sure to unleash revolution and to jeopardize the very existence of capitalism in a number of countries, as was the case in the course of the first imperialist war."[30]

To this initial depiction of a general crisis he subsequently added the formation of a "united and powerful socialist camp confronting the camp of capitalism." The economic consequence of this division of the world into two hostile camps was that "the single all-embracing world market disintegrated, so that now we have two parallel world markets, also confronting one another." The disintegration of the capitalist world market, Stalin concluded, "must be regarded as the most important economic sequel of the Second World War." As a result, the sphere of exploitation of the world's human population has contracted, capitalist industry is operating more and more below capacity because of the failure to find outlets for its products, and the antagonisms among the principal imperialist powers are becoming more acute. Wars continue to be inevitable, because of the "struggle of the capitalist countries for markets and their desire to crush their competitors."[31]

As early as September 1946, Stalin publicly announced that "it was possible to build not merely Socialism but even Communism in a 'single country.'" But not until October 1952 did he come forward with a formal discussion of his contemplated "transition from socialism to communism." His *Economic Problems of Socialism in the USSR* is a landmark of the measures that Stalin promised to introduce gradually, but also "unswervingly and unhesitatingly."[32]

The last of his major works, it reveals a surprising interest in equalization absent from his earlier writings, a concern "to even up conditions of life in town and country," to abolish the surviving nonantagonistic classes of workers and peasants, and also "the essential distinction between mental and physical labor."[33] His concrete measures for improving the condition of labor were expected to contribute to this leveling.

---

[30] Stalin, "Report on the Work of the Central Committee to the Seventeenth Congress," in *Leninism*, 300, 303, 305–306.

[31] Stalin, *Economic Problems of Socialism in the USSR*, 25–26, 30.

[32] Isaac Deutscher, *Stalin: A Political Biography*, 2nd ed. (New York: Oxford University Press, 1967; orig. pub. 1949), 581; and Stalin, *Economic Problems of Socialism in the USSR*, 51, 52–53, 69–70.

[33] Stalin, *Economic Problems of Socialism in the USSR*, 23–24.

Rather than a thaw in party discipline, Stalin was again tightening the screws in preparation for another radical transition in the economy on the foundation already laid by socialism. This time it would be gradual, but nonetheless a forced march "from one form of economy, the economy of socialism, to another, higher form of economy, the economy of communism."[34] Thus Stalin amended both the Manifesto and the "Critique of the Gotha Programme"'s amendment to the Manifesto with respect to the distinction between socialism and communism—no longer regarded as a single economic system but as two distinct modes of production.

Whatever may be said to Stalin's discredit—that he betrayed the Manifesto's communism as a condition of consolidating socialism in the Soviet Union—the evidence suggests that, unlike his successors, he remained faithful to class struggle, to Lenin and the Manifesto, in not reversing the movement toward communism. Indeed, the consensus of his inner circle was that on the eve of his death he was preparing a new purge of the party's slackers along with a new revolutionary upsurge.

According to Isaac Deutscher, it was on the pretext of fighting Trotskyism and Bukharinism that he had decimated and "prevented the managerial groups from consolidation as a social stratum." Like chickens being prepared for slaughter, "Stalin whetted their acquisitive interests and wrung their necks!" It was a Machiavellian stratagem that Trotsky found utterly alien and never understood.[35]

Although Russia dominated all of Eastern Europe and could count on China as a major ally, the hostilities in Korea dragged on and the Cold War threatened to escalate into a nuclear catastrophe—a bizarre inducement to Stalin's grandiose projects as well as paranoid fears of coming destruction. Meanwhile, top members of the party were calling for a relaxation of state controls amid a struggle for succession "over fundamental issues of policy as well as over claims to power…differences between Stalin's successors that were to come to the surface in 1953." Stalin suspected they were plotting his death, which led them to believe that he was preparing their demise.[36] Such was the turbulent background to Stalin's final amendment to the Manifesto.

---

[34] Ibid., 53.

[35] Isaac Deutscher, *The Prophet Outcast. Trotsky: 1929–1940* (New York: Vintage, 1965), 306–307.

[36] Stuart Kahan, *The Wolf of the Kremlin*, 255–264; Martin Malia, *The Soviet Tragedy: A History of Socialism in Russia, 1917–1991* (New York/Toronto: Free Press, 1994), 310–312; and Dmitri Volkogonov, *Stalin: Triumph and Tragedy*, ed. and trans. Harold Shukman (Rocklin, CA: Prima Publishing, 1991), 569, 571.

10. A Humanist Manifesto: Khrushchev and Gorbachev

More than a hundred years ago Karl Marx and Frederick Engels...wrote in the Communist Manifesto: *"A specter is haunting Europe, the specter of communism"*...the system under which the abilities and talents of free man blossom forth and reveal themselves in full.

Nikita Khrushchev, "Report on the Programme of the Communist Party of the Soviet Union" (1961)

Human rights...are an inalienable characteristic of socialism....Our philosophy in this key aspect of the organization of society follows from the famous formula in the *Manifesto of the Communist Party*: "The free development of each is the condition for the free development of all."

Mikhail Gorbachev, *On Progress in Implementing the Decisions of the 27th CPSU Congress and the Tasks of Promoting Perestroika* (1988)

Unlike his three great predecessors, Khrushchev is seldom remembered as a theoretician. Roy Medvedev, the dissident historian who welcomed Khrushchev's liberal reforms, says that Khrushchev "contributed nothing to the theoretical discourse initiated by Lenin or to its successor, that political-theoretical hybrid...known as Stalinism." With Khrushchev begins the era of mediocrities in the Kremlin. Although highly original in some of his epoch-making decisions, they were founded on the facts at hand rather than on knowledge of human history and reflections on the human predicament. "Nevertheless, he often advanced ideas that were bold and fresh, and these stimulated indirectly the development of Marxist theory."[1]

Unquestionably, Khrushchev changed the course of Soviet history. No one but he was responsible for the post-Stalinist "thaw" and its humanist reinterpretation of the *Communist Manifesto* that wormed its way into the new program adopted at the party's Twenty-Second Congress in October 1961. Inspired by the new program, party intellectuals launched a second edition of the most influential manual of communism since the appearance of Bukharin and Preobrazhensky's *ABC of Communism* some four decades

---

[1]   Roy Medvedev, *Khrushchev*, trans. Brian Pearce (Garden City, NY: Anchor, 1984), ix.

earlier. Under the general editorship of Otto Kuusinen, the *Fundamentals of Marxism-Leninism* was revised so as to incorporate the substance of Khrushchev's innovations to which it acknowledged a theoretical debt. "The present, second edition," says the preface, "has been enriched by the valuable new ideas of the most outstanding work of modern Marxist-Leninist thought—the Programme of the Communist Party of the Soviet Union—and by the basic propositions of the other documents of the Twenty-Second Congress of the CPSU."[2]

People's Communism

As a result of the party's updating of Lenin's 1919 program, "Khrushchev's stature abroad was considerably enhanced." His new communist program challenged not only Mao Zedong's brand of communism, but also Mao's claim to leadership of the international communist movement. Having broken with Stalin's practical legacy of purges and persecutions, he reaffirmed Stalin's theoretical legacy. Instead of calling a halt to Stalin's march to a higher stage of communism, he shortened the time-table for arriving there. But how could he possibly accomplish this tour de force without exhorting the Soviet people to endure still further sacrifices?[3]

The irony is that after promising the Soviet people what they wanted in the near rather than remote future, he soon realized that his people's communism was a pipe-dream. Perhaps that explains why he forgot about it, since he barely refers to it in his memoirs. From the beginning, his new program seems to have had mainly propaganda value, much as Stalin's new 1936 liberal constitution. Taken seriously, it would have been discussed at length by the Twenty-Second Congress that endorsed it. Instead, Khrushchev revived the issue of Stalin's crimes and "pushed into the background all discussion of the Communist Party's programme." So when Soviet citizens opened their newspapers they read not optimistic articles

---

[2] O. V. Kuusinen et al., *Fundamentals of Marxism-Leninism*, 2nd rev. ed. (Moscow: Foreign Languages Publishing House, 1963), 13. For a similar assessment of the "'New Communist Manifesto' . . . [as] unquestionably the most important offical document published in Russia since Stalin's death," see Arthur P. Mendel, ed., *Essential Works of Marxism* (New York/London: Bantam, 1965), 313.

[3] Jan F. Triska, ed., *Soviet Communism: Program and Rules* (San Francisco: Chandler, 1962), 13, 14.

about the projected transition from socialism to communism by 1980, but "assessments of the dark days of a quarter of a century before."[4]

The program begins with a quotation from the original manifesto of 1848: "*A specter is haunting Europe, the specter of communism.*" It had long since ceased to be a ghost, we are told. "First dozens and hundreds of people, and then thousands and millions, inspired by the ideals of communism, stormed the old world." Then came the Bolshevik Revolution and the task of building socialism, a promise that "*triumphed in the Soviet Union completely and finally.*" So the next task was to build a society according to the communist principle "From each according to his ability, to each according to his needs."[5]

The new program called itself communist, but was above all a humanist program. The party's new motto was formulated in humanist terms: "Everything in the name of man, for the benefit of man." Thus the chief purpose of communist society is "to provide all its members with material and cultural benefits according to their growing needs, their individual requirements and tastes." Communism is a "system under which the abilities and talents of free man, his best moral qualities, blossom forth and reveal themselves in full"—a system where "everyone will live comfortably," where there will be "greater opportunities of *educating a new man, who will harmoniously combine spiritual wealth, moral purity and a perfect physique*"![6] This was not just a paraphrase of Stalin's slogan "Everything for the masses." It was a political testament for future generations, a humanism redefining communism in unreal terms.

To achieve this humanist goal, certain technocratic conditions were considered necessary. Under communism "*the all-round development of people will be accompanied by the growth of the productive forces through continuous progress in science and technology; all sources of public wealth will gush forth abundantly.*" It was only logical that communist society would exemplify "the unlimited possibilities of scientific progress...[and] the utilization of atomic energy for peaceful purposes." Communism ensures an increase in "labor productivity through rapid scientific and technological progress; it equips man with the best and most powerful machines, greatly increases his power over nature and enables him to control its elemental forces to an ever greater extent." To this the program adds that, through the extension of planned production, "the most effective and rational use is made of the material wealth and labor reserves to meet the growing

---

[4] Medvedev, *Khrushchev*, 208.
[5] Triska, *Soviet Communism*, 23–25.
[6] Ibid., 25, 69–70, 113.

requirements of the members of society." Thanks to technology, "mental and physical labor will merge organically...workers by hand will have risen in cultural and technological standards to the level of workers by brain."[7]

There was even a niche for demoliberalism within the new program. "Communism accomplishes the historic mission of delivering all men from social inequality...and proclaims Peace, Labor, Freedom, Equality, and Happiness for all peoples of the earth." In the original draft the word "Brotherhood" occurs after the word "Equality," so that as initially formulated the new program reaffirmed the bourgeois credo of "Liberty, Equality, Fraternity." Since the dictatorship of the proletariat has become a state of the entire people, an organ expressing the interests and will of the people as a whole, it "has fulfilled its historic mission and has ceased to be indispensable in the USSR." Not just the vanguard but the working class as a whole "plays a leading role...in the period of the full-scale construction of communism" and will continue in this capacity until communism is built and classes disappear. Meanwhile, democracy will expand in scope through the active participation of all citizens in the administration of the state.[8]

With Khrushchev's amendments to the Manifesto in the saddle, there was a deliberate promotion of consumer goods industries with animal consumption in first place. "By 1964 grain for livestock feed outstripped grain for bread, and by the time the Soviet Union collapsed, livestock were eating three times as much grain as humans!" The breadbasket of the Ukraine went to feeding cattle. "All this required greater and greater imports of grain until precious foreign exchange made the Soviet Union the world's second-largest grain importer."[9] Meanwhile, the dietary pattern based on bread gave way to insatiable meat-eating with its toll of heart disease, stroke, and cancer.

As one of seven factors reputedly responsible for the economic slowdown in the USSR during the 1970s and 1980s, the agricultural crisis was among the most decisive. Hard currency needed to import machinery for modernizing Soviet industry had to be earmarked for personal consumption, especially for cattle feed. "Our people," comments Soviet economist Stanislav Menshikov, "love to eat more meat and less bread...but the cattle have to be fed."[10]

---

[7] Ibid., 33, 68–69.

[8] Ibid., 25, 32, 97–98, 101.

[9] Alexander Cockburn, "Beat the Devil: Dead Meat," *The Nation* (22 April 1996), 10.

[10] John Kenneth Galbraith and Stanislav Menshikov, *Capitalism, Communism, and Coexistence: From the Bitter Path to a Better Prospect* (Boston: Houghton Mifflin, 1988), 24–32.

Khrushchev's new communist program had pinpointed grain production as the chief link in the plan for meat production to triple by 1980. The increase in meat consumption was designed to keep pace with the planned growth in real wages over the same period. But Khrushchev was naïve. "He thought that once the Soviet Union...provided this or that amount of meat, we would reach an abundance. It turned out that the better off the people got in terms of income, the more the demand developed." The price one had to pay for the humanist faith that needs should be multiplied was a geared-up technocratic treadmill that did not come to rest when all the basic needs were satisfied. When Khrushchev arrived in power most of them had been met. So he set his sights even higher—on the satisfaction of nonbasic needs.[11]

That the Soviet Union became wrecked on the shores of humanism should be evident not only from the artificially induced agricultural crisis, but also from the new wage policy begun under Khrushchev. Unlike his predecessors, Khrushchev raised real wages, especially the wages of lower-paid labor. What could be wrong with that, especially for a Communist? But "the share of the gross national product that could be used for capital investment became smaller, so, step by step...capital investment went down, and there was an even larger deficit of capital goods." By the 1980s the equipment installed in the 1950s and 1960s was nearing the end of its life cycle. The funds needed to cover additional investment were being eaten up by the consumer goods industries and higher wages. "So, although there was construction of new plants going on, there was a serious problem trying to maintain existing production capacity, let alone creating new capacity."[12]

Like the Manifesto's synthesis of modernist "isms," the new communist program pulled in opposite directions. The humanist multiplication of needs dependent on ever greater production signified that the nearer one got to one's goal the more it receded. Instead of enforced renunciation to put an end to human servitude, Khrushchev chose self-cultivation at the price of remaining on the technocratic treadmill.

As Marx amended the Manifesto in 1875, the revolutionary dictatorship of the proletariat would cover the entire transition period between capitalist and communist society. But we have seen that Stalin amended Marx's amendment by replacing the dictatorship of the proletariat with a dictatorship of the working people. The 1961 program went a step further in replacing even this nominally softened dictatorship with the "leading role" of the working class—an amendment to an amendment of an amendment.

---

[11] Triska, *Soviet Communism: Program and Rules*, 80, 91; and Galbraith and Menshikov, *Capitalism, Communism, and Coexistence*, 16, 33, 36–45.
[12] Galbraith and Menshikov, *Capitalism, Communism, and Coexistence*, 29–30.

For the most part, Khrushchev followed Stalin's guidelines in *Economic Problems of Socialism in the USSR* (1952). But there were three crucial departures from Stalinist orthodoxy. First, contrary to Stalin's thesis that the fundamental contradiction after World War II consisted of interimperialist rivalries, the new program called for a policy of peaceful existence and declared that the "basic contradiction...[is] that between socialism and imperialism." Supposedly, the rapid growth of world socialism was sapping and destroying imperialism, leading to its weakening and collapse. Second, contrary to Stalin's thesis of the inevitability of national and revolutionary wars under imperialism, the new program declared that the main objectives of Communist parties can be realized without world war and in many instances without civil war. The working class can, in other words, "win a solid majority in parliament...and provide the necessary conditions for a peaceful socialist revolution." Third, contrary to Stalin's focus on class and intraclass antagonisms, the new program shifted the focus to what Mikhail Gorbachev would later call universal human values. Thus the struggle for peace was hailed as the *"principal issue of today...to ward off a thermonuclear war, to prevent it from breaking out."*[13]

But to this cautious side of the document was appended the most careless boasting, a feature of Khrushchev's personality that would soon prove his undoing. In the course of the next twenty years, the program predicted that "public consumption funds will total almost half of the aggregate real income." If so, this would make possible the provision at public expense of all the following: free boarding schools for all children; free education at all educational institutions; free and universal medical care; free housing; free transportation; the gradual introduction of free noonday meals for all working people; and other free public services.[14] The perplexing question is what objective conditions in the world balance of power at the time prompted Khrushchev to make an ass of himself.

The Sino-Soviet Imbroglio

The answer hinges on the Sino-Soviet rivalry that came into the open in 1963 and culminated in outright hostilities and border clashes in 1969.[15] With Stalin's death in 1953, Khrushchev's chief rival for leadership in the

---

[13] Triska, *Soviet Communism*, 44, 46, 50–51, 64–66.
[14] Ibid., 96.
[15] Edward Crankshaw, *Khrushchev: A Career* (New York: Viking, 1966), 275–277, 280.

communist world was his Chinese counterpart, Mao Zedong, born only a year earlier in 1893, but the ruler of a population three times that of the Soviet Union. Khrushchev's new communist program was an effort to steal Mao Zedong's fire.

Not to be outdone by Khrushchev's denunciation of Stalin's crimes at the Twentieth Congress in February 1956, Mao launched his own liberalization campaign, "Let a Hundred Flowers Bloom." Although conceived in 1956, it was not implemented until February a year later. Mao anticipated that popular criticism of past and present mistakes by Chinese Communists would help the country along the road to socialism. Instead, it encouraged the same revisionist, anti-Leninist as well as anti-Stalinist tendencies in China that had erupted in Poland and Hungary in 1956 as a consequence of the Soviet thaw. Mao's response to the failure of liberalization was to make a sharp turn to the left known as the "Great Leap Forward" (1958–1960), followed by a change in foreign policy aimed at Soviet as well as Yugoslav backsliding.

Such was the immediate political background to Khrushchev's efforts to emulate Mao by adopting a nominally leftist, new communist program at his party's Twenty-Second Congress in 1961.

Mao's "Great Leap Forward" had put pressure on the Soviet Union because of its ostensible shortcut to communism. Mao called for the creation of supercommunes in the countryside to replace the established agricultural collectives built on the Soviet model. Within a few months of the inception of this People's Commune Program, "some 740,000 recently organized cooperatives had already been consolidated into 26,000 gigantic communes." With such slogans as "Twenty years concentrated into a day!" and "Three years of hard labor—ten thousand years of happy life!" Mao hoped to accomplish the transition to Marx's higher stage of communism during his lifetime.[16]

The drawback from the Soviet point of view was that these supercommunes bordered on "barracks communism." Mao's forced march represented a revival not only of crude workers' communism, but also of pre-Marxist dreams of building communism on a rural agricultural basis before laying the foundations of full industrialization. One can imagine Khrushchev's indignation when he read that the Chinese "who are in their seventies and eighties, even those in their nineties, will live to see the attainment of Communism." After launching his program of forcible collectivization in 1929, it had taken Stalin almost a quarter of a century to

---

[16] Mendel, *Essential Works of Marxism*, 490.

be able to announce the beginning of the transition from socialism to communism. The Chinese were bragging that, owing to the communes and "thought reform," they could bypass capitalism and pass directly to the simultaneous construction of both socialism and communism. This was Mao's most radical amendment to the Manifesto: it was not material abundance created by modern science and technology that was the chief prerequisite of communism, but rather communist ideology.[17]

The system of distribution in the communes combined payment according to work with distribution according to need, thereby bridging the gap between Marx's lower and higher stages of communism. Among the communes' free services were public dining rooms, nurseries, "free dishes," "free tailoring," "free barbering," "free theater tickets," and "free grain." In his "Principles of Communism," Engels envisioned that the commune would become the basic unit of a full communist society. Mao's "people's commune" was the closest approximation yet to Engels' original model.

As a revival of Lenin's communist socialism and equalitarian line, it also exhibited traces of Bakunin's communist legacy. Alone among the great communist leaders of the twentieth century, Mao began his political career under the influence of anarchist circles in Beijing with which he established close ties. He read Bakunin's essays before reading those of Marx. His peasant communism was a Bakuninist nostrum that had absolutely no parallel in either Marx or Lenin's writings.

In his memoirs, Khrushchev recalled his rivalry with Mao for leadership of the world revolution. In a chapter on "Mao Tse-tung and the Schism," he focused on their personal differences. He saw Mao as an Asiatic despot who "played politics with Asiatic cunning, following his own rules of cajoling, treachery, savage vengeance, and deceit...[until] we saw through his tricks." Mao, he reflected, had always been "a master at concealing his true thoughts and intentions." Khrushchev questioned not only the extent of Mao's Marxism, but also his refusal to recognize "any other Communist Party...[as] superior to his own." As early as 1954, Khrushchev had concluded that conflict with China is inevitable. When China launched its "egalitarian reforms," its slogans threatened to "find fertile soil in our own country." As Khrushchev acknowledged, "We had to respond in substance to Mao's assumptions and propositions," although it was not until the Party's Congress in 1961 that "we rejected the main tenets of Mao's

---

[17] Ibid., 491–492.

position."[18] In effect, Khrushchev's nominal communism was designed to replace Mao's real communist program.

That Khrushchev's "communism" was fainthearted became evident during the Cuban missile crisis of October 1961. The Chinese immediately accused him of betraying the Cuban Revolution and of failing to stand up to the United States. Khrushchev had abandoned Stalin's collision course with the West as early as the Twentieth Congress in 1956, and in 1959 he had become the first general secretary of the Communist Party of the Soviet Union to visit the United States—at the cost of a decisive break with China. But it was not until the Cuban crisis that he finally realized where he stood. He had seriously endangered his policy of rapprochement with America by his blustering defiance that might have led to a nuclear holocaust. He apparently realized his mistake. According to one observer, "Khrushchev finally made up his mind that there was one object to which all else must be sacrificed, and that was peace, first for the preservation of the Soviet Union, then for the preservation of the world."[19] From then on, universal human values would be given precedence over the struggle for communism—a flagrant betrayal, according to Chinese Communists, of the principles of the Manifesto.

In March and July 1964, the Chinese Communist party gave its assessment of Khrushchev's program as basically a fraud, a "phoney communism."[20] What was counterfeit was its claim that communism could be built in twenty years by the methods it proposed, by a "party of the entire people" instead of a class party of the proletariat. It further erred in believing that communism could be built without a dictatorship of the proletariat, by a "privileged bourgeois stratum" in control of the party and the government. And its final outrage was to claim that communism could be constructed on the basis of material instead of moral incentives, by "turning all human relations into money relations and encouraging individualism and selfishness."[21]

Instead of defining communism as the abolition of exploitation, Khrushchev depicted it on Austrian Radio and Television (7 July 1960) as "a bowl accessible to all and brimming with the products of physical and mental labor." Its humanist cornucopia took for its model the imperialist

---

[18] Khrushchev, *Khrushchev Remembers*, 1:461–462, 466, 474–475.

[19] Crankshaw, *Khrushchev*, 273.

[20] See the pamphlets by the Editorial Departments of *People's Daily* and *Red Flag*, *The Proletarian Revolution and Khrushchev's Revisionism*, and *On Khrushchev's Phoney Communism and Its Historical Lessons for the World* (Peking: Foreign Languages Press, 1964).

[21] *On Khrushchev's Phoney Communism*, 48–50, 52, 53.

United States of America. "Khrushchev's 'communism' is in essence a variant of bourgeois socialism...indeed 'goulash communism,' the 'communism of the American way of life.'" Predicated on Marx's belief in the endless multiplication of needs, Khrushchev's communism was a tribute to consumerism to the nth degree. As British Prime Minister Douglas-Home declared, "goulash-communism is better than war communism, and I am glad to have the confirmation of our view that fat and comfortable Communists are better than lean and hungry Communists"![22]

By Chinese standards, it was a weak and hypocritical document. Some Western commentators observed as much. "Taken as a whole," wrote Arthur Mendel, "the program seems strikingly moderate and even 'revisionist' in character." Unlike the Chinese, who were being repeatedly told that they must suffer further sacrifices as the price of communism, "Soviet citizens are promised continual improvements in living standards, the rapid acquisition of typically western, 'bourgeois' services and comforts, and a variety of free benefits" to be had for the asking. Whereas the Chinese Communists stressed the role of imperialism and the inevitability of wars and revolutions, the Soviet program hinged on the promise of a new era of world peace and cooperation among nations.[23] Everything considered, Khrushchev's program was not a whit more realistic than Mao's.

From Khrushchev to Gorbachev

Khrushchev's program became the chief inspiration of so-called Reform Communism, the effort "to humanize and liberalize the Stalinist legacy without abandoning...[centralized] planning, collective property, and the leading role of the Party." Khrushchev hailed it, as did Gorbachev after him, as a return to "true Leninist principles"[24]—to the principles of the young Marx and of the *Economic and Philosophic Manuscripts of 1844*. In retrospect, we now know that Gorbachev had quite early in his career come under Khrushchev's influence.

The Soviet writer and dissident Andrei Amalrik recognized in Khrushchev's humanist legacy the most widespread ideology in Soviet society. As he summarized it, Reform Communism signified belief in "partial reforms, the replacement of an old bureaucratic elite by a new one

---

[22] Ibid., 56, 57–58, 59.
[23] Mendel, *Essential Works of Marxism*, 313.
[24] Malia, *The Soviet Tragedy*, 316.

that is more intellectual and endowed with good sense." It held out the hope that these changes would bring about the "humanization of socialism."[25]

Another classic name for Reform Communism was that popularized by the Czech reformers in 1968, "socialism with a human face." But the most famous characterization of it is unquestionably Gorbachev's "perestroika," or demoliberal restructuring predicated on "universally shared values...the centerpiece of the new theory." Lest it be forgotten, the original impetus of political restructuring was to implement much-needed economic reforms. Democratization and liberalization were designed to overcome economic stagnation and inflexible forms and methods of management, to change people's attitudes to work, to increase labor productivity, to eliminate waste, to accelerate economic growth, and to modernize the economy on the basis of the scientific and technological revolution in electronics, information science, computers, and robots. The party's concerted effort to modernize accounts for the intimate connection between Gorbachev's humanism and the new breed of technocrats in the Soviet Union. As Stephen Cohen notes, "'perestroika' contained the seeds of a mixed economy based on market relations."[26]

As Gorbachev recalled in conversation with Margaret Thatcher in the fall of 1995, it was not President Reagan's decision to go ahead with the Strategic Defense Initiative (Star Wars) that brought the Soviet Union to the point of collapse. Domestic issues were the deciding factor and the lack of freedom in particular. "In the eyes of the people, especially the educated, the totalitarian system had run its course morally and politically. People were waiting for reform...[but] we could only do it from above because initiative from below would have meant an explosion of discontent. That was the decisive factor, not SDI." That educated people took the lead in questioning the Soviet system's drive toward communism should come as no surprise. Neither should the new logo of the resurrected Communist Party of the Russian Federation. A book has been added to the traditional hammer and sickle representing an alliance of three classes instead of two, the book

---

[25] Ibid., 405.

[26] Mikhail Gorbachev, "An Ideology of Renovation for Revolutionary Perestroika," *Information Bulletin* (Prague: Peace and Socialism International Publishers, 1988), Vol. 26, No. 8, 21; idem, *Political Report of the CPSU Central Committee to the 27th Party Congress* (Moscow: Novosti Press Agency, 1986), 7, 11, 36–43; and *On the Tasks of the Party in the Radical Restructuring of Economic Management* (Moscow: Novosti Press Agency, 1987), 6, 13, 28–38, 69–71. See Stephen F. Cohen, "Introduction: Ligachev and the Tragedy of Soviet Conservativism," in Yegor Ligachev, *Inside Gorbachev's Kremlin* (New York: Pantheon, 1993), xxiii, xxx.

taking up most of the space.[27] No longer a dictatorship of the hammer, the new logo suggests a preferred place for the educated class in a regime of market socialism.

A disciple of Khrushchev, Gorbachev called for a reform of the Soviet system focused on the recognition of "human rights." The Manifesto had kept a lid on these universal human values. It was one thing to assimilate them on behalf of the communist movement, another to subordinate the movement to humanist imperatives. Gorbachev turned the Manifesto on its head by inverting the priorities.

Perestroika was an amendment to the Manifesto in the name of "true Communist principles." Gorbachev spelled out the implications of his humanism in *Perestroika: New Thinking for Our Country and the World* (1987). By the new thinking he meant the "priority of interests common to all humanity over class interests." Thus winning the battle of democracy is not simply a means to socialism—"socialism and democracy are indivisible."[28]

Both Khrushchev and Gorbachev emphatically rejected both Lenin's principle of equalization and Stalin's periodic purges of the party.[29] But were there no outstanding differences between Khrushchev's and Gorbachev's assessments of their precursors?

According to Khrushchev, the crimes of Stalin against socialist legality contradicted the Manifesto's brief for human freedom and democracy. But he also believed that the period from Stalin's purges against the Old Guard in December 1934 to the denunciation of Stalin's crimes at the Twentieth Congress in February 1956 represented only twenty years of backsliding from the principles enunciated in 1848. Otherwise, he agreed with Stalin's trashing of Lenin's New Economic Policy (NEP) in 1928.[30]

Gorbachev went considerably further. Rather than a twenty-year aberration, the party had passed through a sixty-year hiatus from the abandonment of NEP in 1928 to its effective restoration at the party's

---

[27] Thomas Powers, "Who Won the Cold War," *The New York Review of Books* (20 June 1996), 24; and David Remnick, "Hammer, Sickle, and Book," *The New York Review of Books* (23 May 1996), 48.

[28] Mikhail Gorbachev, "On Progress in Implementing the Decisions of the 27th CPSU Congress and the Tasks of Promoting Perestroika," in *Soviet Life*, special supplement entitled *Documents and Materials: 19th All-Union Conference on CPSU* (Washington DC: Embassy of the Union of the Soviet Socialist Republics, 1988), 42–43, 92; and *Perestroika*, 32, 34, 145.

[29] Khrushchev, *Documents of the 22nd Congress of the CPSU*, 1:130–131 (New York: Crosscurrents Press, 1961); and Gorbachev, *Perestroika*, 45, 100–101.

[30] Roy Medvedev, *Let History Judge: The Origins and Consequences of Stalinism*, rev. ed., ed. and trans. George Shriver (New York: Columbia University Press, 1989), 16.

Twenty-Seventh Congress in 1988. As he reported on June 30 and July 1, 1988, "we have renounced everything that deformed socialism in the 1930s and that led to its stagnation in the 1970s." As another advocate of a return to "true Leninist principles" recalled, "when it comes to real economic success, our golden age was a brief but very effective seven or eight years during the 1920s, from 1921 to 1928."[31]

It remained for Alexander Yakovlev, Gorbachev's principal adviser, to reveal the full intent of Gorbachev's new course in an article entitled "The Humanistic Choice of Perestroika." "One can say that in the USSR, the alliance between the political leaders and the intellectuals was the first political victory of the April 1985 plenary meeting of the CPSU Central Committee." Precisely this alliance provided the "ideological and moral support for democratic change," for the opening to the intelligentsia as a whole and for the legitimization of its open instead of concealed rule.[32]

"For centuries," Yakovlev observes, "prominent humanists called for man's self-improvement," but until the advent of perestroika the Soviet road to self-cultivation lacked both "common sense" and "realism." "The sacred socialist principle of universal equality and social justice was manipulated to produce crude egalitarianism...[which] degenerated into a mechanism that held back creative efforts, initiative, and competence." Thanks to perestroika, the goal of furthering man's self-improvement was for the first time tackled intelligently through the determination to "reward hard work, creative attitudes, and talent as much as possible."[33]

Yakovlev claims that the degeneration of the Soviet Union dates from the "1929 switch from NEP and from Lenin's flexible strategy of gradually shaping the foundation of socialism to Stalin's policy of accelerated communist construction." Beginning in 1929, "Instead of promoting the value of good work...Stalin encouraged crude egalitarianism [*sic*] in the party and in society, thus fomenting an envious and politically distrustful attitude toward competent workers." Instead of Lenin's and the Comintern's policy of "cautious compromise and bridge-building in relation with the Social Democrats...he [Stalin] suggested 'stepping up the struggle against right-wing elements in the communist parties and called for new class battles' without which 'victory over social democracy was unthinkable.'"

---

[31] Gorbachev, "On Progress in Implementing the Decisions of the 27th CPSU Congress," 90; and Nikolai Shmelev, "Moving Toward the Market," in Robert J. Kingston, ed., *Perestroika Papers* (Dubuque, IA: Kendall/Hunt, 1988), 21.
[32] Yakovlev, "The Humanistic Choice of Perestroika," in *World Marxist Review* (February 1989), 13.
[33] Ibid., 8–10.

Thus "Stalin not only revised the theoretical accomplishments of Marxism but also purged it of its humanistic essence." Because of his "high-handed attitude to talent," his "anti-intellectualism," and his "unnatural opposition contrasting the interests of socialist development to the creative interests of the intelligentsia," he failed to understand that "Socialism *is* Knowledge"—a knowledge society ruled by intellect![34]

These charges are not altogether unfounded. They are predicated on Stalin's April 1929 speech to the party's Central Committee. Entitled "The Right Deviation in the Communist Party of the Soviet Union," it launched the forced march toward socialism.[35] But this picture omits the other side of Stalin's complex political personality and policies—the pacification of the new Soviet intelligentsia and of international Social Democracy during the Popular Front period that followed.

Stalinism was not as Gorbachev and Yakovlev portray it—except for the brief period from 1929 to 1934—nor was Lenin's NEP as they construed it. The period from 1921 to 1928 was a retreat based on a strategy closely tied to the historical conditions at the time; the period from 1929 to 1934 marked an advance culminating in the establishment of socialism in one country. The shapers of perestroika called a retreat an advance, and an advance a retreat. By focusing on the Manifesto's humanism, Gorbachev not only misinterpreted the Soviet past, but also reversed the movement toward communism in the USSR. The Manifesto shares part of the blame.

---

[34] Ibid., 10–13.

[35] Joseph Stalin, "The Right Deviation in the Communist Party of the Soviet Union," *Leninism: Selected Writings*, 89–107.

Conclusion: Assessing the Manifesto

> The Manifesto of Marx and Engels begins with the balance sheet of historical evolution at the threshold of the crucial year 1848. A new balance sheet is called for today.
>
> Lucien Laurat, *Le Manifeste communiste de 1848 et le monde d'adjourd'hui* (1948)

How has the Manifesto stood the test of time? As Engels proudly observed, "the history of the Manifesto reflects, to a great extent, the history of the modern working class movement." Besides hope for the toiling masses—albeit a false hope—he believed that it had opened their eyes to the reality underlying the surface of modern society. *Would* that it were so!

Looking backward, one is struck by two sides to the Manifesto's ledger. On one side, it appealed to workers and intellectuals alike, as the German Social Democratic and the Bolshevik parties gained adherents. On the other side, its popularity was ephemeral, as seen by the loss of interest in the Manifesto after these parties enjoyed their stint in power.

After 150 years of the Manifesto, its eclipse stares us in the face. Neither the humanist highroad nor the egalitarian low road to communism turned out to be passable. There is, however, a third communist alternative—an expanding public sector of free goods and services—a pacifier of the discontented and a sanctuary for the insecure.

For almost a century and a half, the Manifesto has been the centerpiece of communist ideology, the leading manual of international communism. It still ranks as one of the modern world's most consequential political documents. It helped to establish the first mass-based socialist parties in the 1860s and 1870s, and it paved the way to the 1917 Bolshevik Revolution. As one of America's leading historians notes, "the Russian Revolution...[was] arguably the most important event of the century," while its repercussions "would be felt in every corner of the globe."[1] If the Russian Revolution was that important, then no less consequential was the *Communist Manifesto* that fueled it.

The Manifesto's invaluable service to the communist movement was to transform it from a sect into the secular equivalent of a church, a worldwide

---

[1]   Richard Pipes, *The Russian Revolution* (New York: Vintage, 1991), xxi.

mass movement whose only rivals in greatness, numbers of adherents, and geographical expansion were Islam and Christianity. Just as St. Paul's Christology helped to sanitize the spiritualized communism of Jesus and the Apostles, so Marx's humanism helped to defang the secular communism of Babeuf, Buonarroti, Blanqui, and their disciples. And as Christianity took the heart out of the messianic doctrine of the carpenter from Nazareth, so Marxism toned down the revolutionary communism of Blanqui's German followers with the socialist humanism of the Manifesto.

If communist extremists were ever to join forces with trade unionists in struggles for the workers' daily bread, it was necessary for communists to moderate their demands. Wrote Kautsky in the first major updating of the Manifesto, *The Class Struggle* (1892), an exposition of the Erfurt Program of German Social Democracy: "In their [Marx and Engels'] *Communist Manifesto*...they laid the scientific foundation of modern socialism. They transformed the beautiful dreams of well-meaning enthusiasts into the goal of a great and earnest struggle."[2]

As a public relations coup, the Manifesto was a success; like the religious faiths it resembled, it came to mean all things to all men. It thus offers a prime illustration of Machiavelli's dictum that "the great majority of mankind are satisfied with appearances."[3] Bakunin's and Lenin's readings of the Manifesto made a brief for relentless class struggle, but its humanist and demoliberal readings justified Khrushchev's reforms and Gorbachev's perestroika, leading to the eventual breakup of the Soviet Union.

The Manifesto was meant to be open-ended, to be continually revised in response to economic changes and the appearance of new political forces. Yet in 1872 Marx and Engels decided it was a "historical document which we have no longer any right to alter." So their amendments to it were not incorporated into the text. It was superseded in 1891 by the Erfurt Program of German Social Democracy and again in 1919 by the program of the Communist Party of the Soviet Union. But German Social Democrats and Russian Communists could not agree on whether the Russian Revolution was a bastard or a "legitimate child of *The Communist Manifesto*." If illegitimate, then the Manifesto did not represent a rupture with the liberal democratic tradition in the West; otherwise it did.[4]

---

[2]   Karl Kautsky, *The Class Struggle (Erfurt Program)*, trans. W. E. Bahn (New York: Norton, 1971; orig. pub. 1892), 199.
[3]   Machiavelli, *The Prince* and *The Discourses*, 182; from *The Discourses*, 1:25.
[4]   Marx and Engels, "Preface to the German Edition of 1872," in Bender, 44; and Harrington, "The Democratic Essence of Socialism," in Bender, 109.

Wherever Socialist and Communist parties have contended for power, the Manifesto has outshone all rivals on the Left. But once entrenched, those parties favored their own manuals of revolution at the Manifesto's expense. Paradoxically, the Manifesto's eclipse is correlated rather with the strength than with the weakness of the parties it represented.

Before the turn of the century there had been more German editions than English and French ones combined. Between the time of the first Russian translation in 1869 and half a century later in 1919, however, there were more than twice as many editions in the former Czarist Empire and its Soviet successor than in Germany during the same period. The Manifesto topped its original record of six German editions in 1848 on at least three occasions. In 1899 and again in 1905 and 1917, the number of new Russian editions reached two digits.[5] For the most backward and despotic regime in all of Europe was on the eve of a combined liberal-democratic revolution that would soon match the Great French Revolution of 1789.

It is hardly surprising that both 1905 and 1917 saw the publication of a record number of editions. The first Russian revolution occurred in 1905. Although it failed, it was followed by a second, this time successful, revolution in February 1917 and by the Bolshevik seizure of power eight months later.

But why was the Manifesto such a big hit in 1899? That was the year of the first student general strike. Despite its innocent origins, that strike came under the leadership of an "organizing committee"—militants of the new Russian Social-Democratic Labor party founded in 1898. The student strike has been aptly described as the "prelude to the Russian Revolution."[6] Thanks to the work of the "organizing committee," Russia's restive students and burgeoning intellectuals began rallying behind the *Communist Manifesto*.

The high point in the Manifesto's reception was reached in 1905–1906, and that point was nearly attained again in 1917–1918. Then the Manifesto began facing stiff competition from N. Bukharin and E. Preobrazhensky's *The ABC of Communism*—a commentary on the Communist party's new 1919 program. A few years later, in his bid for power after Lenin's premature death in 1924, Stalin published his best-selling *Foundations of Leninism*, which soon overtook the Manifesto in total sales.

Stalin's book reigned supreme until 1938, when it was displaced by the *History of the Communist Party of the Soviet Union (Short Course)*, drafted

---

[5] Bert Andréas, *Le Manifeste Communiste de Marx et Engels* (Milan: Feltrinelli, 1963), Appendix: Tableaux Synchronoptique (1848–1919), 380–382.
[6] Pipes, *The Russian Revolution*, 6–7.

by a commission of the Party's Central Committee under Stalin's active supervision. As many as twelve million copies of the Russian edition and another two million in the other languages of the Soviet Union were initially published in October. A decade later, some two hundred editions had appeared in more than sixty languages, amounting to some thirty-four million copies. The distribution of the *Short Course* so dwarfed the circulation of the *Communist Manifesto* that at the Party's Eighteenth Congress in March 1939, Stalin's presumptive heir, Andre Zhdanov, announced that "since the inception of Marxism, no Marxist book has ever had such wide circulation."[7]

The Manifesto would never recover from this literary coup. Two decades later it was again overshadowed, this time by the *Short Course*'s successor, *Fundamentals of Marxism-Leninism*. Under the general editorship of Otto V. Kuusinen, the new manual responded to the Bolshevik party's change of line beginning with the Twentieth Party Congress in 1956. When the first edition was followed in 1963 by a second revised edition, the Manifesto continued to lose ground.

The successive revisions and adaptations of the Manifesto point to failures as well as successes on the part of those who attempted to translate its precepts into practice. When the Communist League in 1852 and the International Working Men's Association in 1872 failed to live up to the Manifesto's program and strategy, Marx scuttled both organizations. When the Socialist International during World War I refused to implement the 1912 Basel Manifesto's reaffirmation of the Manifesto's opposition to national wars and imperialism, it too fell apart. Lenin founded the Communist International in 1919 with the aim of implementing the Manifesto's program, but Stalin dissolved it during World War II under pressure from the Soviet Union's Western allies—when it, too, was no longer an asset to socialism but a liability.

Contrary to expectations, socialism made the Manifesto's communism increasingly irrelevant. The Manifesto was a huge success as a socialist manifesto. But the hopes raised by Stalin's second Bolshevik Revolution were dashed when Khrushchev's communism failed to deliver the goods, when Gorbachev's humanism proved to be a mirage, and when Soviet citizens regretfully concluded that socialism had not lived up to its promises. So the Manifesto had outlived its usefulness, save for the boondocks and backwaters of world civilization.

---

[7] Paulo Spriano, *Stalin and the European Communists*, trans. Jon Rothschild (London: Verso, 1985), 79, 80.

During the Bolshevik struggle for power, the Manifesto provided the rationale for a grand alliance of workers, peasants, and petty bourgeois toward the ultimate conquest of the state. But once in power, the alliance dissolved. The same Manifesto that had furthered the unified and concerted action of the parties of discontent became a cause of dissension. Universal self-development was supposed to flourish with the extension of civil liberties to all, followed by the institution of universal suffrage and the replacement of private property in the means of production by collective ownership. But socialism under Bolshevik leadership began by trashing the humanist and demoliberal legacies and then reviving them. In effect, a Leninist revolution built the Soviet Union, and a Marxist counterrevolution destroyed it. The Manifesto cut both ways.

Lenin placed a lid on humanism and its demoliberal offspring by giving precedence to uncivil "Reds" over civil "Pinks," by loosening the reins on equalizing tendencies, and by attempting to build socialism and communism simultaneously instead of sequentially. Stalin succeeded in abolishing capitalism and fulfilling the promise of socialism in the Soviet Union, but at the same time offered nominal support to humanism, liberalism, and democracy. Khrushchev's new program gave a major impetus to humanism, liberalism, and democracy, but prepared the ground for Gorbachev's betrayal that nullified communism altogether.

Such was the logic of unintended consequences that took its toll *beginning* with Khrushchev's and *ending* with Gorbachev's phoney communism. In both instances the contradiction between personal and collective fulfillment was resolved by the path of least resistance. By then the Manifesto had lost most of its appeal. Although Khrushchev made one last effort to salvage it, Gorbachev looked to the Western legal tradition for inspiration.

We have seen that the Manifesto is not just a communist manifesto; it can be read as a humanist, demoliberal, technocratic, and socialist manifesto, and as a set of guidelines to a future anarchism. By preserving part of this ideological heritage, the Manifesto effectively compromised its goal of communist revolution.

In view of the foregoing, is it feasible to rewrite the Manifesto, to revive its ailing body? Or should one give it a decent burial? Bernstein claimed that neither the Marxist building nor its scaffolding was any longer salvageable. More recently, Lucien Laurat notes that it is time "to oppose [to Paleomarxism] a new synthesis embodying the scientific socialism of our times...[since a] new balance sheet is called for today." But if Laurat is correct in claiming that the managerial elites share power with the capitalists, then his updating of the Manifesto's socialist program would tend to play into the hands of Bakunin's nonmanagerial elites.[8]

The Achilles heel of the Manifesto was its assimilation of the so-called progressive ideologies that competed with communism—the humanist credo of the supreme worth of the individual, the demoliberal legacy of civil rights and majority rule, the technocratic utopia of salvation through scientific and material progress, and the socialist class struggle against the bourgeoisie. This constellation of social preferences virtually defines modernism in political philosophy.

The Manifesto's communism is obsolete because of its modernist premises. Unrestrained economic growth on behalf of universal self-cultivation leads up a blind alley. More work implies less leisure for those on the industrial treadmill. Technocracy represents a threat to communism, because the producers of the economic surplus can be made to produce more when the screws are tightened, not loosened. To push at once for optimum economic growth and for the abolition of exploitation is to push in opposing directions. Thus far, the former push has been the more forceful; for the latter requires immense outlays for welfare and education that cut into the reserves set aside for research and development. The Manifesto, however, suggests we can have the best of both possible worlds!

The multiplication of needs in response to increasing wealth means that the more one gets, the more one wants. That is not to say that the Manifesto favors consumption for its own sake. Marx's humanism makes a brief for high-quality over low-quality consumption, the enjoyment of music, art, and literature rather than the enjoyment of material possessions. But he set no limit to the educational treadmill other than the vacuous condition that the free development of each must be compatible with the free development of all. Why vacuous? Because "free development" opens the door to privileged shares in the economic surplus needed to defray the higher costs of a liberal arts education at its higher levels.

The Manifesto's cult of self-development claims to be universally applicable. To become fully literate in the arts and sciences, however, their devotees must become industrially exempt and give priority to what is higher instead of lower on the scale of being. Lenin loved the theater, according to his wife Krupskaya, but he was driven to sacrifice the liberal arts for the sake of ordinary literacy. His urge for personal fulfillment did not stop him from trying to close down the pride and joy of Russia's

---

[8]   Laurat, "If One Were to Rewrite the *Communist Manifesto* Today," in Bender, 146, 147.

intellectual and artistic circles—the Bolshoi Theater. As he instructed Vyasechslav Molotov: "I propose the Politburo issue the following orders...keep just a few dozen artistes for Moscow and Peter[sburg] to perform (as singers and dancers on a self-financing basis), that is, avoid any large expenditure on scenery....Give not less than half the billions thus saved for the liquidation of illiteracy and [for] reading rooms." As one hostile critic observed, "a lowering of the nation's intellect would be the price for raising the general population's awareness."[9]

Although the Manifesto's goal of free development is utopian, it can be achieved on a limited scale. For those unwilling to wait for communism prior to their own emancipation, however, humanism becomes a sanction for egoism under conditions of exploitation. It is this humanist-sanctioned selfishness that communists find intolerable. The Manifesto's slogan, "The proletarians have nothing to lose but their chains," is a communist slogan, but it hardly fits the Manifesto's goal of the free development of all.[10]

The vicious side of humanism has been traditionally concealed by a veil of hypocrisy. Britain's governing classes, according to Bernard Shaw, consist of "people who, though perfectly prepared to be generous, humane, cultured, philanthropic, public spirited and personally charming, are nonetheless unalterably resolved to have money enough for a handsome and delicate life." For that purpose they will "batten in the doors of their fellow-men, sweat them in fetid dens, shoot, stab, hang, imprison, sink, burn and destroy them in the name of law and order...for a sufficient income is indispensable to the practice of virtue."[11]

Marx's claim to fame was that he made communism credible. Instead of Babeuf's "principle of equalization" to be achieved by leveling downward, he proposed to raise ordinary workers to the status of a literate communist like himself. He believed that self-cultivation, a patrician ideal, was what every proletarian secretly wanted.

This is what theologians mean by original sin. In the Biblical account of the fall, Eve is tempted to eat of the forbidden fruit because of the serpent's prodding. Lucifer, the Light-Bearer, assures her that her eyes will be opened, that she will become wise like the gods (Gen. 3:4–6). Eve then shares the fruit with Adam. Did Lucifer lie? On the contrary, God confirms the

---

[9] Volkogonov, *Lenin*, 356, 357.

[10] See my *Socialist Humanism: The Outcome of Classical European Morality* (St. Louis: Warren H. Green, 1974), 281–315, 330–337.

[11] George Bernard Shaw, "Preface" to *The Irrational Knot*, in *The Works of Bernard Shaw* (London: Constable, 1930–38). Cited by Paul A. Hunwert, *Bernard Shaw's Marxian Romance* (Lincoln: University of Nebraska Press, 1973), 10.

serpent's words: "Behold, the man has become as one of us" (Gen. 3:22). But as punishment for aspiring to divine heights, they must thereafter suffer the consequences by being driven from paradise.

Man's fate, according to Milton, is to aspire to a higher form of life, to human self-fulfillment, not just to knowledge of good and evil. But "This higher degree of life...cannot be but to be Gods, or Angels, [i.e.] Demigods."[12] For Milton, paradise is lost because Adam and Eve want to be more than merely human, to be superman and superwoman—a godlike condition with a style of life inaccessible to the immense, underlying population. But like Icarus in the Greek myth, when they fly too close to the sun, the wax melts on their wings and they plunge to their death in the sea. For man's cardinal sin, no less than Lucifer's, is to set himself in glory above his peers.

Renaissance man claimed nothing less. Castiglione's "Courtier" not only was a perfect horseman for every saddle, but also "set all his delights and diligence to wade in everie thing a little farther than other men." To what purpose? For the sake of excellence. Socrates' lover, the great Alcibiades, "excelled...everie man in the thing that he had most skill in. So shall this our Courtier passe other men, and everie man in his owne profession."[13]

This Renaissance credo is thinly disguised in Marx's celebrated Manifesto: "In place of the old bourgeois society...we shall have an association in which the free development of each is the condition for the free development of all"—a condition at the opposite extremity from "universal asceticism and social leveling in its crudest form." But how in this world of irremediable scarcity is the multiplication and refinement of one person's needs to be prevented from infringing on the needs of others?

Milton was right. Humanism is the offspring of presumption and self-adulation compounded by the most insidious and unrestrained selfishness. It is but a short distance from "Man is the measure of all things" to the tempting but deceptive conclusion that, since I am a man, "I am the measure of all things." Remember Faust! There is no more a limit to the craving for knowledge—the apple of discord—than there is to the desire for money or other tangible assets needed for fulfillment. In the Marx-Engels correspondence between 1844 and 1855, one finds references to the great literary figures of both the ancient and modern worlds, but not a single line on Milton. Evidently, the father of literate communists had not studied Milton; or, if he had, he found nothing in Milton's work worth citing.

---

[12] John Milton, *Paradise Lost*, ed. Merritt Y. Hughes (New York: Odyssey, 1935), 9:934–937.

[13] Ibid., 1:39; and Castiglione, *The Book of the Courtier*, 41.

Like wealth, knowledge is a form of power. Wrote Mencius (390–305 BC): "There are those who use their minds and there are those who use their muscles. The former rule; the latter are ruled. Those who rule are supported by those who are ruled."[14] Evidently, nothing has changed in this respect some 2,300 years later! There's *progress* for you!

For Marx, man's goal is to become rich in needs rather than rich in the sense of wealthy, as if money were not a condition of both. It is clear from his early writings that a mature communism aims to sever the link between cultivation of the personality and the accumulation of material wealth. It is unrealistic, however, to believe that riches, and therefore freedom from time-consuming cares and the burdens and frustrations of everyday life, are *not* conditions of human excellence. Although one can enjoy music, art, and literature without "owning" them, ownership is a mighty boon to enjoying them.

Like precious jewels, books filled with knowledge do not come cheaply. What the ancient Cynic, Lucian of Samosata (ca. 125–180 AD), said about luxuries that have become necessities applies to books as well as to jewels: "All that costly array of means of enjoyment which you so gloat over is obtained only...through how many men's blood and death and ruin. To bring these things to you many seamen must perish; to find and fashion them many laborers must endure misery."[15]

No wonder that the pampered will be punished—if only in the hereafter! With 2,000 years of hindsight and another 2,000 years of foresight, Lucian spelled out what they deserved. "Whereas many lawless deeds are done in life by the rich who plunder and oppress and in every way humiliate the poor: Be it resolved by the Senate and people [of Hades] that when they [the pampered] die...their souls be sent back into life and enter into donkeys until they have passed two hundred and fifty thousand years in the said condition, transmigrating from donkey to donkey, bearing burdens and being driven by the poor." *There's* a communist for you—with a vengeance![16]

Louis-Ferdinand Céline, the French misanthrope and cynic, was not one to take the doctrine of original sin and divine punishment as sacred truth. But he astutely recognized its usefulness in unmasking Marx and the

---

[14] John M. and Patricia Koller, *A Sourcebook in Asian Philosophy* (New York: Macmillan, 1991), 483.

[15] Lucian of Samosata, "Cynicus," as cited by Farrand Sayre, ed., *Diogenes of Sinope* (Baltimore, MD: J. H. Furst, 1938), 8.

[16] Lucian of Samosata, "A Journey to Hades," as cited by John Jay Chapman, ed., *Lucian, Plato and Greek Morals* (Boston: Houghton Mifflin, 1931), 334. For a contemporary equivalent of this communist transmigration of souls, see Hodges, *Sandino's Communism*, 126–140, 182–186.

Marxists' humanist hoax. At least the Church says we are inherently vile and acquisitive, unlike Marxists who believe in human perfectibility and a classless society. The one good thing about Christianity, he told his Soviet hosts in 1936, is that it acknowledges human beings to be the greatest scum on earth. But Marxist humanists have the gall to dress up a turd and call it a caramel.[17]

Marx objected to communism for being crude and ascetic. But precisely those features define its perennial nature. The ideas of equality, sharing, and caring owe their existence to a memory of what used to be, "a small voice left over from our kindergarten experience, a sort of super ego or conscience...to a memory buried deep in the primitive brain, a memory of things past when sharing and loving were much more in vogue than in contemporary life." At the dawn of civilization, people who were barely human learned to survive through solidarity and group action, through what Kropotkin called "mutual aid." Primitive communism is a "natural phenomenon in the sense that the sharing, equality, and caring which characterized it flowed out of the extended family network on which the tribe was based."[18]

However, primitive or fraternal communism is irretrievably naïve. It demands more of both workers and their leaders than either is prepared to deliver. To expect leaders of a Marxist party to risk their necks in a struggle from which they would not emerge as beneficiaries is to expect too much. To suppose that a Marxist party in power would act on the few hints of communism in the Manifesto is tantamount to "expecting the Catholic Church to preach and practice the tenets of primitive communism held by the first Christian communities."[19]

Pre-Marxist communism suffers from an ascetic virus and the voluntarist foible of believing in a "new man" capable of renouncing the good things of life, in a "new era" to be ushered in by acts of heroism and the sheer discipline of will. Experience shows that it, too, is slated for defeat, not just from without but also from within. Since subtracting from human needs is as self-destructive as multiplying them, communism is the loser either way.

The vain and interminable search for individual happiness, according to Céline, is the bête noire of communism. "That's what makes life so difficult!

---

[17] Cited by Florence King, *With Charity Toward None: A Fond Look at Misanthropy* (New York: St. Martin's Press, 1992), 131.

[18] James R. Ozinga, *The Recurring Dream of Equality: Communal Sharing and Communism Throughout History* (Lanham/New York/London: University Press of America, 1996), 1–2. See Piotr Kropotkin, *Mutual Aid, A Factor of Evolution* (London: William Heinemann, 1915), 11–62.

[19] Nomad, *Rebels and Renegades*, 119.

What makes people so poisonous, disgusting, intolerable....It's out of happy people that the best damned are made!" A genuine communism, he believed, would not sacrifice the spirit of fraternity to the selfish pursuit of personal well-being—especially since one cannot honestly have both. "Communism, above all, is much more the sharing of all troubles than the sharing of wealth." But it demands also that wealth be shared, really shared, instead of the socialist principle of rewarding each according to his work. "I'm all in favor, me, of sharing! I've never wanted anything else! There! My four halfpennies on the table!...I'll put all I have on the table. If there's a *total* share-out." But that is not what the masses want.[20]

The typical proletarian, says Céline, is infected with ambition. He emulates his social betters. The most ardent working-class militant "has about as much desire to share with his luckless brother worker as has the winner in the national lottery." One becomes a communist not only out of self-interest, but also because of deep feelings for others. Communists are born, not made. "Communism is a quality of the soul. A spiritual state which can't be acquired." As he lays down the conditions of his egalitarian and ascetic—but also eminently aesthetic—communism: "Income...to be based on what is necessary to provide for the basic needs of each human being, and *not* on the kind of work performed *nor* on the degree of responsibility." In this way the absence of differences due to unequal incomes would make possible the total reform of the nation, as a "*family* whose members care for one another."[21]

By appealing to human selfishness and by relying on material instead of moral incentives to get workers to produce more, Céline concludes, Soviet communism was a monstrous imposture. But are ordinary people as yet ready for communism? On the contrary, they are too depraved to appreciate it. No matter! "What is attractive in communism, its great advantage if truth be told, is that it sets out to unmask man at last." Like the Fathers of the Church, it promises happiness not in this world, but in the New Jerusalem that never arrives. It tells us that original sin is not a myth, that man is basically a rat. As in George Orwell's *1984*, in a real pinch most people will betray their closest friends. "Do it to Julia! Not me!"[22]

---

[20] Merlin Thomas, *Louis Ferdinand Céline* (London/Boston: Faber & Faber, 1979), 126, 127, 140. Cited from Céline's pamphlet, *Mea Culpa* (1936), and *Bagatelles pour un massacre* (1937).

[21] Ibid., 157 and 169. From Céline's *L'Ecole des cadavres* (1938).

[22] Ibid., 125–126. From Céline's pamphlet *Mea Culpa*; and George Orwell, *1984* (New York: Signet, 1950), 197, 215, 218.

Céline offers no hope for humankind. But is such an ultra-degree of cynicism warranted? We have seen that the Scylla and Charybdis of modern communism are respectively its sectarianism and its ecumenicism—the pre-Marxist legacy and Marx's revision of this legacy in the Manifesto. It would be stretching credibility to claim that either one is feasible. But like Odysseus, cannot communists steer a middle course between the wreckage on both shores?

Indeed, traces of a third communist project may be found in the Manifesto. As Marx interpreted the Manifesto's "Communistic abolition of buying and selling," the cooperative economy that replaces capitalism includes—besides the exchange of goods for labor certificates that do not circulate and therefore do not function as money—a welfare sector for the common satisfaction of needs, such as schools, health care, and relief for those unable to work. In the lower stage of communism the exchange sector prevails in matters of distribution; but with the progress of industry and the overcoming of scarcity the sector of free goods and services expands until it becomes the dominant sector. Hence, "To each according to his needs"![23]

The Manifesto's transitional program favors a "community of goods" to be achieved in conjunction with income redistribution. It combines upward and downward leveling through a set of halfway measures, including gradual socialization, the restriction of wage labor, the application of rents to public purposes, a progressive income tax, and the abolition of the right of inheritance. Having ridiculed the identification of communism with Babeuf's Republic of Equals and the placing of the principal stress on equality, Marx's communist alternative was to raise the welfare sector to the leading position in the cooperative economy.

The future of communism and the future of welfare *are* thus closely connected. Escalating pressures from below combined with grudging concessions from above have made welfare the least objectionable road to social peace. Since "all modern market economies are to some degree welfare economies,"[24] the Manifesto's prognosis of a future communism has borne fruit without, as well as with, the direct intervention of Communist parties.

The modern Welfare State first took root in Marx's Germany. The term "Wohlfahrsstaat" was coined by journalists to describe Bismarck's comprehensive program of workers' insurance against sickness and accidents in a series of laws in 1883, 1884, and 1885; and another in 1889

---

[23] Marx, "Critique of the Gotha Programme," *Selected Works*, 2:22–24.

[24] George N. Halm, *Economic Systems: A Comparative Analysis*, rev. ed. (New York: Holt, Rinehart and Winston, 1961), 270–271.

insuring the aged and disabled. "Bismarck, the revolutionary against his will," wrote Engels, became the first European statesman to introduce "Staatssozialismus" (State Socialism)—later, a model for every other country in Europe.[25]

What led to this startling innovation? In order to curb the growing influence of German Socialists under the influence of the revived 1848 Manifesto, Bismarck relied on the age-old strategy of the carrot and the stick. The stick was the Anti-Socialist Law (1878–1890); the carrot was the Welfare State. As the Iron Chancellor declared in 1884, "assure him [the workingman] of care when he is sick and maintenance when he is old...*then* if the state will show a little more Christian solicitude for him, the Socialists will sing their songs in vain."[26]

Welfare communism is defined by a sector of free goods and services either completely or partially subsidized by the state. With the emergence of strong Labor and Social Democratic parties in the early twentieth century, public welfare made impressive gains in Germany, Austria, France, the United Kingdom, the British Dominions, and Scandinavia. In response to the worldwide depression of the 1930s, World War II, and the postwar economic boom, the United States and the other market economies in Europe developed similar but more modest welfare programs.

Welfare communism also had a counterpart in the former Soviet Union and in Eastern Europe, and in still larger measure in both China and Cuba during the 1960s. In both countries efforts were made to bridge the gap between Marx's lower and higher stages of communism by reducing wage differences and by gradually withdrawing goods from commercial circulation.[27]

Contrary to popular belief, communism is not just an ideal, myth, utopia, ideology, political movement, or any combination of these. Although no longer a "historical movement going on under our very eyes," communism is a fact of life common to all contemporary societies. As a spin-off of the Manifesto's communism, it has become feasible in miniature—especially when the sector of subsidized goods is not acknowledged as communist.

Although whittled down and partly scuttled in the new Russia and in Eastern Europe under post-Communist rule, welfare communism is here to

---

[25] See Engels' letters of 23 April and 13 November 1885 in Marx and Engels, *Selected Correspondence*, 460, 464.

[26] Cited by Walter Phelps Hall and William Stearns Davis, *The Course of European History Since Waterloo*, 4th ed. (New York: Appleton-Century-Crofts, 1957), 310.

[27] On the guiding principles and prospects of these Communist "heresies," see Donald C. Hodges, *The Bureaucratization of Socialism* (Amherst: University of Massachusetts Press, 1981), 155–160, 163–168, 168–173.

stay. However, welfare has an underside; it is not what it appears. It leaves intact the social status of Mister Drudge Forlyfe, Esquire. First, it is a token communism—like "Bread and Circuses" in the ancient world—marginal to and overshadowed by the private and public sectors where buying and selling are the rule. Second, it is a communism that has passed its zenith, that is currently eroding under pressure from the technocrats concerned with making their firms and national economies "competitive." Third, it is a Machiavellian device for managing social unrest, for preventing social explosions under both late capitalist and postcapitalist conditions, "a political response to political disorder." That is the *sinister* reality of communist welfare—a device for regulating the poor.[28] Thus the welfare carrot serves the interests of old and new masters, not just working stiffs.

Far from attaining the final abolition of buying and selling, the Manifesto has to its credit only socialism and welfare in small and easily digested doses. Socialism was no ordinary achievement. But was exploitation abolished—other than capitalist-induced misery? On the contrary, the Manifesto contributed to making revolutions, but the exploited and oppressed got only a token share of the benefits.

For the semiprivileged but exploited workers—those earning more than the minimum but less than the average wage—conditions have markedly improved. On this score, Céline is mistaken. But for those at the bottom of the social pit, Céline is right. For the Lazarus-layers of society there are only degrees of Hell.

When not inventing heavenly kingdoms, people fabricate earthly substitutes. The various forms of communism are witness to this extravagant levity among communist thinkers. After 150 years of trial, the Manifesto's communism is in agony almost everywhere. Yet it would be hazardous to predict the long-range outcome. The communist phoenix does more than self-destruct; it has a two-thousand-year history of rising from the ashes.[29]

---

[28] Frances Fox Piven and Richard A. Cloward, *Regulating the Poor: The Functions of Public Welfare* (New York: Pantheon, 1971), 3–8, 104–111, 196–198; and Hodges, *America's New Economic Order*, 154–163.

[29] A revival of interest in the Manifesto occurred in anticipation of its 150th anniversary. See Karl Marx, *The Communist Manifesto*, Introd. by Mick Hume (Chicago: Pluto Press, 1996); K. Marx and F. Engels, *The Communist Manifesto*, Introd. by A.J.P. Taylor (Harmondsworth: Penguin, 1997); Karl Marx, *The Communist Manifesto*, Introd. by Eric Hobsbawm (London: Verso, 1998); and Mark Cowling, ed., *The Communist Manifesto: New Interpretations*, trans. Terrell Carver (New York: New York University Press, 1998).

Postscript

The French novelist André Gide, like his compatriot Ferdinand Céline, visited the Soviet Union in the mid-1930s, only to become disenchanted with the outcome of the Manifesto's communism.

He had come as an enthusiast, totally convinced, and was prepared to embrace the New World with open arms. But the comrades offered him seductions of various kinds—the prerogatives of the Old World he abominated.

"But you don't understand," declared his host. "Communism is opposed only to the exploitation of man by man." Once it is abolished as in the Soviet Union, you can become as rich as you like—as long as you acquire your fortune by your own hard work!

Gide had no reply.

"In your scorn and hatred for wealth and possessions," his host continued, "I detect a very regrettable trace of your early Christian ideas."

"That may well be."

"Which, let me tell you, have nothing in common with Marxism."

"Alas!"[1]

---

[1] From André Gide, "Second Thoughts on the USSR" (1937), in Edith Kurzweil, ed., *A Partisan Century: Political Writings from Partisan Review* (New York: Columbia University Press, 1996), 9–10. Acknowledgment is due to Professor Larry Lustig at the University of Maryland Asian Division in Seoul, Korea, for drawing my attention to Gide's reminiscences and for editing the final manuscript.

Bibliography

Selections from the anthologized, selected, and collected works of the principal authors—Engels, Marx, Marx and Engels, Bakunin, Lenin, Trotsky, and Stalin—are not listed separately but are cited with the sources in the text.

Adler, Max. "Socialism and Communism." In *Karl Marx. The Communist Manifesto*. Ed. Frederic L. Bender. New York/London: Norton, 1988.

Althusser, Louis, et al. *Polémica sobre marxismo y humanismo*. Trans. Marta Harnecker. Mexico City: Siglo XXI, 1968.

"Analysis of the Doctrine of Babeuf by the Babouvists." In *Socialist Thought: A Documentary History*, rev. ed. Ed. Albert Fried and Ronald Sanders. New York: Columbia University Press, 1992.

Andréas, Bert. *Le Manifeste Communiste de Marx et Engels*. Milan: Feltrinelli, 1963.

Annenkov, Pavel. "Memoires." In *Reminiscences of Marx and Engels*. Ed. Institute of Marxism-Leninism. Moscow: Foreign Languages Publishing House, 1957.

Avineri, Shlomo. *The Social and Political Thought of Karl Marx*. New York: Cambridge University Press, 1968.

Avrich, Paul, ed. *The Anarchists in the Russian Revolution*. Ithaca, NY: Cornell University Press, 1973.

Babeuf, François Noël. "Babeuf's Defense." In *Socialist Thought: A Documentary History*, rev. ed. Ed. Albert Fried and Ronald Sanders. New York: Columbia University Press, 1992.

———. "Le Manifeste des plébéiens." *Textes Choisis*. Paris: Editions Sociales, 1965.

Bakunin, Michael. *Marxism, Freedom and the State*. Ed. and trans. K. J. Kenafick. London: Freedom Press, 1950.

———. "To the International Workingmen's Association of Locle and Choix-de-Fonds." In *Socialist Thought: A Documentary History*, rev. ed. Ed. Albert Fried and Ronald Sanders. New York: Columbia University Press, 1992.

Baring-Gould, S., ed. "Clementine Recognitions and Homilies." In *The Lost and Hostile Gospels*. London: Williams and Norgate, 1874.

Barruel, Augustin de. *Mémoires pour servir a l'histoire du jacobinisme*. 5 vols. Hamburg: Fauche, 1798–1799.

Bender, Frederic L., ed. *Karl Marx. The Communist Manifesto*. New York/London: Norton, 1988.

Bernstein, Eduard. *Evolutionary Socialism*. Trans. Edith C. Harvey. New York: Schocken, 1961; orig. pub. 1899.

Billington, James H. *Fire in the Minds of Men: Origins of the Revolutionary Faith*. New York: Basic Books, 1980.

Black, C. E., ed. *Rewriting Russian History*. New York: Praeger, 1956.

Blanqui, Louis Auguste. "The Man Who Makes the Soup Should Get to Eat It." In *Socialist Thought: A Documentary History*, rev. ed. Ed. Albert Fried and Ronald Sanders. New York: Columbia University Press, 1992.

———. "Oath of Membership into the Société des Saisons." In *Before Marx: Socialism and Communism in France, 1830–48.* Ed. Paul E. Corcoran. New York: St. Martin's Press, 1983.

Bosmajian, Haig A. "A Rhetorical Approach to the *Communist Manifesto.*" In *Karl Marx. The Communist Manifesto.* Ed. Frederic L. Bender. New York/London: Norton, 1988.

Buonarroti, Philippe (Filippo). *Babeuf's Conspiracy for Equality.* Trans. Bronterre O'Brien. New York: Augustus M. Kelley, 1965; orig. pub. 1828.

Canterbery, E. Ray. *The Literate Economist.* New York: HarperCollins, 1995.

Castiglione, Baldassare. *The Book of the Courtier.* Trans. Sir Thomas Hoby. London: J. M. Dent & Sons/New York: Dutton, 1948; orig. pub. 1528.

Chapman, John Jay, ed. *Lucian, Plato and Greek Morals.* Boston: Houghton Mifflin, 1931.

Cockburn, Alexander. "Beat the Devil: Dead Meat." *The Nation* (22 April 1996).

Cohen, Stephen F. *Bukharin and the Bolshevik Revolution: A Political Biography 1888–1938.* New York: Vintage, 1975.

———. "Introduction: Ligachev and the Tragedy of Soviet Conservativism." In *Inside Gorbachev's Kremlin* by Yegor Ligachev. New York: Pantheon, 1993.

Cohn, Norman. *The Pursuit of the Millennium.* New York: Harper, 1961.

Collins, Henry, and C. Abramsky. *Karl Marx and the British Labour Movement. Years of the First International.* London: Macmillan, 1965.

Corcoran, Paul E., ed. *Before Marx: Socialism and Communism in France 1830–1848.* New York: St. Martin's Press, 1983.

Crankshaw, Edward. *Khrushchev: A Career.* New York: Viking, 1966.

Crossan, John Dominic. *Jesus: A Revolutionary Biography.* New York: HarperCollins, 1994.

Davidson, Rondel V. "Reform versus Revolution: Victor Considérant and the *Communist Manifesto.* In *Karl Marx. The Communist Manifesto.* Ed. Frederic L. Bender. New York/London: Norton, 1988.

Deutscher, Isaac. ed. *The Age of Permanent Revolution: A Trotsky Anthology.* New York: Dell, 1964.

———. *The Prophet Outcast. Trotsky: 1929–1940.* New York: Vintage, 1965.

———. *Stalin: A Political Biography,* 2nd ed. New York: Oxford University Press, 1967; orig. pub. 1949.

Dolgoff, Sam, ed. and trans. *Bakunin on Anarchy.* Montréal: Black Rose Books, 1990.

Dommanget, Maurice. *Babeuf et la conjuration des egaux.* 2nd ed. Paris: Spartacus, 1969.

Draper, Hal. *Karl Marx's Theory of Revolution.* 4 vols. New York: Monthly Review Press, 1977–1990.

Easton. L. D. "August Willich, Marx, and Left-Hegelian Socialism." In *Cahiers de l'Institut de Science Economique Appliquée.* August 1965.

Editorial Departments of *People's Daily* and *Red Flag. On Khrushchev's Phoney Communism and its Historical Lessons for the World.* Peking: Foreign Languages Press, 1964.

———. *The Proletarian Revolution and Khrushchev's Revisionism.* Peking: Foreign Languages Press, 1964.

Eisenstein, Elizabeth L. *The First Professional Revolutionist: Filippo Michele Buonarroti (1761–1837)*. Cambridge: Harvard University Press, 1957.

Engels, Frederick. *Anti-Dühring*, 2nd ed. Moscow: Foreign Languages Publishing House, 1959; orig. pub. 1878.

——. *Ludwig Feuerbach*. New York: International Publishers, 1941.

Fedoseyev, P. N., et al., eds. *Karl Marx: A Biography*. Trans. Yuri Sdobnikov. Moscow: Progress Publishers, 1973.

Feuerbach, Ludwig. *The Essence of Christianity*. Trans. Marian Evans from the 2nd German ed. London, 1893; orig. pub. 1841.

Fried, Albert, and Ronald Sanders, eds. *Socialist Thought: A Documentary History*, rev. ed. New York: Columbia University Press, 1992.

Friedrich, Carl, ed. *The Philosophy of Hegel*. New York: Modern Library, 1953.

Galbraith, John Kenneth, and Stanislav Menshikov. *Capitalism, Communism, and Coexistence: From the Bitter Path to a Better Prospect*. Boston: Houghton Mifflin, 1988.

Gide, André. "Second Thoughts on the USSR." In *A Partisan Century: Political Writings from Partisan Review*. Ed. Edith Kurzweil. New York: Columbia University Press, 1996.

Gorbachev, Mikhail. "An Ideology of Renovation for Revolutionary Perestroika." In *Information Bulletin*, vol. 26, no. 8. Prague: Peace and Socialism International Publishers, 1988.

——. "On Progress in Implementing the Decisions of the 27th CPSU Congress and the Tasks of Promoting Perestroika." In *Soviet Life*, special supplement entitled *Documents and Materials: 19th All-Union Conference on CPSU*. Washington DC: Embassy of the Union of the Soviet Socialist Republics, 1988.

——. *On the Tasks of the Party in the Radical Restructuring of Economic Management*. Moscow: Novosti Press Agency, 1987.

——. *Perestroika: New Thinking for Our Country and the World*. New York: Harper, 1987.

——. *Political Report of the CPSU Central Committee to the 27th Party Congress*. Moscow: Novosti Press Agency, 1986.

Guillaume, James. "On Building the New Social Order." In *Bakunin on Anarchy*. Ed. and trans. Sam Dolgoff. Montréal: Black Rose Books, 1990.

Hacker, Andrew. *Political Theory: Philosophy, Ideology, Science*. New York: Macmillan, 1961.

Hall, Walter Phelps, and William Stearns Davis. *The Course of European History Since Waterloo*, 4th ed. New York: Appleton-Century-Crofts, 1957.

Halm, George N. *Economic Systems: A Comparative Analysis*, rev. ed. New York: Holt, Rinehart and Winston, 1961.

Harding, Neil. *Lenin's Political Thought: Theory and Practice in the Democratic and Socialist Revolutions*. 2 vols. Atlantic Highlands, NJ: Humanities Press, 1983.

Harrington, Michael. "The Democratic Essence of Socialism." In *Karl Marx. The Communist Manifesto*. Ed. Frederic L. Bender. New York/London: Norton, 1988.

Heitman, Sidney. "New Introduction." In *The ABC of Communism* by N. Bukharin and E. Preobrazhensky. Ann Arbor: University of Michigan Press, 1962.

Hobsbawm, Eric. "Lenin and the 'Aristocracy of Labor.'" In *Lenin Today: Eight Essays on the Hundredth Anniversary of Lenin's Birth*. Ed. Paul M. Sweezy and Harry Magdoff. New York/London: Monthly Review Press, 1970.

Hodges, Donald C. *America's New Economic Order*. Aldershot UK/Brookfield USA: Avebury-Ashgate, 1996.

——. *The Bureaucratization of Socialism*. Amherst: University of Massachusetts Press, 1981.

——. "Engels' Contribution to Marxism." In *The Socialist Register 1965*. Ed. R. Miliband and J. Saville. London: Merlin Press, 1965.

——. *Philosophy of the Urban Guerrilla: The Revolutionary Writings of Abraham Guillén*. New York: William Morrow, 1973.

——. *Sandino's Communism: Spiritual Politics for the Twenty-First Century*. Austin: University of Texas Press, 1992.

——. *Socialist Humanism: The Outcome of Classical European Morality*. St. Louis: Warren H. Green, 1974.

Hook, Sidney. *From Marx to Hegel: Studies in the Intellectual Development of Karl Marx*. New York: Humanities Press, 1958; orig. pub. 1936.

——. "Introduction." In *Evolutionary Socialism,* by Eduard Bernstein. Trans. Edith C. Harvey. New York: Schocken, 1961; orig. pub. 1899.

Horowitz, Irving Louis. *Radicalism and the Revolt Against Reason*. London: Routledge and Kegan Paul, 1961.

Hunwert, Paul A. *Bernard Shaw's Marxian Romance*. Lincoln: University of Nebraska Press, 1973.

Hutchins, John Maynard, ed. Great Books of the Western World, *Vol 50, Marx*. Chicago: Encyclopedia Britannica, 1990; orig. pub. 1952.

Hutton, Patrick H. *The Cult of the Revolutionary Tradition: The Blanquists in French Politics, 1864–1893*. Berkeley/Los Angeles/London: University of California Press, 1981.

Institute of Marxism-Leninism. *Reminiscences of Marx and Engels*. Moscow: Foreign Languages Publishing House, 1957.

Johnstone, Monty. "Marx and Engels and the Concept of the Party." In *The Socialist Register 1967*. Ed. R. Miliband and J. Saville. London: Merlin Press, 1967.

Kahan, Stuart. *The Wolf of the Kremlin*. New York: William Morrow, 1987.

Kautsky, Karl. *The Class Struggle (Erfurt Program)*. Trans. W. E. Bahn. New York: Norton, 1971; orig. pub. 1892.

——. "The *Communist Manifesto* after Six Decades." In *Karl Marx. The Communist Manifesto*. Ed. Frederic L. Bender. New York/London: Norton, 1988; orig. pub. 1906.

——. *The Labour Revolution*. Trans. H. J. Stenning. New York: Dial Press, 1925.

Kenafick, K. J. *Michael Bakunin and Karl Marx*. Melbourne: A. Maller, 1948.

Khrushchev, Nikita S. "Report on the Program of the Communist Party of the Soviet Union." In *Documents of the 22nd Congress of the CPSU*. 2 vols. New York: Crosscurrents Press, 1961.

——. *Khrushchev Remembers*. 2 vols. Ed. and trans. Strobe Talbott. Boston: Little Brown, 1970, 1974.

King, Florence. *With Charity Toward None: A Fond Look at Misanthropy*. New York: St. Martin's Press, 1992.

Kingston, Robert J. ed. *Perestroika Papers*. Dubuque, IA: Kendall/Hunt, 1988.

Koller, John M., and Patricia. *A Sourcebook in Asian Philosophy*. New York: Macmillan, 1991.

Kropotkin, Piotr. *Mutual Aid, A Factor of Evolution*. London: William Heinemann, 1915.

Kuusinen, O. V. et al. *Fundamentals of Marxism-Leninism*. 2nd rev. ed. Moscow: Foreign Languages Publishing House, 1963.

Laurat, Lucien. "If One Were to Rewrite the *Communist Manifesto* Today." In *Karl Marx. The Communist Manifesto*. Ed. Frederic L. Bender, New York/London: Norton, 1988.

Lehning, Arthur. *From Buonarroti to Bakunin*. Leiden: Brill, 1970.

Lenin, V. I. *Collected Works*. 18 vols. New York: International Publishers, 1930.

——. *Marx, Engels, Marxism*. 5th English ed. Moscow: Foreign Languages Publishing House, 1953.

——. *The National-Liberation Movement in the East*. Moscow: Foreign Languages Publishing House, 1962.

——. *Selected Works*. 3 vols. New York: International Publishers, 1967.

Lichtheim, George. *The Origins of Socialism*. New York: Praeger, 1969.

Liebman, Marcel. "Lenin in 1905: A Revolution that Shook a Doctrine." In *Lenin Today: Eight Essays on the Hundredth Anniversary of Lenin's Birth*. Ed. Paul M. Sweezy and Harry Magdoff. New York/London: Monthly Review Press, 1970.

Lucian of Samosata. "A Journey to Hades." In *Lucian, Plato and Greek Morals*. Ed. John Jay Chapman. Boston: Houghton Mifflin, 1931.

——. "Cynicus." In *Diogenes of Sinope*. Ed. Farrand Sayre. Baltimore, MD: J. H. Furst, 1938.

Machiavelli, Niccolò. *The Prince* and *The Discourses*. Trans. Luigi Ricci. Revised by E. R. P. Vincent. New York: Modern Library, 1940; orig. pub. 1532.

Malia, Martin. *The Soviet Tragedy: A History of Socialism in Russia, 1917–1991*. New York/Toronto: Free Press, 1994.

Maréchal, Sylvain. "Manifesto of the Equals." In *Socialist Thought: A Documentary History*. rev. ed. Ed. Albert Fried and Ronald Sanders. New York: Columbia University Press, 1992.

Marshall, Alfred. *Principles of Economics*. 8th ed. New York: Macmillan, 1948; orig. pub. 1920.

Marx, Karl. *Capital*. Vol. 1. Ed. Frederick Engels. New York: Modern Library, n.d.

——. *Capital*. Vols. 2–3. Ed. Frederick Engels. Moscow: Foreign Languages Publishing House, 1961–1962.

——. *A Contribution to the Critique of Political Economy*. Chicago: Charles Kerr, 1904.

——. *The Communist Manifesto*. Introd. by Eric Hobsbawm. London: Verso, 1998.

——. *The Communist Manifesto*. Introd. by Mick Hume. Chicago: Pluto Press, 1996.

——. *The Communist Manifesto: New Interpretations*. Ed. Mark Cowling. Trans. Terrell Carver. New York: New York University Press, 1998.

——. *Letters to Dr. Kugelmann*. New York: International Publishers, 1934.

Marx, Karl, and Frederick Engels. *Collected Works*. 46 vols. New York: International Publishers, 1975–1992.

——. *The Communist Manifesto*. Introd. by A. J. P. Taylor. Harmondsworth: Penguin, 1997.

——. *Das Kommunistische Manifest*. Ed. Thomas Kuczynski. Trier: Karl-Marx-Haus, 1995.

——. *Selected Correspondence*. Moscow: Foreign Languages Publishing House, 1953.

——. *Selected Works*. 2 vols. Moscow: Foreign Languages Publishing House, 1958.

Maximoff, G. P., ed. *The Political Philosophy of Bakunin: Scientific Anarchism*. Glencoe, IL: Free Press, 1953.

Medvedev, Roy. *Khrushchev*. Trans. Brian Pearce. Garden City, NY: Anchor, 1984.

——. *Let History Judge: The Origins and Consequences of Stalinism*, rev. ed. Ed. and trans. George Shriver. New York: Columbia University Press, 1989.

Mendel, Arthur P., ed. *Essential Works of Marxism*. New York/London: Bantam, 1965.

Miliband, R., and J. Seville, eds. *The Socialist Register 1965*. London: Merlin Press, 1965.

——. eds. *The Socialist Register 1967*. London: Merlin Press, 1967.

Milton, John. *Paradise Lost*. Ed. Merritt Y. Hughes. New York: Odyssey, 1935.

Miranda, José Porfirio. *Comunismo en la biblia*. Mexico City: Siglo XXI, 1981.

Moore, Stanley. *Marx on the Choice between Socialism and Communism*. Cambridge: Harvard University Press, 1980.

——. *Three Tactics: The Background in Marx*. New York: Monthly Review Press, 1963.

Morelly. "Code of Nature." In *Socialist Thought: A Documentary History*. rev. ed. Ed. Albert Fried and Ronald Sanders. New York: Columbia University Press, 1992.

Nettlau, Max. "Mikhail Bakunin: A Biographical Sketch." In *The Political Philosophy of Bakunin*. Ed. G. P. Maximoff. Glencoe, IL: Free Press, 1953.

Nomad, Max. *Apostles of Revolution*. New York: Collier Books, 1961; orig. pub. 1933.

——. *Aspects of Revolt*. New York: Bookman, 1959.

——. *Rebels and Renegades*. Freeport, NY: Books for Libraries, 1968; orig. pub. 1932.

Orwell, George. *1984*. New York: Signet, 1950.

Ostergaard, G. N., and A. H. Halsey. *Power in Cooperatives: A Study of the Internal Politics of British Retail Societies*. Oxford: Basil Blackwell, 1965.

Ozinga, James R. *The Recurring Dream of Equality: Communal Sharing and Communism Throughout History*. Lanham/New York/London: University Press of America, 1996.

Palmer, R. R. *Twelve Who Ruled: The Year of Terror in the French Revolution*. Princeton: Princeton University Press, 1989; orig. pub. 1941.

Paul, Eden and Cedar, trans. "Program of the Communist Party of Russia" (1919). In *The ABC of Communism* by N. Bukharin and E. Preobrazhensky. Ann Arbor: University of Michigan Press, 1962.

Peacham, Henry. *Peacham's Compleat Gentleman*. Oxford: Clarendon Press, 1906; orig. pub. 1622.

Pipes, Richard. *The Russian Revolution*. New York: Vintage, 1991.

Piven, Frances Fox, and Richard A. Cloward. *Regulating the Poor: The Functions of Public Welfare*. New York: Pantheon, 1971.

Polan, A. J. *Lenin and the End of Politics*. Berkeley/Los Angeles: University of California Press, 1984.

Powers, Thomas. "Who Won the Cold War." *The New York Review of Books* (20 June 1996).

Proudhon, P. J. *What Is Property?* Trans. Benjamin R. Tucker. London: William Reeves, n.d.; orig. pub. 1840.

Pyziur, Eugene. *The Doctrine of Anarchism of Michael A. Bakunin.* Milwaukee, WI: Marquette University Press, 1955.

Remnick, David. "Hammer, Sickle, and Book," In *The New York Review of Books* (23 May 1996).

Rizzi, Bruno. *The Bureaucratization of the World.* Trans. Adam Westoby. New York: Free Press, 1985; orig. pub. 1939.

Roberts, J. M. *The Mythology of the Secret Societies.* London: Secker & Warburg, 1972.

Robison, John. *Proofs of a Conspiracy.* Boston: Western Islands, 1967; orig. pub. 1798.

Rose, B. *Gracchus Babeuf: The First Revolutionary Communist.* Stanford: Stanford University Press, 1978.

Rousseau, Jean-Jacques. *The Social Contract* and *Discourses.* Trans. G. D. H. Cole. New York: Dutton, 1950.

Rubel, Maximilien. "Marx's Concept of Democracy." *Democracy,* Fall 1983.

Rubel, Maximilien, and Margaret Manale. *Marx Without Myth: A Chronological Study of His Life and Work.* New York: Harper, 1976.

Ryazanoff, David V. *The Communist Manifesto of Karl Marx and Friedrich Engels.* Trans. Eden and Cedar Paul. New York: Russell & Russell, 1963; orig. pub. 1922.

Saint-Simon, Henri Comte de. *Selected Writings.* Ed. and trans. F. M. H. Markham. Oxford: Blackwell, 1952.

Sayre, Farrand, ed. *Diogenes of Sinope.* Baltimore, MD: Furst, 1938.

Sazonov, V. *On the "Manifesto of the Communist Party" of Marx and Engels.* Moscow: Progress Publishers, 1984.

Scanlan, James P. "From Samizdat to Perestroika: The Soviet Marxist Critique of Soviet Society." In *The Road to Disillusion: From Cultural Marxism to Postcommunism in Eastern Europe.* Ed. Raymond Taras. Armonk, NY: M. E. Sharpe, 1992.

Schumpeter, Joseph A. "The *Communist Manifesto* in Sociology and Economics." In *Karl Marx. The Communist Manifesto.* Ed. Frederic L. Bender. New York/London: Norton, 1988.

Seidman, Steven. *Liberalism and the Origins of European Social Theory.* Berkeley/Los Angeles: University of California Press, 1983.

Seigel, Jerrold. *Marx's Fate: The Shape of a Life.* Princeton: Princeton University Press, 1978.

Shaw, George Bernard, ed. *Fabian Essays.* London: George Allen & Unwin, 1948; orig. pub. 1889.

——. "Preface." In *The Irrational Knot. The Works of Bernard Shaw.* London: Constable, 1930–1938.

Shevardnadze, Eduard. *The Future Belongs to Freedom.* Trans. Catherine Fitzpatrick. New York: Free Press, 1991.

Shmelev, Nikolai. "Moving Toward the Market." In Robert J. Kingston, ed. *Perestroika Papers.* Dubuque, IA: Kendall/Hunt, 1988.

Sorel, Georges. "The Decomposition of Marxism," trans. Irving Louis Horowitz. Appended to Irving Louis Horowitz, *Radicalism and the Revolt Against Reason*. London: Routledge and Kegan Paul, 1961.

Spitzer, Alan B. *The Revolutionary Theories of Louis Auguste Blanqui*. New York: Columbia University Press, 1957.

Spriano, Paulo. *Stalin and the European Communists*. Trans. Jon Rothschild. London: Verso, 1985.

Stalin, Joseph V. *Anarchism or Socialism?* New York: International Publishers, 1953; orig. pub. 1906–1907.

——. *Economic Problems of Socialism in the USSR*. New York: International Publishers, 1952.

——. *Foundations of Leninism*. Tenth Anniversary Edition. New York: International Publishers, 1934.

——. *Leninism: Selected Writings*. New York: International Publishers, 1942.

——. *Problems of Leninism*. New York: International Publishers, 1934; orig. pub. 1926.

——. *Works*. 16 vols. Moscow: Foreign Languages Publishing House, 1954–55.

Strong, Anna Louise, trans. "The New Constitution of 1936." Appended to Sidney and Beatrice Webb, *The Truth About Soviet Russia*. New York/London: Longmans, Green, 1942.

Struik, Dirk. *The Birth of the Communist Manifesto*. New York: International Publishers, 1971.

Svanidze, Budu. *My Uncle Joseph Stalin*. Trans. Waverly Root. New York: Putnam's Sons, 1953.

Sweezy, Paul M., and Harry Magdoff, eds. *Lenin Today: Eight Essays on the Hundredth Anniversary of Lenin's Birth*. New York/London: Monthly Review Press, 1970.

Taras, Raymond, ed. "The 'Meltdown' of Marxism in the Soviet Bloc." In *The Road to Disillusion: From Critical Marxism to Postcommunism in Eastern Europe*. Armonk, NY: M. E. Sharpe, 1992.

Thomas, Merlin. *Louis Ferdinand Céline*. London/Boston: Faber & Faber, 1979.

Thomas, Paul. *Karl Marx and the Anarchists*. London/Boston: Routledge & Kegan Paul, 1980.

Triska, Jan F., ed. *Soviet Communism: Program and Rules*. San Francisco: Chandler, 1962.

Trotsky, Leon. *In Defense of Marxism*. New York: Pioneer, 1942.

——. *The First Five Years of the Communist International*. 2 vols. New York: Pioneer, 1945.

——. *My Life*. New York: Charles Scribner's Sons, 1931.

——. *The Permanent Revolution* and *Results and Prospects*. New York: Pathfinder, 1974.

——. *The Revolution Betrayed*. New York: Merit, 1965; orig. pub. 1937.

Tucker, Robert C., ed. *The Lenin Anthology*. New York: Norton, 1975.

——. ed. *The Marx-Engels Reader*, 2nd. ed. New York/London: Norton, 1978.

Ulam, Adam B. *The Bolsheviks: The Intellectual and Political History of the Triumph of Communism in Russia*. New York: Collier, 1965.

Varlamov, Volodymy. "Bakunin and the Russian Jacobins and Blanquists." In *Rewriting Russian History*. Ed. C. E. Black. New York: Praeger, 1956.

Vigor, P. H. *A Guide to Marxism and its Effects on Soviet Development*. New York: Humanities Press, 1966.

Volkogonov, Dmitri. *Lenin: A New Biography*. Ed. and trans. Harold Shukman. New York and London: Free Press, 1994.

——. *Stalin: Triumph and Tragedy*. Ed. and trans. Harold Shukman. Rocklin, CA: Prima Publishing, 1991.

Wagner, Y., and M. Strauss. "The Theoretical Foundations of the *Communist Manifesto's* Economic Program." In *Karl Marx. The Communist Manifesto*. Ed. Frederic L. Bender. New York/London: Norton, 1988.

Walicki, Andrzej. *Marxism and the Leap to the Kingdom of Freedom*. Stanford: Stanford University Press, 1995.

Webb, Sidney. "The Basis of Socialism: Historic." In *Fabian Essays*. Ed. George Bernard Shaw. London: George Allen & Unwin, 1948; orig. pub. 1889.

Webb, Sidney, and Beatrice. *The Truth About Soviet Russia*. New York/London: Longmans, Green, 1942.

Weeks, Albert L. *The First Bolshevik: A Political Biography of Peter Tkachev*. New York: New York University Press, 1968.

Weitling, Wilhelm. *The Poor Sinner's Gospel*. Trans. Dinah Livingstone. London: Sheed & Ward, 1969.

Yakovlev, Alexander. "The Humanistic Choice of Perestroika." *World Marxist Review*. February 1989.

Index

Abramsky, C., 47
Achilles heel (of the Manifesto), 190
Adoratsky, V., 17
Althusser, Louis, 68
Amalrik, Andrei, 180
anarcho-Marxism, 5, 129
Anti-Socialist Law, 108, 131, 197
Areopagites, 22
Aristotle, 2
artisans, 81, 135, 150
Babeuf, François Noël, 42–43, 78, 80,
    116; assailed by Proudhon, 118;
    Bakunin influenced by, 124;
    conspiratorial uprising of, 17;
    egalitarian credo of, 20–21, 24, 25,
    26, 27; Machiavellian and Jesuitical
    practice of, 150; Marx's critique of,
    186, 196; opposed to humanism,
    liberalism, and democracy, 45; as a
    revolutionary communist, 6; Trotsky
    influenced by, 155
Babouvism, 17
Bakunin, Michael, 102, 131, 138, 186,
    190; amendments to the Manifesto,
    119-121, 122-123, 124-125, 126-127,
    146; criticism of Marxists by, 115;
    criticizes universal suffrage, 122;
    distrusts Marx's communism, 116-
    117, 137, 157; egalitarianism of,
    116; father of anarcho-Marxism, 5,
    113; on fourth governing class, 92,
    120-121, 135; influences on, 115-
    117, 119; Lenin's indebtedness to,
    129-130, 145, 149; as a libertarian
    communist, 118; Machajski
    influenced by, 154; Mao indebted to,
    178; Marx's differences with, 102;
    redefines Marx's "proletariat," 119-
    120; reliance on invisible
    dictatorship, 78; Rizzi influenced by,
    158; on social liquidation, 114-115;
    on state and church as props of
    capital, 115; targets Capital as main

evil, 114; translates the Manifesto
    into Russian, 7, 129
Ball, John, 4
Barruel, Abbé, 23
Basel Program, 147, 188
Bentham, Jeremy, 43
Bernstein, Eduard: amendments to the
    Manifesto, 137–139; criticizes Marx's
    theory of economic development,
    134–136, 189; decommunizes
    socialism, 150; disputes Manifesto's
    reliance on violent revolution, 7,
    131–132, 138; liberal and democratic
    credo of, 132, 134; rejection of
    utopian residues in Marxism, 132,
    136, 137; shelves socialism as remote
    goal, 162; underestimates the
    democratic essence of the Manifesto,
    133
Bernsteinians, 144, 145
Bible, 3, 4, 7, 128, 133, 160, 162
Bizmarck, Otto von, 131, 197
Blanc, Louis, 56
Blanqui, Auguste, 42, 61, 74;
    communism of 25–26, 75, 150, 186;
    followers of, 20; Manifesto indebted
    to, 132; partisan of revolutionary
    violence, 138; transmitter of
    Buonarroti's legacy, 18; Trotsky's
    indebtedness to, 154; use of Biblical
    sources, 24
Blanquism, 131
Bolshevik(s), 11, 13, 61, 138, 142; and
    Babeuf's legacy, 155; hierarchical and
    quasi-military organization of, 143;
    left wing, 12; precursors of, 6; purge
    of Old, 163; Revolution, 137, 173,
    185, 187; struggle for power, 189
Bolshoi Theater, 191
Bonaparte, Louis, 94, 95–96
Bonapartism, 95, 96, 97
bourgeoisie: industrial, 72, 73, 88, 114,
    133, 135; nonindustrial, 73;
    progressive, 88; radical, 43

MAJOR CONCEPTS IN POLITICS
AND POLITICAL THEORY

This series invites book manuscripts and proposals on major concepts in politics and political theory—justice, equality, virtue, rights, citizenship, power, sovereignty, property, liberty, etc.—in prominent traditions, periods, and thinkers.

Send manuscripts or proposals, with author's vitae to:

Garrett Ward Sheldon
General Editor
Clinch Valley College
of the University of Virginia
College Avenue
Wise, VA 24293